Those who analyze public opinion have long contended that the average citizen is incapable of recounting consistently even the most rudimentary facts about current politics; that the little the average person does know is taken strictly from what the media report, with no critical reflection; and that the consequence is a polity that is ill prepared for democratic governance. And yet social movements, comprised by and large of average citizens, have been a prominent feature of the American political scene throughout American history and have experienced a resurgence in recent years. William Gamson asks, how is it that so many people become active in movements if they are so uninterested and badly informed about issues?

The conclusion he reaches in this book is a striking refutation of the common wisdom about the public's inability to reason about politics. Rather than relying on survey data, as so many studies of public opinion do, Gamson reports on his analysis of discussions among small groups of working people on four controversial issues: affirmative action, nuclear power, Arab–Israeli conflict, and the troubles in American industry. Excerpts from many of these discussions are transcribed in the book. In addition, Gamson analyzes how these same issues have been treated in a range of media material, from editorial opinion columns to political cartoons and network news programs, in order to determine how closely the group discussions mimic media discourse.

He finds that the process of opinion formation is more complex than it has usually been depicted and that people condition media information with reflection on their own experience or that of people they know. The discussions transcribed in this book demonstrate that people are quite capable of conducting informed and well-reasoned discussions about issues, and that although most people are not inclined to become actively involved in politics, the seeds of political action are present in the minds of many. With the appropriate stimulation, this latent political consciousness can be activated, which accounts for the continual creation of new social movements.

Talking politics

Talking politics

William A. Gamson
Boston College

CAMBRIDGE
UNIVERSITY PRESS

Published by the Press Syndicate of the University of Cambridge
The Pitt Building, Trumpington Street, Cambridge CB2 1RP
40 West 20th Street, New York, NY 10011-4211, USA
10 Stamford Road, Oakleigh, Melbourne 3166, Australia

© Cambridge University Press 1992

First published 1992
Reprinted 1994, 1995, 1996

Printed in the United States of America

Library of Congress Cataloging-in-Publication Data is available.

A catalog record for this book is available from the British Library.

ISBN 0-521-43062-3 hardback
ISBN 0-521-43679-6 paperback

To SAM FINKELSTEIN,
pushing ninety and still arguing about politics.

Contents

Contents

Figures and tables

Figures

Tables

Preface

Issues of political consciousness bridge the study of movements and media. One might imagine that with thousands of studies of people's voting preferences and attitudes on every conceivable issue, we would thoroughly understand how people think and talk about politics. Indeed, we do understand a lot about the end product – the content of the opinions they express. But on how they get there, on what the issues mean to people and how they reach their conclusions, we are still groping.

Surveys of political attitudes frequently ask people about issues on which there is a rich public discourse, presented selectively in mass media accounts and commentaries. Most students of public opinion assume that this media discourse is somehow reflected in the attitudes people express but would be hard pressed to specify exactly how it is used in thinking and talking about the issues. Media discourse is clearly not the only resource that most people use to construct meaning on political issues. Faced with a cacophony of media clatter, popular wisdom, and knowledge from their own experience, whether and how they make sense of it all remains a substantial mystery.

For social movement activists, it is frequently a frustrating mystery. Armed with powerful analyses that suggest that people are being exploited or injured by various state or corporate policies and actions, we must ruefully acknowledge that the very people most affected often miss the meanings we find in events. There are many explanations to account for quiescence and "false consciousness," but less convincing accounts of how it is that ordinary people sometimes do develop ways of understanding issues that support collective action for change.

Unraveling the mystery begins with recognizing consciousness as arising from the interplay of culture and cognition. The mass media are a system in which active agents with specific purposes are constantly engaged in a process of supplying meaning. Rather than thinking of them as a set of stimuli to which individuals respond, we should think of them as the site of a complex symbolic contest over which interpretation will prevail. This cultural system encounters thinking individuals, and political consciousness arises from the interweaving of these two levels.

This book unites my long-standing interests in mass media and social movements. The interest in political communication goes back to my undergraduate days at Antioch College, where it was nurtured by Heinz Eulau, who first stimulated my interest in political language and symbolism. Those early encounters with the ideas of Harold Lasswell and Walter Lippmann never quite left me, even while I was pursuing other questions in my research on social movements.

My interest in the mass media was kept alive by my frustrations in teaching undergraduates about what social scientists had to say on the subject. I remember dutifully informing them, in the early 1960s, how their beliefs about the influence of the mass media were greatly exaggerated; the real action was elsewhere, in enduring predispositions and social location. They, as dutifully, told me this was so on examinations, but they unconsciously demonstrated in their comments and observations that they felt something was missing. I was dismayed not because students did not really believe what the professor was telling them – an old story – but because I did not believe it myself.

These social science accounts were so unconvincing that, for a dozen years, I stopped teaching about the mass media and public opinion. My interest was recaptured by a new stream of work reflecting a social construction tradition on which this book draws. Under the impetus of work by Murray Edelman, Michael Schudson, Herbert Gans, and Todd Gitlin, among others, I rediscovered my teaching interest in this area in the late 1970s.

Concerns about the construction of meaning were percolating in my research as well. Working with Bruce Fireman, Stephen Rytina, and others on *Encounters with Unjust Authority* (1982), I found myself focusing heavily on the development of injustice frames in analyzing the process by which people organize for rebellious collective action. Framing was only one part of the story, but this interactive process of constructing meaning was clearly a critical ingredient in how our groups of participants handled the dilemmas of compliance that they confronted.

With the completion of this study of micromobilization processes, I began the inquiry reported here in collaboration with Andre Modigliani in the early 1980s at the University of Michigan. My interest in social movements was relatively muted at this early stage as we sought to trace the ebb and flow of how the mass media framed a series of issues historically. We intended to couple this analysis with focus group conversations of people discussing the same issues and carried out a pretest of several groups.

When I moved to Boston College in 1982, I started the Media Research and Action Project (MRAP), a continuing seminar on movements and media. The participants in this seminar, mostly graduate students in Boston College's program in Social Economy and Social Justice, are activist-scholars oriented to the concrete problems involved in mobilizing people for collective action. Participants are or have been involved in the Central American solidarity movement, the nuclear freeze movement, the movements for more equitable health care and decent housing, the labor movement, the movement against nuclear power, and others. Members of the seminar write papers, run workshops, and consult on media strategy for various movement organizations, as well as conduct research.

Academic studies of social movements in the 1980s were also reflecting a revival of interest in political consciousness. They frequently focused attention on the development of collective action frames, a particular type of political consciousness. The questions we pursued as the research continued at Boston College came to focus more and more on the ways in which people's understanding of the issues supported or failed to support collective action.

Both the original and developing concerns are reflected in this book. In the first part, I focus on collective action frames, exploring the presence of their individual elements in how issues are framed in the mass media and in how people talk about them. The process of constructing meaning is broader than collective action frames, however, and I step back from these concerns in the second half of the book to explore how people generally use the media along with other resources in understanding public issues.

This has been a long project, with many people to acknowledge. When Andre Modigliani and I began at Michigan, we started a continuing research seminar on Political Culture and Political Cognition. The sampling and preliminary content analysis of mass media materials were begun there. Linda Kaboolian did an outstanding job coordinating a massive data collection operation, and Catherine Rice did much of the work and supervised an array of work-study undergraduates who were involved in compiling and coding. Various graduate and postdoctoral students made important intellectual contributions, including Celeste Burke, Vic Burke, Jerry Himmelstein, Kathy Lasch, Rob Simmons, Marc Steinberg, and Daniel Steinmetz.

At Boston College, a new group of graduate students assumed various roles. Sharon Kurtz took on the heroic task of organizing some forty peer group conversations, with the endless logistics involved, and was unflagging in her commitment to quality control. Her intellectual integrity and uncompromising standards were a constant check on my temptation to become sloppy. Betsy Wright organized the first extensive pilot study of our peer group conversations in the Boston area. Bill Hoynes, Mary Murphy, and Jackie Orr worked extensively with the transcription and coding of the conversations, and their interpretations are frequently reflected in the points made in this book. Idella Hill did a skillful job as facilitator in the black groups. Charlotte Ryan, whose own work on media strategies for activists influenced the questions asked in this study, helped to draw out the emphasis on collective action frames. Other MRAP members including Patty Bergin, David Croteau, Paulo Donati, Janice Fine, Hannah Herzog, David Meyer, Ted Sasson, Cassie Schwerner, David Stuart, and James Vela-McConnell spent many hours discussing the design issues involved and reviewing earlier drafts of the chapters.

I circulated a very uneven first draft to colleagues at other universities. Responding to such requests is one of those collegial favors that requires making considerable time in an already busy schedule. Many of them made marginal comments, as well as writing long letters with suggestions and criticisms, most of which I took to heart. I am particularly grateful to Lance Bennett, Paul Burstein, Philip Converse, Zelda Gamson, Herbert Gans, Doris Graber, Jerry Himmelstein, Shanto Iyengar, Doug McAdam, Carol Mueller, Sidney Tarrow, and Charles Tilly for going beyond what I could reasonably expect in providing such detailed and thorough comments.

I am indebted to the National Science Foundation for supporting an unorthodox study with an unconventional methodology through a series of grants (SES80–1642, SES83–09343, SES85–09700, and SES86–42306). Finally, I owe an incalculable debt to the 200 people whose conversations ground the arguments presented here. I have changed their names to protect their anonymity, but their voices animate the pages of this book.

Chilmark, Massachusetts   William A. Gamson

1

Political consciousness

Place: A home in Mattapan, a town in the greater Boston area. Five adults, all of them black, are seated in a circle in the living room. A tape recorder and microphone rest on a table in their midst.
Time: February 1987
Characters:

Aretha, in her thirties, a facilitator hired by researchers at Boston College.
Vanessa Scott, in her forties, a teacher's aid.
Mr. B., in his fifties, the owner of a small restaurant.
Roy, in his twenties, a food service worker at a hospital.
Nicole, in her twenties, a manager at a fast food chain.

Aretha: Another topic in the news is the issue of affirmative action – programs for blacks and other minorities. There's a disagreement over what kind of programs should we have, if any, to increase the hiring, the promotion, and the college admissions of blacks and other minorities. When you think about the issue of affirmative action, what comes to mind?

Mr. B: Ms. Scott, you always like to lead off. [*laughter in group*] I love listening to your voice.

Vanessa: When I think about the issue of affirmative action, what comes to mind? Well, basically, affirmative action, the affirmative action programs were instituted to redress past wrongs, right? All right. And I think that – was it in the, was the sixties when Martin Luther King and his movement? [*nods from others*] Okay. I think that the gains that Martin Luther King made during that time have all been taken away. And now they've come out with this thing about, what is it –

Roy: Reverse discrimination.

Vanessa: *Reverse* discrimination – meaning that because there were certain slots of certain programs allocated for black people to bring up the quotas in certain positions, and so on and so forth – it's discriminating against white people. But you have to understand that for centuries, black people have been discriminated against, all right. And the only way that you can redress that – address that issue – *is* to set aside slots for black people or for minority people, where they can at least, you know, be on par somewhat with the larger society. When I say larger society, I mean white people.

The way I see it now, all the gains that we have made and all the things that we have fought for have been taken away by your president, Ronald Reagan. All right. And I see black people now going back to the time of slavery. Because that's what it – it's institutional slavery. I mean, we're no longer – we don't have signs on doors that say "Black here" and "White here." We don't lynch black people anymore. But it's institutionalized. We go to get a job, we can't get it.

And now we can't even get into college anymore, because the Reagan administration has really – he has – what is – cut down on the – eliminated the financial aid, which makes it impossible for poor people, and black people in particular, to even get into these institutions. Which means that if we cannot get the education, we cannot get the jobs. All right. So I see the doors being slammed in our faces again, and we're going back to the time of slavery.

Aretha: Any other –

Mr. B: – Ms. Scott?

Aretha: – Mr. B?

Mr. B: It couldn't have been said no better.

Vanessa: Why, thank you.

Roy: I agree with Vanessa's views, too. 'Cause if you look at some of Reagan's appointments to the Supreme Court, for instance Chief Justice William – [*pause*]

[*whispers*] Rehnquist.

Roy: Rehnquist – some of his views that – some of the things that he stood for – he was a very, I mean he *is* a very racist person. And I don't think he should have been nominated for the Chief Justice.

Vanessa: When you look at, you know, the Bakke decision. You know, this man brought charges that he was discriminated on the basis that he was white because he could not get into a medical school,

> okay – and that because they have set aside certain slots for
> black people. And when you read the information on this man –
> he was turned down from five medical schools, not because he
> was white but because the man was just not competent. Okay?
> Nicole: Not qualified.
> Vanessa: That was a whole turnaround, when that Bakke decision. That
> was the first time they brought a case about reverse discrimi-
> nation. How in the world can something be reversed when we've
> been discriminated against all our lives? It cannot be reversed.

This play is unrehearsed, with the characters playing themselves, writing the script as they proceed. Here we watch them attempting to make sense of a complex issue that has been the subject of public discourse since the late 1960s. And, in my judgment, succeeding quite well.

I say this not because I agree with the general thrust of their opinions on affirmative action – which I do. Even if I disagreed, I would acknowledge the coherence of their discussion. The conversation is informed and shaped by an implicit organizing idea or *frame*. This REMEDIAL ACTION frame (see Gamson and Modigliani, 1987) assumes that racial discrimination is not a remnant of the past but a continuing presence, albeit in subtle form. It rests on the abstract and difficult idea of institutional racism, which Vanessa skillfully articulates and makes understandable and concrete. In this frame, affirmative action programs are an expression of an ongoing, incomplete struggle for equal opportunity in American society.

Vanessa is clearly the senior author of this part of the script, but there is evidence that her frame is collective and a property of the group. She is prompted and encouraged at various points, and others express agreement and attempt to develop her remarks, working within the same frame. Notice how readily Roy presents the correct prompt, "reverse discrimination," a catch phrase from the public discourse on affirmative action, when Vanessa falters with a vague "this thing."

No one disagrees during this segment or introduces some alternative way of framing the affirmative action issue. Later on, some disagreements arise and the group discusses the plight of poor whites with some sympathy, but in ways that are consistent with the REMEDIAL ACTION frame.

In the segment quoted here and in other parts of the conversation, the group members draw on media-generated knowledge about affirmative action. Vanessa is able to invoke the Supreme Court's Bakke decision, which took place more than eight years earlier, and Roy alludes to information featured in William Rehnquist's recent confirmation hearing. Vanessa's rhetorical question about reverse discrimination does not sound very different from that of Benjamin Hooks, executive director of the National Association for the Advancement of Colored People (NAACP), on *CBS News* (July 4, 1978), who asked, "How can there be reverse discrimination when the black and brown population of California is 25 percent but the [minority] medical school population is only 3 percent?"

But the mass media are not the only source the players use in writing this script. In other parts of the conversation, they bring in the experiences of friends who cannot afford to go to college, as well as their own and others' work experiences. They draw on shared subcultural knowledge and popular wisdom about race relations in America. Mass media commentary is an important tool in their framing of affirmative action, but it is not the only one.

This book focuses on a particular kind of political consciousness, one that supports mobilization for collective action. It is a fleeting thing at best in this conversation, but one can see elements of it. First, the frame presented here has a strong injustice component, one that breeds a sense of moral indignation. It is carried in terms and phrases such as *institutional slavery, racism,* and *doors being slammed in one's face.* Furthermore, there is a sympathetic allusion to the civil rights movement, with its images of people acting collectively to bring about change, acting as agents and not merely as objects of history. Their conversation is divorced from an action context, and the civil rights movement is history; nevertheless, their frame has important collective action components.

Central themes

Three themes run throughout the analyses of political talk in this book:

a.   People are not so passive,
b.   People are not so dumb, and
c.   People negotiate with media messages in complicated ways that vary from issue to issue.

The phrases *not so passive* and *not so dumb* refer to the way mass publics frequently appear in social science portraits. Of course, this is another case of whether the glass is half-empty or half-full. One could read the script quoted earlier to make different points. Vanessa's grasp of history is so weak that she is unsure of the decade in which the civil rights movement reached its peak. Roy does not remember the name of the chief justice of the Supreme Court without prompting. The full transcript from which the excerpt is taken contains plenty of evidence of gaps in knowledge, confusion, and passivity if one is looking for them.

The story told here is a selective one, intended to correct or balance a misleading picture that emerges from much of the literature on public understanding of politics. "The problem of what the political world means to the average American citizen has been fairly well resolved in the minds of many political scientists," Bennett (1975, 4) writes in a book that challenges the conventional wisdom. "The consensus seems to be that political issues and events do not make much sense to most people." Neuman (1986) calls "the low level of political knowledge and the pervasive inattentiveness of the mass citizenry" a fundamental given of American electoral behavior. Converse (1975, 79) comments that "Surely the most familiar fact to arise from sample surveys in all countries is that popular levels of information about public affairs are, from the point of view of the informed observer, astonishingly low."

The mystery, for those who accept this conventional wisdom, is how people manage to have opinions about so many matters about which they lack the most elementary understanding. "The challenge of public opinion research," Iyengar (1991, 7) writes, "has been to reconcile the low levels of personal relevance and visibility of most political issues with the plethora of issue opinions . . . that large proportions of the population profess to hold. How do people manage to express opinions about civil rights legislation, economic assistance for the newly-freed nations of Eastern Europe, or President Bush's performance at the international drug summit, when these matters are so remote from matters of daily life and so few citizens are politically informed?"

If the mass citizenry appear as dolts in mainstream social science, they hardly fare better in critiques of American political institutions and culture. The critics, of course, don't blame people for their false consciousness and incomprehension. They are victims of a consciousness industry that produces and encourages a conveniently misleading and incomplete understanding of their world. The victims, in fact, make few appearances in analyses that emphasize the power of the sociocultural forces that put scales on their eyes. The implicit message seems to be: Of course people are confused and unable to make adequate sense of the world; what can you expect?

When critical accounts do take notice of the victims, they attend to the cognitive and linguistic incapacity of working people. Mueller (1973), drawing heavily on Habermas and other critical theorists, describes different forms of "distorted communication." *Constrained communication* denotes the successful attempts by corporate and governmental actors "to structure and limit public communication in order that their interests prevail." *Arrested communication,* however, refers to the "limited capacity of individuals and groups to engage in political communication because of the nature of their linguistic environment (a restricted speech code) and not because of any apparent political intervention" (Mueller, 1973, 19). This time, it is not the consciousness industry that victimizes them, but a class structure that denies them the linguistic and conceptual ability to discern the political nature of problems that are disguised as individual or technical ones. In sum, critics and defenders of American society argue over who is to blame for the ignorance of working people – but the message in this book is that they aren't so dumb.

I do not deny the handicaps or argue that people are well served by the mass media in their efforts to make sense of the world. The limitations that media critics have pointed out are real and are reflected in the frames that people are able to construct on many issues. Frames that are present in social movement discourse but are invisible in mass media commentary rarely find their way into their conversations. Systematic omissions make certain ways of framing issues extremely unlikely. Yet people read media messages in complicated and sometimes unpredictable ways, and draw heavily on other resources as well in constructing meaning.

Collective action frames

As a student of and a participant in various social movements, I have had a continuing concern with the development of a particular type of political consciousness – one that supports participation in collective action. There are many political movements that try in vain to activate people who, in terms of some allegedly objective interest, ought to be up in arms. Like many observers, I watch in dismay as people ignore causes that are dear to my heart, obstinately pursuing their daily lives rather than making history.

I know, of course, that collective action is more than just a matter of political consciousness. One may be completely convinced of the desirability of changing a situation while gravely doubting the possibility of changing it. Beliefs about efficacy are at least as important as understanding what social changes are needed. Furthermore, we know from many studies of social movements how important social networks are for recruiting people and drawing them into political action with their friends. People sometimes act first, and only through participating develop the political consciousness that supports the action.

Personal costs also deter people from participating, notwithstanding their agreement with a movement's political analysis. Action may be risky or, at a minimum, require foregoing other more pleasurable or profitable uses of one's time. Private life has its own legitimate demands, and caring for a sick child or an aging parent may take precedence over demonstrating for a cause in which one fully believes.

Finally, there is the matter of opportunity. Changes in the broader political structure and climate may open or close the chance for collective action to have an impact. External events and crises, broad shifts in public sentiment, and electoral changes and rhythms all have a heavy influence on whether political consciousness ever gets translated into action. In sum, the absence of a political consciousness that supports collective action can, at best, explain only one part of people's quiescence.

Lest we be too impressed by the inactivity of most people, the history of social movements is a reminder of those occasions when people do become mobilized and engage in various forms of collective action. In spite of all the obstacles, it occurs regularly and frequently surprises observers who were overly impressed by an earlier quiescence. These movements always offer one or more *collective action* frames. These frames, to quote Snow and Benford (1992), are "action oriented sets of beliefs and meanings that inspire and legitimate social movement activities and campaigns."[1] They offer ways of understanding that imply the need for and desirability of some form of action. Movements may have internal battles over which particular frame will prevail or may offer several frames for different constituencies, but they all have in common the implication that those who share the frame can and should take action.

This book looks carefully at three components of these collective action frames: (1) injustice, (2) agency, and (3) identity. The *injustice component* refers to the moral indignation expressed in this form of political consciousness. This is not merely a cognitive or intellectual judgment about what is equitable but also what cognitive psychologists call a *hot cognition* – one that is laden with emotion (see Zajonc, 1980). An injustice frame requires a consciousness of motivated human actors who carry some of the onus for bringing about harm and suffering.

The *agency component* refers to the consciousness that it is possible to alter conditions or policies through collective action. Collective action frames imply some sense of collective efficacy and deny the immutability of some undesirable situation. They empower people by defining them as potential agents of their own history. They suggest not merely that something can be done but that "we" can do something.

The *identity component* refers to the process of defining this "we," typically in opposition to some "they" who have different interests or values. Without an adversarial component, the potential target of collective action is likely to remain an abstraction – hunger, disease, poverty, or war, for example. Collective action requires a consciousness of human agents whose policies or practices must be changed and a "we" who will help to bring the change about.

It is easy to find evidence of all of these components when one looks at the pamphlets and speeches of movement activists. This book asks about their broader cultural presence in understanding public affairs. Looking closely at four quite different issues, it asks about the presence of these collective action components in both mass media commentary and the conversations of working people about them. To what extent do the dominant media frames emphasize injustice, for example? To what extent do the frames constructed in conversations emphasize this component? The answers to these questions tell us both about the mobilization potential in popular understanding of these issues and about the contribution of media discourse in nurturing or stifling it.

The four issues

Each of the four issues is the subject of a long and continuing public discourse: affirmative action, nuclear power, troubled industry, and Arab–Israeli conflict. Each is enormously complex in its own way and quite different from the others. Arab–Israeli conflict is relatively remote from the everyday experience of most people compared to affirmative action. Troubled industry and affirmative action have a high potential for tapping class and ethnic identifications, but nuclear power does not appear to engage any major social cleavage in American society. Nuclear power, more than the other issues, includes claims of privileged knowledge by technical experts.

In the course of the research, I learned what I should have known from the outset: These apparent characteristics of issues that my colleagues and I used in selecting them were our own social constructions and not an intrinsic property of the issues. Whether an issue touches people's daily lives, for example, depends on the meaning it has for them. One person's proximate issue is remote for the next person; with a vivid imagination or a convincing analysis of structural effects, an issue that might initially appear remote can be brought home to one's daily life. Similar observations can be made about the other dimensions as well. Whether an issue is technical or not is a matter of how it is framed, not an intrinsic characteristic; the relevance of social cleavages is a matter of interpretation.

This complicates the analysis but, in general, the issues did provide substantial variety. Our a priori construction of meaning on these issues was close to the mark for most people, in spite of a few surprises. The issues we thought most likely to engage social cleavages did; the ones that we guessed would be most proximate tended to tap people's daily experiences more than did the foreign policy issue. Most important, there was substantial variety in the appearance of collective action frames and in how people used mass media materials from issue to issue. The story of how people construct meaning is, in fact, a series of parallel stories in which patterns emerge through juxtaposing the process on different issues.

Labeling these issues is itself an act of framing. *Affirmative action* is not a neutral term to define this domain but reflects a labeling success by supporters of affirmative action programs.[2] The positive connotation of the label suggests the REMEDIAL ACTION frame described earlier. But once a term becomes established in public discourse, it is difficult even for those with a different frame to avoid it. To do so runs the risk that the listener won't know what one is talking about. Those with a different frame may try to distance themselves from such a label by the use of *so-called* and quotation marks, but if they want to communicate their subject matter to a general audience, they find it difficult to avoid established labels.

Hence, labels frequently and appropriately become the target of symbolic contests between supporters of different ways of framing an issue domain. Affirmative action programs developed out of the efforts of the civil rights movement, and the movement was successful in establishing its label in public discourse. Neoconservative and other challengers entered the fray later and sponsored an alternative label, *reverse discrimination*. But it was too late for this term to appear as a neutral description of the subject matter instead of as advocacy of a particular position on a controversial issue. *Affirmative action,* through conventional usage in public discourse as a descriptive phrase, had become the official label in spite of its lack of frame neutrality.

This is not an advocacy exercise, and frame-neutral labels are best for analytical purposes – to the extent that they exist. *Arab–Israeli conflict* and *nuclear power* are relatively problem-free labels. Those who see the Israeli–Palestinian conflict as the heart of the former issue might prefer to call it the *Arab–Israeli–Palestinian conflict,* but the label chosen here does not contradict such a framing. Similarly, those who see nuclear power and nuclear weapons production as integral parts of the same more general issue are not discouraged from doing so by the label chosen.

Troubled industry, on the other hand, is a more problematic label. There is no generally accepted term in the public discourse about this issue domain. We might have labeled it *plant closings,* for example, since this concrete manifestation is the form in which it frequently arises in media commentary and conversations. Perhaps the term used here already implies some form of industrial policy frame, plus a grand overview that diverts attention from the human consequences of the troubles. To mitigate this problem, when people were asked to discuss *troubled industries,* we provided three concrete examples of what the label was intended to cover – including the closing of a shipyard at Quincy, Massachusetts, the problems in the domestic automobile industry, and the closing of shoe and clothes factories in New England (see Appendix A for fuller details).

What follows

In order to follow the story, the reader needs to know more about the nature of the media materials and conversations examined here. Chapter 2 describes the media samples, the participants in the conversations, and the circumstances and setting in which their interaction took place. The media products are varied, including visual imagery as well as words, with television accounts and editorial cartoons as well as more conventional print media. The conversants are a broad and heterogeneous group of working people without higher education credentials and with only an average interest in public affairs. The methodological detail that professional scholars need to evaluate or replicate this work or to use it in their own research is included in Appendix A. This chapter attempts to establish both the generalizability and the limits of what I am claiming about political talk.

Part I explores the presence of collective action frames and their components in media discourse and popular conversations about the four issues. Chapter 3 addresses the presence of ideas of injustice and targets of moral indignation. There is a strong overall relationship between the prominence of injustice frames in media and popular discourse. On affirmative action, where the injustice theme is central and highly visible in the most prominent media frames, it is equally central and visible in the attempts of working people to make sense of the issue. On nuclear power and Arab–Israeli conflict, where injustice frames have low prominence in media discourse, conversations about these issues rarely express moral indignation. The causal relationship, however, is complicated and indirect.

Chapter 4 explores the ways in which the idea of grass-roots action by working people appears (or fails to appear) in media and popular discourse. The conversations examined provide abundant evidence of cynicism about politics and government, belief in its domination by big business, and the impossibility of working people like themselves altering the terms of their daily lives. Again, there is enormous variability among issues. Media coverage frequently and inadvertently keeps alive and helps transmit images of group protest. On nuclear power, in particular, there is a strong case that media discourse has been more of a help than a hindrance to the antinuclear movement. Media-amplified images of successful citizen action on one issue can be generalized and transferred to other issues. Despite the differences in media discourse, sympathetic discussions of collective action occur at least as often on troubled industry as they do on nuclear power.

Chapter 5 examines the extent to which media and popular discourse analyze issues in collective terms and, more specifically, the extent to which adversarial frames are emphasized. The foremost concerns of working people are with their everyday lives, but this does not mean that they think only as individuals and family members in making sense of political issues. Nor does the fact that they strongly affirm every person as a unique individual who should be judged as such preclude them from thinking collectively. A variety of larger collective identities are brought into play as they talk about politics. Chapter 6 examines the relationship among the three components of collective action frames and explores the implications of the findings for political mobilization.

Studying collective action frames forces one to recognize that, in many cases, one is dealing with more basic processes of constructing meaning. Part II explores these more generic issues about how people make sense of the news. Chapter 7 looks at the strategies they employ and, more specifically, how they combine (or fail to combine) media discourse, experiential knowledge, and popular wisdom in constructing an integrated frame. Which of these resources they rely on most varies from issue to issue.

On issues such as nuclear power and Arab–Israeli conflict, people almost always begin with media discourse; often they bring in popular wisdom as well, but they rarely integrate media frames with their experiential knowledge. On affirmative action, in contrast, they tend to begin with experiential knowledge but, in due course, bring in supporting media discourse as well.

Chapter 8 explores the importance of broader cultural resonances in enabling people to integrate different resources in support of the same overall framing of an issue. More specifically, it looks at broader cultural themes – for example, the cultural belief in technological progress and mastery over nature. Such themes are invariably linked to counterthemes: In this example, harmony with nature and technology run amok. When the framing of a particular issue draws on popular wisdom that resonates with themes or counterthemes, it is easier for people to connect media discourse with their own experiential knowledge. Furthermore, it is especially the more adversarial counterthemes rather than the mainstream ones that are central for working people's understanding on three of the four issues.

Chapter 9 explores the complicated connection between issue proximity and engagement and their relationship to the resource strategy used to understand an issue. Proximity, it turns out, is only one factor in promoting issue involvement, and an interest that is stimulated by media discourse can lead to increased attention to proximate consequences.

Chapter 10 attempts to weave together the different threads of the argument. More specifically, a resource strategy that integrates direct experiential knowledge and media discourse facilitates the adoption of an injustice frame. The injustice component, in turn, facilitates the adoption of other elements of a collective action frame.

2

Conversations and media discourse

Who are the people whose political talk is quoted throughout this book? What is the context of their conversations? What is the nature of the mass media discourse to which their conversations are being compared? These questions need to be answered before the reader can actively judge if the interpretations offered here make sense.

Working people

We conducted thirty-seven peer group conversations among 188 participants.[1] The following profile is based on information they provided in a questionnaire filled out in advance of the discussion. They are heterogeneous in race and gender but less so in age. Slightly more than half are white (54 percent) and female (56 percent). More than three-fourths are between the ages of twenty-five and forty-nine, with a median age of thirty-three, and only 1 percent are over sixty-five. In terms of religion, they are a mix of Catholics, Protestants, and those with no preference (plus one Jewish participant). Irish is the most frequent ethnicity among the whites, but they comprise only 15 percent of the total sample.

Almost 90 percent are currently employed in the paid labor market, with only 4 percent unemployed and 3 percent who are full-time homemakers. About 30 percent are in service jobs of some sort, and another 24 percent are clerical and office workers; only 12 percent work in manufacturing jobs. Cooks and kitchen workers, bus drivers, medical and lab technicians, nurses, firefighters, and auto service workers are some of the specific job categories that include five or more people.

For reasons discussed later, we deliberately tried to exclude from the sample people who were current students or college graduates. Groups were formed by recruiting a contact person, who then invited three to five friends. Although the contact person was not a college graduate or currently enrolled student, we could not fully control whom they invited. Hence, some 6 percent of the total sample are college graduates, but 58 percent have no education beyond high school or trade school. About one-third have some college or post–high school technical training short of a baccalaureate.

Labeling the sample population

Analysts concerned with a similar population have used a variety of terms, including *middle Americans, middle mass, mass public, working class, lower middle class,* or (the label I will use) *working people.* The population here is both broader and narrower than what Gans (1988) includes in his description of "middle Americans." In socioeconomic terms, Gans describes them as a combination of working-class and lower-middle-class families. "Middle Americans are . . . ranked above the lower class of poorly paid service workers, laborers, and the jobless poor, but below the upper middle class of generally affluent professionals, managers, and executives, as well as the upper class of top executives and coupon clippers" (1988, 7–8). In Gans's vision, this population is mainly white, since "many blacks and other racial minorities cannot yet afford its individualistic goals." For Gans, the category is more cultural than socioeconomic, defined in part by the values he attributes to it.

The target population we hoped to represent was somewhat less middle and more colorful than Gans's middle Americans. We made conscious efforts to include substantial numbers of black participants, and there are many poorly paid service workers in our sample, although very few jobless persons or members of a putative urban underclass. Nor did we make any a priori assumptions about individualistic goals or other values in defining the boundaries.

Structurally, our target population is *working class* in the sense that Wright (1985) uses the term. They are people who do not own the means of production, who sell their labor power and do not control the labor power of others. There are two reasons for not using the class label. First, from historic usage, it conjures up an image of industrial factory workers engaged in primary production, but this is a misleading way of describing our sample. Most of them are in the secondary labor market, engaged in service or office jobs rather than in manufacturing.

An even more compelling reason is the evidence that the class term is not one they would be most likely to use to describe themselves. Halle (1984) observed and interviewed workers in a New Jersey chemical plant. "Blue collar [male] workers in America," Halle writes (1984, 204), "refer to themselves as 'working men' but rarely as 'working class.' " When they used the term *class,* they focused on their life outside of the workplace – especially where they live, their standard of living, and their lifestyle. Since these were well-paid industrial workers, they tended to live in middle-class neighborhoods with other people of similar income, only a minority of whom were blue-collar workers.

The distinction is less sharp in our sample, where the working people are less affluent and many live in neighborhoods they might think of as working class, but they more often refer to themselves as "working people" than as "working class." Since I am attempting to understand how the world looks from their standpoint, it seems wise to begin by using their own natural language to label the population segment they represent.

Typicality

In Appendix A, I discuss various methodological issues concerning how well we succeeded in representing working people in the Boston area. The most important bias is the underrepresentation of an apolitical stratum who simply don't attend to politics at all.[2]

Certain contextual issues would remain even if we had a perfect random sample of all Boston area working people. Boston has its own special history and set of geographical factors that influence the issues studied. Residents of cities that did not experience the bitter racial clashes over school busing in the 1970s would not necessarily discuss the affirmative action issue in the same way; strong regional differences are central to the history of race relations in the United States. The Seabrook and Pilgrim nuclear reactors are close to Boston and received much local publicity for a number of years, creating a special context for the discussion of nuclear power. The unemployment rate in the Boston area was only 4 percent at the time of these conversations on troubled industry.

The timing of these conversations played a role on all issues. They occurred soon after the Chernobyl nuclear accident and at a moment when affirmative action was under challenge by the Reagan administration; before the *intifada* but not long after the *Achille Lauro* hijacking and the bombing of Libya. These contextual characteristics of time and location influence the extent to which results can be generalized, independently of the representativeness of the sample.

Recruiting participants

We recruited contact people at multiple sites and ended up with participants from thirty-five different neighborhoods or separately incorporated communities in the Boston metropolitan area. We chose public sites where a recruitment table for the project was not out of place, and where it was possible to carry on a conversation and establish some rapport with potential recruits. This led us to focus on neighborhood and community events of various sorts – festivals, picnics, fairs, and flea markets, for example. We also posted notices of the research, with a phone number to contact us at various neighborhood and work sites. We avoided recruiting at any event or site associated with a political cause or tendency, since we were eager to avoid any kind of political atypicality.

To minimize the chances of obtaining a sample biased toward those with a special interest in discussing "issues in the news," we paid people enough to make the monetary incentive attractive. The desire to earn a little money, we reasoned, was a better motive for participating than the more atypical motive of a special interest in politics. Judging from the combination of self-reported interest on the questionnaire and the discussions themselves, there is no evidence that our participants were unusually high in political interest, but there is good reason to suspect that we lost the apolitical end of the spectrum. Only 2 percent of our sample claimed that they follow the news "hardly at all." For some people, the risk of embarrassment or humiliation inherent in talking about politics for a gallery of university researchers isn't worth the modest payment involved.

Conversations as the unit

The unit used here is always the group conversation rather than the individual. Beginning with a contact person and including his or her friends did not always produce a homogeneous group. American society being what it is, it should come as no surprise that the race of the contact person generally determined the racial composition of the group and that more than 90 percent of our groups were racially homogeneous; of the thirty-seven groups, seventeen were all white, seventeen were all black, and only three were interracial.

Both men and women, however, tended to produce mixed gender groups, with only four exclusively male and eight exclusively female groups among the thirty-seven. Another eight had only a single male or a single female, but the numbers here are small enough to limit the extent to which we can detect gender differences in the conversations being analyzed. On other variables, a limited number of other groups may have shared an occupation, a neighborhood, or some other salient characteristic, but none of these patterns occurred with sufficient frequency to provide a separate category for analysis.

Context of the conversations

Most people do not spontaneously sit down with their friends and acquaintances and have a serious discussion for more than an hour on different issues in the news. We can still learn a great deal from people's efforts to deal with an unfamiliar situation, but it requires us to be sensitive to the norms governing it and how they differ from other similar social situations in which working people commonly find themselves. Some norms are carried over from other interaction settings and apply here as well, but others are distinctive to this particular type of conversation and their generalizability to other settings is more problematic.

The peer group conversations used here are a variant of the more generic technique of *focus groups*. The strengths and weaknesses of this method are discussed in detail in Appendix A. The greatest advantage is that it allows us to observe the process of people constructing and negotiating shared meaning, using their natural vocabulary.

We were concerned with the threatening nature of the task for working people who do not normally carry on a sustained conversation about public issues. By going to participants instead of having them come to us, we hoped to put the interaction with the facilitator on a more equal footing. Most of the groups were run in people's homes, where our facilitator and observer were present as guests, even though the participants were being paid and did not control the topic of conversation.

We were also concerned that a university or other bureaucratic setting might inadvertently cue a particular style of technomanagerial discourse embodied, for example, in cost–benefit analysis. By holding discussions on the participants' own turf among people they knew and felt comfortable with, we hoped to minimize some of the constraints in the situation and to make the participants less fearful that they would expose themselves as political incompetents.

To encourage conversation rather than a facilitator-centered group interview, the facilitator was instructed to break off eye contact with the speaker as early as politeness allowed and to look to others rather than responding herself when someone finished a comment. We relied mainly on two facilitators, both women, matching their race with that of the participants. When substitutes were occasionally necessary, we kept the race and gender of the facilitator constant to avoid introducing extraneous variables that might influence the course of the conversations.

If a discussion got off the track, the facilitator moved it back on by going to the next question on the list. But we encouraged a conservative approach to what was considered off the track since, in negotiating meaning on any given issue, participants typically brought in other related issues. Decisions on what is or is not relevant are intimately tied to how an issue is framed, and the facilitator tried to avoid imposing or suggesting any particular frame except when presenting the relevant cartoons (see the following discussion and Appendix B).

Because of our concern with inadvertently suggesting frames to participants, the facilitators were instructed to follow a standard script, especially in describing each issue under discussion (see Appendix A for details). They aimed for a discussion of approximately twenty minutes on each issue, using a series of follow-up questions to the open-ended one with which we began each discussion. Once most people had responded to a question and no one else sought the floor, the facilitator moved to the next question on the list. These follow-up questions also served as a reminder of the issue in the event that a discussion had rambled.

One follow-up question asked whether people were personally affected by the issue, a second asked whether larger groups stood to gain or lose, and a "cartoon" question showed them a series of four or five cartoons on each issue (see Appendix B). Each cartoon represented a different way of framing the issue in public discourse. Finally, they were asked for their judgment of what should be done about the issue.[3]

The transcripts of these discussions provided the basic texts that are analyzed, along with media discourse, in the remainder of this book. Written transcriptions involve several levels of data transformation. Being there, one uses body language, facial expression, and other nonverbal cues to supplement the meaning of the words used; even videotape loses much of this detail. Audiotape, which we used, captures voice intonations and emphasis, much of which is lost in a written transcript. I felt the limitations of written transcripts especially strongly in attempting to capture expressions of moral indignation, but the losses are less relevant for many other variables.

Interaction norms

Morgan (1988, 16) argues that "the single largest disadvantage of focus groups in comparison to participant observation [is this]: [T]hey are fundamentally unnatural social settings." But if one looks at this distinction between "natural" and "unnatural" from the standpoint of participants, it is by no means clear. Most people are aware of the existence of a set of interactions between members of the public such as themselves and political pollsters, market researchers, survey research interviewers, journalists, and talk show hosts. Many have been involved in such interactions in the past.

We introduced ourselves to them as researchers from Boston College who were doing public opinion research on people's views on various issues in the news. From their standpoint, the researchers in this project were part of a broad category of people who, for a variety of reasons, want some kind of information from people like themselves. All of these interactions are "unnatural" in the sense that they do not occur spontaneously without the contrivance of a researcher. But work-based interactions do not occur either without some employer who contrives to bring people together to do a job.

The best way to approach this issue is to put aside the red herring of "naturalness," analyzing the special features of an interaction situation to determine the particular norms operating. The relevant norms are those that might be influencing the phenomena under study and vary as the focus of research changes.

Sociable public discourse

The essence of public discourse is the sense of speaking to a gallery. People who respond to a survey are not just telling the interviewer their opinions but recognize that they are speaking to a broader audience who will be presented with the survey results. The interviewer is a medium to this gallery. Even a personal diary, when written with some thought of eventual publication, is a form of public discourse in this sense.

The peer group conversations that we conducted clearly have this element of public discourse. The situation was defined as producing a conversation for a gallery, and the fact was underlined by the presence of a tape recorder and the payment the participants received for their effort. If they asked what would be done with the information being collected, they were told that "the sociology professor who is carrying out the research intends to write a book about it but he won't use anyone's name."[4]

There are frequent comments that indicate an awareness by participants that they are speaking on the record, frequently in the context of using obscenities. This does not act as much of a general inhibitor, but it changes what is emphasized; certain remarks that people might make in a strictly private discourse violate norms of public discourse. Other remarks are so clearly addressed to the gallery that they would be completely inappropriate in private discourse.

This difference is clearest with respect to affirmative action discussions. In black groups, for example, even though everyone present was black, including the facilitator and the observer, participants were very much aware of a white gallery. They knew the research was being carried out at

Boston College, a university with about a 2 percent black enrollment. This means, for example, that criticism of black people that they might have felt free to make among themselves may seem disloyal in this context.

Similarly, in white groups, the presence of a gallery was likely to constrain overt expressions of racism. Racial epithets that might be used in strictly private discourse and might even be normative in some subgroups are generally recognized as inappropriate in public discourse. Remarks that might be interpreted by an unseen gallery as prejudiced are more likely to be prefaced by disclaimers or additional remarks to make such an interpretation less likely.

Although the interaction setting has these elements of public discourse, it also has many of the elements of a sociable interaction. These working people have few occasions to participate in public discourse but many in which they converse with familiar acquaintances or friends at work, parties, and other social settings. They have practical knowledge from these settings of how to carry on a sociable conversation that is jointly maintained by the participants and an implicit awareness of the norms governing such conversations. They quickly discover that many of the same conversational techniques and resources that they use in these other settings work here as well and that they are collectively quite competent in the task we have set for them. Hence, the peer group conversations are really a combination: *sociable public discourse.*[5]

The conversations are held in a living room setting with refreshments, thereby cueing norms of sociability. At the same time, some of the norms of social interaction are clearly violated. Sociable talk among familiar acquaintances typically excludes serious conversation about public affairs. In sociable interaction, the conversation is a resource for expressing self and group solidarity and for achieving conviviality, not an end in itself.[6] Rapid changes of topic occur because any single topic is likely to exclude some people or give them insufficient opportunity to express themselves.

The conversations produced here are constrained by the requirement of collectively producing a serious conversation on topics that are not of the participants' own choosing. Within that constraint, however, they are left to their own devices, many of which transfer from sociable interaction among familiar acquaintances. Eisenstadt (1984) suggests two important ones that seem especially likely to apply to the conversations here:

1. Legendary conversational style. Serious public discourse is oriented to arguments that marshall facts and weigh the advantages and disadvantages of alternatives; it claims to represent an external reality accurately and objectively. Sociable interaction is oriented to fantasy and play, and much that is said is not intended to be taken literally.

Eisenstadt and her colleagues have identified a third style of conversation, combining elements of both, which they labeled *legendary*. In this style, "facts and interpretations of facts were blended to give a pattern of belief which was dramatic, satisfying, consistent with other legends, and more or less true; but truth was not particularly relevant. The power of a legend depended not upon its referential accuracy, but upon the extent to which it could generate consensus and enlist the imaginative energies of participants" (1984, 41). Pointing out inaccuracies in the facts utilized in legends is conversationally inappropriate and likely to be regarded as nit-picking that misses the point.

This legendary style, Eisenstadt argues, is especially likely to be used among familiar acquaintances. Furthermore, the combination of sociable and public discourse would appear especially likely to trigger it, since it falls between the playful style of the former and the serious style of the latter. As we will see in the chapters that follow, it makes frequent appearances in the conversations studied here.

2. Cynical chic. This term comes from Eliasoph (1991), who credits it to the Rev. F. Forrester Church. "Cynical chic speakers," she writes, "capitalize on ignorance and powerlessness, making them seem intentional, even exaggerating them. They strenuously, though sometimes with subtlety, assert that they do not care, that they have not been fooled into wasting their time on something they cannot influence. . . ."

Eliasoph recorded on-the-street interviews with people on the Iran-Contra affair and other issues and found many respondents who adopted this irreverent style. Their purpose in the interaction, she argues, was "in showing distance between themselves and the world of politics; in saving face as individuals; in absolving themselves of responsibility for what they saw as the absurdity and corruption of political life." The tone was ironic, providing a safe distance and an air of condescension toward politicians and public life.[7]

Because of its self-defensive function, cynical chic is more common among familiar acquaintances than among close friends and intimates. And it seems especially likely to be present in sociable public discourse, where there is a risk of being taken in and of looking foolish in front of a gallery. Hence, our peer group conversations actively encourage this discourse style compared, for example, to private conversation among close friends.

Participant assessments

At the end of the long discussion, we asked participants about their reactions. Almost 90 percent of the groups made some comment expressing
positive feelings about the experience. The exceptions did not express
negative feelings but stuck to specific suggestions without offering a more
general assessment. Norms of politeness to guests may help to account for
some of the reassurance they provided, but their comments typically reflect
satisfaction with their own performance in the task of producing a good
conversation.

About 20 percent of the groups also described some initial nervousness
or anxiety, but all but one explicitly indicated that these feelings passed
as they "got into it." Several groups mentioned that talking to people they
knew in familiar surroundings was very helpful in making them feel comfortable in the discussion. They often compared it with other public or
sociable discourse situations such as discussions in church or union groups,
discussions on a bus or in a barroom, or classroom discussions. The following excerpts, from three different groups, reflect a widely shared, consensual view of the experience.

> *Characters:*
>
> *Carol, a bookkeeper, in her thirties.*
> *Lil, a data entry clerk, in her twenties.*
> *Cissy, a bus driver, in her forties.*

Carol: As far as a group like this is concerned, it's much more relaxing
       'cause you know everybody.
Lil: Yeah, that's true.
Carol: Don't have to worry about anybody looking at you, and making –
Cissy: – say the wrong words. And we all go on the same level.

> *Characters:*
>
> *Bill, a firefighter, in his forties.*
> *Ken, a firefighter, in his thirties.*
> *Larry, a firefighter, in his fifties.*
> *Ron, a firefighter, in his forties.*
> *Paul, a firefighter, in his fifties.*
> *Joe, a firefighter, in his fifties.*

Bill: It's interesting. I've never had – um – such intriguing conversation.
       For quite a while. I don't socialize that much, other than in the
       firehouse. It's nice to sit down and express different views on –

Ken: You're on tape and the feds are going to get everything you said.
(laughter)

Larry: It was a first time for me, but I sort of enjoyed it.

Ron: I felt comfortable.

Bill: I've been enlightened.

Paul: I enjoyed it.

Ken: I didn't pull any punches anyways, so it's nice to be able to get other people –

Joe: You didn't throw any either.
(laughter)

Characters:

Ida, a bookkeeper, in her late sixties.
Nancy, a secretary, in her forties.
Arlene, a bookkeeper, in her forties.
Ruth, an office supervisor, in her fifties.

Ida: This was wonderful.

Nancy: Invite us back on different topics. This is really interesting because I tell you, I hate to go out and sit around and talk because most conversations with the people I chum with are totally boring.

Ida: Oh, poor baby.

Nancy: It's usually gossip, and I hate gossip.

Arlene: That is boring.

Nancy: This was the most intelligent night for a long time –

Ruth: I'm left with a definite feeling of how inadequate my knowledge is on any of those topics, and maybe you've accomplished something on that tonight. Maybe the next time I pick up the paper, I'll look at whatever the article is a little differently.

Nancy: Um hum.

In sum, the peer group conversations used here represent a hybrid form of social interaction: sociable public discourse among familiar acquaintances. The public discourse component means that participants are aware of speaking for a gallery, not merely to the other people in the room. Furthermore, this is an educated gallery represented by university researchers, and, for the black groups, they are conscious of speaking to an unseen *white* public.

The purpose of creating a conversation for others clearly marks it as different from a purely sociable interaction. Norms about choosing and changing the topic of conversation that normally apply are suspended here.

But other norms of sociable interaction among familiar acquaintances are carried over. For example, a *legendary* style that combines elements of serious and playful conversation in a complex amalgam seems especially appropriate for sociable public discourse; similarly, a cynical chic posture that allows speakers to distance themselves from politics lends itself to this legendary style and is encouraged by the norms of this interaction.

Participants' comments support the idea that they view the situation as combining familiar and unusual elements. Obviously, their typical sociable interactions are not constrained in the way these are, but this has some positive aspects. Norms against serious conversation may have some elements of pluralistic ignorance, and it comes as a relief to some people when this particular norm is suspended. Furthermore, awareness of a gallery increases the sense of being taken seriously by others, and with good reason. University researchers have sought them out, come to their homes, and are paying them to express their views.

Media discourse

Each policy issue has a relevant public discourse – a particular set of ideas and symbols that are used in various public forums to construct meaning about it. This discourse evolves over time, providing interpretations and meanings for newly occurring events. An archivist might catalog the metaphors, catch phrases, visual images, moral appeals, and other symbolic devices that characterize it. The catalog would be organized, of course, since the elements are clustered and held together by a central organizing frame.

This discourse is carried on in many forums – conferences, speeches, hearings, books and magazines, television, movies, and newspapers. It does not confine itself neatly to entities labeled "news and public affairs," but rudely enters advertising and entertainment as well. A wide variety of media messages can act as teachers of values, ideologies, and beliefs and provide images for interpreting the world, whether or not the designers are conscious of this intent.

National, general audience media are only one set of forums, but their discourse dominates the terms in which the issue is discussed. They serve a complex dual role. On the one hand, they are producers of the discourse. Journalists contribute their own frames and invent their own clever catch phrases and metaphors, drawing on a popular culture that they share with their audience. On the other hand, they are also, to quote Gurevitch and

Levy (1985, 19), "a site on which various social groups, institutions, and ideologies struggle over the definition of social reality."

Media discourse is represented in this book by four national media forums: television network news, national news magazine accounts, syndicated editorial cartoons, and syndicated opinion columns.[8] Since media frames are conveyed indirectly through visual imagery as much as through information, it was important to include various modes, not simply words.

Public discourse must be studied historically; the discourse of the moment cannot be understood outside of this necessary context. Media discourse on each issue is a continuing story that develops over time. Only in looking at the whole story can we see ways of thinking and assumptions, once taken for granted, that are now contested.

Stories have beginnings and ends, but real life is not so simple. The story on these issues ends in the present – a temporary stopping place, since all of these issues remain on the public agenda. The research extended over a decade and "the present" kept moving forward, forcing us to collect additional materials on three of our four issues to keep up with these unending sagas. The apparatus that we originally assembled to collect materials was no longer intact, and we were inevitably forced to compromise on less complete samples as we updated.

The beginning of the story posed problems of a different sort. The point at which a story begins is very much a question of how the issue is framed. Does the story of Arab–Israeli conflict, for example, begin 2,000 years ago with the Judean wars against the Roman Empire and the subsequent dispersion of the Jews, or in the nineteenth century with the beginning of the Zionist movement, or in 1948, or 1967, or at some other point? How one answers this question reflects particular ways of framing the issue, and choices of when to begin a story are never frame neutral.

In this case, the research purpose made the choice only slightly less arbitrary. We were interested in public discourse within the life experience of adults living in the mid-1980s, and this led us to go back no further than the end of World War II for the nuclear power and Arab–Israeli conflict issues. For affirmative action, we began the story with President Lyndon B. Johnson's 1965 executive order, and our troubled industry story began only in 1971, when the Lockheed Aircraft Company sought help from the federal government.

Having chosen a beginning and an end, we would have preferred a continuous sample, a movie of the ongoing public discourse over the entire period. Since we also sought several different types of media texts to offset the idiosyncracies of any particular medium, this would have created overwhelming practical obstacles. Our compromise solution was to focus on what Chilton (1987) calls "critical discourse moments" that make discourse on an issue especially visible. They stimulate commentary in various public forums by sponsors of different frames, journalists, and other observers.

On nuclear power, for example, we sampled in December 1953, when President Dwight D. Eisenhower addressed the United Nations on nuclear power, presenting what media discourse labeled his "atoms for peace" speech. In it, he proposed to make American nuclear technology available to an international agency that would attempt to develop peaceful uses for nuclear energy. There were no critical discourse moments on nuclear power in the 1960s. In the 1970s, we sampled a period in 1977 in which two relevant events coincided: President Jimmy Carter's initiative to gain international support for controlling the spread of nuclear technology and the arrest and detention for two weeks of more than 1,400 antinuclear demonstrators who occupied the site where the Seabrook, New Hampshire, nuclear reactor was being constructed. Our most recent critical discourse moments included the accidents at Three Mile Island in 1979 and at Chernobyl in 1986. The complete set of critical discourse moments used for the four issues studied here is included in Appendix A.

Critical discourse moments are especially appropriate for studying media discourse. With continuing issues, journalists look for 'pegs' – that is, topical events that provide an opportunity for broader, more long-term coverage and commentary. These pegs provide us with a way of identifying those time periods in which efforts at framing issues are especially likely to appear.

Critical discourse moments create some perturbation. Sponsors of particular frames feel called upon to reassert them and to interpret the latest development in light of them. This characteristic allowed us to focus our sampling on periods when commentary was especially dense. But it has a disadvantage as well: We ended with a small series of snapshots of media discourse at irregular intervals instead of the more desirable movie.[9]

If the media discourse sampled here does a reasonably good job of representing the public discourse on these issues, it is irrelevant that the people carrying on the conversations may have encountered only a tiny fraction of it at best. They do not confine themselves to national media coverage of an issue but draw from many other issues, from advertising and movies, from local media, and from media-generated stories relayed by friends in a two-step or multistep flow.

I have no idea of where Vanessa learned about the Supreme Court's Bakke decision, for example, but her exact source is not relevant for the questions addressed in this book. The Bakke decision is a much discussed critical moment in the public discourse on affirmative action, and Vanessa is drawing on this public discourse, regardless of the mechanism by which she first encountered it.

Media discourse, then, is a meaning system in its own right, independent of any claims that one might make about the causal effect on public opinion. Certain ways of framing issues gain and lose prominence over time, and some assumptions are shared by all frames. National media discourse, although only one part of public discourse, is a good reflection of the whole. We need to understand what this public discourse says about an issue, since it is a central part of the reality in which people negotiate meaning about political issues.

I

Collective action frames

This part explores the presence of collective action frames in media discourse and in conversations about the four issues. Chapter 3 examines the presence of ideas of injustice and targets of moral indignation. An injustice frame requires a consciousness of motivated human actors who carry some of the onus for bringing about harm and suffering.

Chapter 4 explores the consciousness that it is possible to alter conditions or policies through collective action. Collective action frames deny the immutability of some undesirable situation and define people as potential agents of their own history. They suggest not merely that something can be done but that "we" can do something. More specifically, this chapter examines the ways in which the idea of grass-roots action by working people appears (or fails to appear) in media discourse and conversations.

Chapter 5 explores the process of defining a "we" in opposition to some "they" who have different interests and values. It examines the extent to which media and popular discourse define issues in collective terms and, more specifically, the extent to which adversarial frames are emphasized. Finally, Chapter 6 looks at the relationship among the three components of collective action frames and considers the implications of the findings for collective action.

3

Injustice

Students of social movements with different orientations emphasize a strong injustice component in the political consciousness that supports collective action. Turner and Killian (1987, 242) argue that "a movement is inconceivable apart from a vital sense that some established practice or mode of thought is wrong and ought to be replaced. . . . The common element in the norms of most, and probably all, movements is the conviction that existing conditions are unjust."

Moore (1978, 88) agrees. "Any political movement against oppression has to develop a new diagnosis and remedy for existing forms of suffering, a diagnosis and remedy by which this suffering stands morally condemned." Similarly, McAdam (1982, 51) argues that "before collective action can get underway, people must collectively define their situations as unjust. . . ."

The main challenge on this point comes from those who accept that a sense of grievance is necessary but argue that it is so ubiquitous that it lacks any explanatory value. Hence, Oberschall (1973, 133–4) concedes that sentiments of "being wronged are . . . frequently present in the lower orders" but aren't very important, since they "can be easily linked with the more elaborate ideologies and world views." McCarthy and Zald (1977, 1215) suggest that there is always enough unhappiness to supply the grassroots support for a movement and, hence, the only explanatory power is in how "grievances and discontent may be defined, created, and manipulated by issue entrepreneurs and organizations."

But the cynical view that grievances have little explanatory value, since it is so easy for leaders or organizations to link more elaborate world views with the sufferings of the "lower orders," has not prevailed. Most contemporary analysts treat it as no simple matter to explain how the indignities of daily life are sometimes transformed into a shared grievance with a focused target of collective action.

Different emotions can be stimulated by perceived inequities – cynicism, bemused irony, resignation. But injustice focuses on the righteous anger that puts fire in the belly and iron in the soul. Injustice, as I argued earlier, is a hot cognition, not merely an abstract intellectual judgment about what is equitable.

The heat of a moral judgment is intimately related to beliefs about what acts or conditions have caused people to suffer undeserved hardship or loss. The critical dimension is the abstractness of the target. Vague, abstract sources of unfairness diffuse indignation and make it seem foolish. We may think it dreadfully unfair when it rains on our parade, but bad luck or nature is a poor target for an injustice frame. When we see impersonal, abstract forces as responsible for our suffering, we are taught to accept what cannot be changed and make the best of it. Anger is dampened by the unanswerable rhetorical question: Who says life is fair?

At the other extreme, if one attributes undeserved suffering to malicious or selfish acts by clearly identifiable persons or groups, the emotional component of an injustice frame will almost certainly be there. Concreteness in the target, even when it is misplaced and directed away from the real causes of hardship, is a necessary condition for an injustice frame. Hence, competition over defining targets is a crucial battleground in the development or containment of injustice frames.

More specifically, an injustice frame requires that motivated human actors carry some of the onus for bringing about harm and suffering. These actors may be corporations, government agencies, or specifiable groups rather than individuals. They may be presented as malicious, but selfishness, greed, and indifference may be sufficient to produce indignation.

An injustice frame does not require that the actors who are responsible for the condition be autonomous. They may be depicted as constrained by past actions of others and by more abstract forces – as long as they have some role as agents in bringing about or continuing the wrongful injury. From the standpoint of those who wish to control or discourage the development of injustice frames, symbolic strategies should emphasize abstract targets that render human agency as invisible as possible. Reification helps to accomplish this by blaming actorless entities such as "the system," "society," "life," and "human nature."

As Sennett (1980, 180) points out, "The language of bureaucratic power is often couched in the passive voice, so that responsibility is veiled." Any given agent of an authority system can disclaim responsibility easily by passing the buck. For subordinates, "I'm only following the rules; I don't make them" is the classic ploy. Even those at the top can externalize a "system" that binds them as well as all other participants and is beyond anyone's ability to alter.

The late Saul Alinsky pinpoints the problem for organizers in his *Rules for Radicals* (1972, 130–1):

In a complex urban society, it becomes increasingly difficult to single out who is to blame for any particular evil. There is a constant, and somewhat legitimate, passing of the buck.... One big problem is a constant shifting of responsibility from one jurisdiction to another – individuals and bureaus one after another disclaim responsibility for particular conditions, attributing the authority for any change to some other force.

If reification does not prevent the development of an injustice frame, a second line of defense involves accepting human agency but diverting the focus to external targets or internal opponents. Righteous anger cannot always be prevented, but it may still be channeled safely and perhaps even used to further one's purposes.

For those who would encourage collective action, these strategies of social control provide a formidable dilemma. The conditions of people's daily lives are, in fact, determined by abstract sociocultural forces that are largely invisible to them. Critical views of "the system," however accurate, may still encourage reification just as much as benign ones as long as they lack a focus on human actors.

The antidote to excessive abstraction has its own problems. In concretizing the targets of an injustice frame, there is a danger that people will miss the underlying structural conditions that produce hardship and inequality. They may exaggerate the role of human actors, failing to understand broader structural constraints, and misdirect their anger at easy and inappropriate targets.

There is no easy path between the cold cognition of an overdetermined structural analysis and the hot cognition of misplaced concreteness. As long as human actors are not central in understanding the conditions that produce hardship and suffering, we can expect little righteous anger. Targets of collective action will remain unfocused. As long as moral indignation is narrowly focused on human actors without regard to the broader structure in which they operate, injustice frames will be a poor tool for collective action, leading to ineffectiveness and frustration, perhaps creating new victims of injustice.

To sustain collective action, the targets identified by the frame must successfully bridge abstract and concrete. By connecting broader sociocultural forces with human agents who are appropriate targets of collective action, one can get the heat into the cognition. By making sure that the concrete targets are linked to and can affect the broader forces, one can make sure that the heat isn't misdirected in ways that will leave the underlying source of injustice untouched.

Injustice in media discourse

Media practices have a double-edged effect, both stimulating and discouraging injustice frames. As we will see shortly, the extent to which they do one or the other differs substantially from issue to issue. But some framing practices cut across issues and operate more generally.

Some encouragement of injustice frames is built into the narrative form that dominates news reporting. Most journalists understand that news writing is storytelling, but sometimes it is made explicit. Epstein (1973, 241) describes a memo that Reuven Frank sent to his staff at NBC News. "Every news story should, without any sacrifice of probity or responsibility, display the attributes of fiction, of drama." Stories were to be organized around the triad of "conflict, problem, and denouement," with "rising action" building to a climax.

This dependence on the narrative form has implications for promoting an injustice frame. Narratives focus attention on motivated actors rather than structural causes of events. As new events unfold and changes appear in the conditions of people's daily lives, human agents are typically identified as causal agents in a morality play about good and evil or honesty and corruption. The more abstract analysis of sociocultural forces favored by social scientists is deemphasized, if it enters the story at all.

Media emphasis on narrative form, then, tends to concretize targets in ways that would appear to abet injustice frames. Far from serving the social control needs of authorities in this instance, media coverage frequently gives people reasons to get angry at somebody. Of course, that "somebody" need not be the real source of grievance at all but merely some convenient surrogate. Nevertheless, however righteous indignation may get channeled, media discourse on many issues inadvertently helps to generate it by providing concrete targets. Hence, it is an obstacle to social control strategies that diffuse a sense of injustice by moving the causes of undeserved hardship beyond human agency.

At the same time, the personalization of responsibility may have the effect of blurring broader power relations and the structural causes of a bad situation. Many writers have argued that the total media experience leads to the fragmentation of meaning. News comes in quotations with ever shorter sound bites. The preoccupation with immediacy results in a proliferation of fleeting, emphemeral images that have no ability to sustain any coherent organizing frame to provide meaning over time. The "action news" formula adopted by many local news programs packs thirty to forty short, fast items to fill a twenty-two-and-a-half-minute "newshole." "One minute-thirty for World War III," as one critic described it (Diamond, 1975).

Bennett (1988) analyzes the news product as a result of journalistic practices that combine to produce fragmentation and confusion. "The fragmentation of information begins," he argues, "by emphasizing individual actors over the political contexts in which they operate. Fragmentation is then heightened by the use of dramatic formats that turn events into self-contained, isolated happenings." The result is news that comes to us in "sketchy dramatic capsules that make it difficult to see the connections across issues or even to follow the development of a particular issue over time." Hence, the structure and operation of societal power relations remain obscure and invisible.

Iyengar (1991) provides experimental evidence on how the episodic nature of media reporting on most issues affects attributions of responsibility. He contrasts two forms of presentation – the "episodic" and the "thematic." The episodic form – by far the more common one – "takes the form of a case study or event-oriented report and depicts public issues in terms of concrete instances." In contrast, the much rarer thematic form emphasizes general outcomes, conditions, and statistical evidence.

By altering the format of television reports about several different political issues as presented to experimental and control groups, Iyengar shows how people's attributions of responsibility are affected. More specifically, he shows that exposure to the episodic format makes viewers less likely to hold public officials accountable for the existence of some problem and less likely to hold them responsible for alleviating it.

The implication of this line of argument is that if people simply relied on the media, it would be difficult to find any coherent frame at all, let alone an injustice frame. The metanarrative is frequently about the self-reforming nature of the system, operating to get rid of the rotten apples that news media have exposed. If moral indignation is stimulated by fingering the bad guys, it is quickly and safely assuaged by their removal.

These complicated and offsetting characteristics invite us to look closely at how media discourse treats the injustice theme on different issues. All of the issues considered here contain hardship and suffering as part of the story. On troubled industry, workers lose their jobs, and their families and communities suffer along with them. On affirmative action, people may experience discrimination and lose jobs or educational opportunities. On nuclear power, people may risk harm from radiation and be forced to evacuate their homes. On Arab–Israeli conflict, which so often takes a violent form, death, injury, and dislocation are constant features. Every frame has the task of interpreting the source of these sufferings and considering how they can be mitigated or eliminated. Only by examining each issue in turn can we understand the extent to which media discourse encourages or discourages specific injustice frames.

Injustice in conversations

When working people talk about the actors who dominate the news, they constantly judge and, most of the time, condemn them. There are very few heroes in these conversations. But the implicit and explicit judgments are not necessarily about injustice – that is, the belief that individuals or organizations are operating in a way that warrants righteous indignation.

There are many ways of short-circuiting the connection between the belief that people are being undeservedly wronged by human agents and the emotional response of indignation. Corruption, for example, rarely seems to trigger it. A cynical chic view of politics leads to the expectation that greed and the pursuit of narrow self-interest are typical and, perhaps, even part of human nature. To learn that yet another rich businessman has colluded with government officials to rip off the taxpayers is so normal, in this view, that apathy and boredom are more likely to be triggered than outrage.

But a countertendency operates as well. There is enough pain and hardship in the daily lives of many of these working people to produce quite a bit of anger. They draw on these feelings when some aspect of an issue under discussion makes these emotions relevant. In this sense, injustice frames offer potential hooks to which people can attach their anger over the hardships and indignities that they experience in their daily lives. Since this coupling of the cognition of unfairness in the larger society with the emotion of indignation does not happen easily or automatically, we can learn by taking a close look at how it occurs in these conversations.

Here, I must acknowledge the importance of a methodological limitation discussed in Chapter 2. Something is lost with each transformation of this conversation – from being there, to videotape or audiotape, to written transcript. This "something" centers on the intensity and nature of the emotions being expressed. We used audiotape, which loses all of the critical visual cues, although it at least preserves voice intonations.

Most of the vocal cues are lost in the written transcriptions, in spite of our inclusion of some transcribing conventions to indicate emphasis. Our coders flagged "high-intensity moments" using audiotapes, but these included a much broader range of emotions than indignation and never reached satisfactory levels of reliability. Hence, the measure of injustice in these conversations relies on an impoverished expression of it – a written transcript – that may underestimate its presence.

When indignation does spill over into words, it may well be only the tip of the iceberg. It seems likely that the more visible part is not very different from the less easily visible in revealing which perceived injustices seem to make working people angry as they talk about these issues. My search for injustice frames focused on explicit moral condemnations: "That is just wrong," "That's unfair," "That really burns me up," and "That pisses me off," for example.

The mere words, however, are not sufficient to make a segment of conversation qualify as expressing moral indignation. Sometimes the word *wrong* is used in the sense of a mistake, not in the sense of a moral wrong – for example, "They think they have this nuclear power under control, but they're wrong." The context must make the moral nature of the injustice claim clear. However, even when the moral dimension is clear, it is quite common for other speakers to challenge the target of indignation, suggesting that the emotion is either misdirected or not justified.

Finally, speakers sometimes qualify their own statements in ways that explicitly break the potential link between the unfairness claim and indignation. They say, "It's unfair, *but* . . . " and the "but" may include either the fatalism of "that's life" or more explicit arguments that offset or justify the unfairness.

Injustice frames are measured here by explicit moral condemnation, unqualified by offsetting arguments and unchallenged by other group members. The following excerpt provides a good example of such a discussion.

Characters:

Marjorie, a waitress, in her forties.
Judy, a data entry clerk, in her thirties.
Several others who don't speak in this scene.

(The group is near the end of a discussion of nuclear power):
Marjorie: They should have taken all that money to nuclear power and everything – and you've got kids starving in America.
Judy: Yeah.
Marjorie: You've got homeless people. Where's your values? (pause) They suck. They really do suck.
Judy: You're on tape.
(laughter)
Marjorie: I don't care what I'm on. Still – it's obvious – when you pay

millions and millions of dollars in nuclear plants when people in
America are starving –

Judy: – Right.

Marjorie: And you've got homeless people, no matter what they are –
whether they're drunks or they're – whatever they are. Mentally ill
people and you've got them living on a street. And you've got a
family of five people – I worked for Legal Services of Greater Boston and I had people in the Milner Hotel, mothers with five kids in
one room. Living. And we don't have places for them, but we have
places to build nuclear plants. That's garbage. That's garbage!

Troubled industry

Two of the critical discourse moments in our media sample centered on
large corporations seeking government help to avoid bankruptcy. In 1971
the Lockheed Aircraft Company, a major defense contractor, sought and
received guarantees from the Nixon administration for a $250 million loan;
in 1979, the Chrysler Corporation sought and received similar guarantees
for a $1.5 billion loan from the Carter administration.

Media accounts generally framed the controversy as a contest between
pragmatists who focused on the hardships created by the closing of such
large companies and the ideologues who objected on principle to public
bailouts of failing private enterprises. What intrigued most commentators,
however, was the central irony that apostles of free enterprise were seeking
government handouts. Supporters of the loans, as Rep. Bella Abzug put
it, believed in "Socialism for the rich and capitalism for the poor."

This theme of a hypocritical double standard was repeated again and
again. In 1971, a full 50 percent of the thirty-six cartoons and 39 percent
of the thirty-three opinion columns played on it. The phrases *socialism for
the rich* and *welfare for the rich* occurred repeatedly, and Lockheed was
frequently depicted as a fat ne'er-do-well looking for an easy handout.
Many commentators contrasted the help proposed for Lockheed with the
neglect of the poor. The following Herblock cartoon expresses the central
irony very well.

The same theme of a hypocritical double standard remained central in
commentary on the $1.5 billion Chrysler loan eight years later. Some 31
percent of twenty-six relevant cartoons and columns presented some version of it. A column by Art Buchwald, "Giving a Broken-Down Bum a
Break" (Nov. 8, 1979), captures it most fully; reprinted with permission
from Art Buchwald:

'It makes my blood boil to see those people getting government handouts'

Cartoon 3.1.   Troubled industry. (Herblock, *Washington Post*, July 25, 1971. From HERBLOCK'S STATE OF THE UNION (Simon & Shuster 1972). Reprinted by permission.)

"Hey, mister, could you spare a billion and a half dollars to get me through 1980?"

"Out of my way, you bum. Why don't you get a job like everyone else?"

"I have a job making Chrysler cars."

"Then why are you standing here with a tin cup asking decent folks for money?"

"Nobody seems to want to buy my cars."

"In the capitalist system, my good man, it is the survival of the fittest. If you can't sell a product, then you don't deserve to be in business. Suppose I do give you a billion and a half dollars. How do I know you won't use it for drink instead of building better cars?"

"Don't worry about that, mister. You give me the money and I'll go right to the plant and produce one of the most beautiful automobiles you've ever seen."

"Why didn't you produce one before if you know how to do so?"

"That's a long story." . . .

"This is ridiculous. I don't approve of panhandlers, even if they make automobiles."

"Don't think it's much fun being out here on the street, mister. But panhandling for car money is all I can do. The banks won't give me none, and a lot of people think I'm a loser. But if I can just get a little nest egg, you won't see me on this corner again." . . .

"If I give you a billion and a half dollars, what will you do differently?"

"I have great plans for the new models. I even have an updated slogan: 'Buy the car that is guaranteed by the United States Treasury.' How does that grab you?" . . .

"I guess I'm always a sucker for a hard-luck corporation story. You know, if you had been a little guy I'd have let you starve to death."

"I appreciate that, sir. The minute I saw you walking down the street I said to myself. 'There's a man who cares about the big guy when he gets in trouble.' "

The other critical discourse moments on this issue focused on problems in the steel industry during 1976 and 1977. The double standard theme did not emerge in this coverage, since steel companies sought different forms of federal aid – especially the relaxation of environmental and safety regulations, import restrictions, and tax breaks. This time, the hardships for laid-off workers, their families, and their communities were a current rather than a future prospect.

Of the twenty-seven attributions of blame for this suffering, only one put the onus on the workers themselves. Some 63 percent focused on Japan or other countries as the primary culprits. *Time* magazine's coverage (Dec. 5, 1977) was especially inflamatory, speaking of "a relentless assault from cut-rate foreign competitors" and a "foreign invasion [that] has caused shutdowns of old mills, forcing more than 60,000 workers out of jobs." An accompanying picture showed a steel mill in Fukuyama, Japan, captioned "Cut-rate competition routs U.S. rivals." Three of the five cartoons told people to blame the Japanese for their troubles. The following Sargent cartoon provides a good example.

Critics of deindustrialization who emphasized management decisions such as the milking of Youngstown Sheet and Tube by the Lykes Corporation (see Chapter 4, "Troubled Industry") and the failure to modernize production received scant attention. Steel companies themselves received only 12 percent of the blaming attributions, a number equaled by the environmental movement and the "Nader juggernaut," which allegedly forced costly antipollution and health regulations on the struggling industry.

There is a sharp contrast here with the discourse on the Lockheed and

Cartoon 3.2. Troubled industry. (Sargent, *Austin American-Statesman*, December 8, 1977. Reprinted by permission.)

Chrysler loans. When a company was in trouble, media discourse emphasized management responsibility. Lockheed received 46 percent and Chrysler 54 percent of the blaming attributions when the critical discourse moment focused on their plight. But when the problems were industrywide, management responsibility almost disappeared in a discourse that emphasized other causal agents.

In sum, media discourse on troubled industry offered two potential injustice frames. First, there was the unfairness implicit in the double standard of government welfare for the rich and powerful, and neglect for the poor and weak. Second, there were foreign agents, with their cheap and docile labor force and their lack of environmental and safety constraints, who exploit these and other unfair advantages to force American workers out of jobs. Potential sources of injustice flowing from global capitalism, with multinational corporations as the human agents, rarely appeared, and one would need to go beyond national media discourse to be aware of such frames.

Injustice frames in conversations

Injustice frames occurred in less than one-third of the conversations on troubled industry. The double-standard theme of welfare for the rich came up explicitly in about one-sixth of the groups – but instead of the amused irony of the editorial cartoonists, it was linked to moral indignation.

> *Characters:*
>
> *Don, a construction worker, in his early twenties.*
> *Pam, a secretary, in her late twenties.*
> *Alice, an administrator at a state agency and college graduate, in her thirties.*
>
> *(The group is discussing the government loan to Chrysler):*

Don: That one gets me mad, you know.

Pam: I think it all boils down to politics. It's the bottom line. It's politics.

Don: The almighty buck. It's an economic decision.

Pam: It's politics. Enough of us could see that, at the lower level, the little level.

Don: Chrysler was at that point where they had to play ball, because they were going down the drain. And now he, he just come out and said, "hey, whatever you want, how much you want? You can have it, just make me number one."

Alice: Oh, come on, Lee Iacocca when he needed it –

Don: And they said, "Don't worry, Lee. We'll get you a book, we'll write you a book, we'll put your name on the cover and you'll be all set."

Alice: You know what burns me is, they spend, I don't think a lot of money to aid people, but then they go and they give the Contra aid. And here they won't give people in our country, they're cutting social services.

Don: Now that's another subject –

Alice: The real kick in the ass is that they say, "Now we're going to displace all these workers, and we're going to throw you a little 75 mill. to do a training program, but we'll give you an incentive and we'll let you have 10 percent of that for displaced workers." Thank you very much! I mean, you know, "train all the people that we put out of work." We helped Chrysler people go back to work, but Chrysler people had to take a cut in pay and that was fine. They didn't tell you the second year they got a bonus.

The two-thirds of the groups that expressed no explicit moral indignation on troubled industry frequently expressed sympathy for the hardships of the unemployed and their families. They complained freely about companies, unions, government, the decline of the work ethic, and the direction in which society is headed. This unfocused general griping did not lead them to indignation but to a cynicism that accepts that politics and justice are distant acquaintances, if indeed they have ever met.

Affirmative action

In 1969, the conflict over affirmative action centered on the construction industry. Major demonstrations had taken place in several cities by black workers demanding entry into the building trades, and these stimulated counterdemonstrations by white workers in Chicago and Pittsburgh. The major vehicle for affirmative action was the Philadelphia Plan, named for the first city in which a Labor Department agreement with federal contractors had been reached. The plan set specific numerical goals for each of the building and construction trades, based on the extent of current minority employment and the availability pool. Labor Department officials announced that "because of the deplorably low rate of employment among members of minority groups" in the industry, they would set up similar plans in other major cities.

Media discourse offered a clear target of moral indignation: unions, especially in the building trades. Opponents were typically symbolized in cartoons, for example, by a construction worker in hard hat or sometimes by AFL-CIO head George Meany. The recurrent theme in all eight of the cartoons from this period was the hypocrisy and covert racism of opponents of affirmative action. The cartoonists all took for granted that blacks were unfairly excluded from the building trades and lampooned the opposition.

The media's "other side" in this case was represented by quoting union leaders or rank-and-file workers who were undisguisedly racist. *Newsweek,* for example, presented a construction worker: "We do all the work. The niggers have got it made. They keep closing in, working their way into everything. Last 3 or 4 months you can't even turn on the damn TV without seeing a nigger. They're even playing cowboys" (Oct. 6, 1969, 57).

Ten years later, at the time of the Supreme Court's Weber decision, there was a dramatic change. Brian Weber was a worker at a Kaiser Aluminum and Chemical plant in Gramercy, Louisiana. The company, in an agreement with the United Steelworkers Union, had instituted a program to correct a racial imbalance among its craft workers. Blacks were to be given half of the openings in a training program until the imbalance was corrected. The result of this program was that some blacks were accepted who had less seniority than several white applicants who were rejected. Weber, who was one of these, claimed that his exclusion was racial discrimination, prohibited by the Civil Rights Act.

This time there was no media heavy at all, no clear-cut target of moral indignation. Supporters of affirmative action relied more and more on the abstract and complex idea of institutional racism: Race-conscious programs are necessary because of the continuing structural effects of past discrimination. But none of the players in the Weber story were carrying on that legacy.

Opposition to affirmative action was no longer represented by workers complaining that blacks were getting undeserved advantages but by articulate neoconservatives who objected to race-conscious programs as a violation of individual rights. The opponents of affirmative action competed directly with proponents over claims of victimization and the moral indignation to which those who have been wronged are entitled. By 1979, the affirmative action story in the media had competing victims and would-be redeemers but, as villains, only ghosts from the past.

By the middle of the Reagan administration, this situation had changed again. Affirmative action discourse was more polarized, with two strong competing frames, each with influential sponsors. Each of the major protagonists – the Reagan administration and the network of civil rights advocates – was a potential target of indignation, depending on the frame being displayed. Victimization had become an equal opportunity job, available to whites, blacks, and other minorities alike. Two competing frames both offered their own reasons for getting angry.

Boston, of course, has its own special racial history that is not reflected in this national media discourse. For months at a time during the 1970s, local media attention was heavily focused on the bitter controversy over de facto segregation in the Boston public school system. Unlike the national discourse during the 1970s, which blurred potential targets for an injustice frame, the Boston school busing controversy offered clear-cut and personalized targets.

Although de facto school segregation and affirmative action are not the same issue, reference to the busing conflict comes up repeatedly in the affirmative action discussions of both white and black groups in our Boston sample. Since the local and national discourses are quite different in presenting targets for injustice frames, one can't rely exclusively on national discourse for this part of the analysis.

In sum, national media discourse on affirmative action combined with local discourse on the school busing controversy has consistently presented concrete targets of moral indignation for use in injustice frames. In the late 1960s, these were provided mainly for supporters of affirmative action, but from the 1970s to the present, injustice claims abound with concrete targets on all sides at which to point a finger of accusation.

Injustice frames in conversation

Affirmative action conversations, far more than any other issue, were heavily permeated with injustice frames. For almost all of the black groups and half of the white groups, affirmative action requires that they reconcile a moral conflict. Black groups either took for granted or explicitly pointed out the continuing disadvantages of blacks in American society. But, as we will see in Chapter 5 ("Affirmative Action"), the majority of them also asserted that a person should be judged as an individual, independently of group membership. Hence, they acknowledged the possibility that individual whites may suffer unfairly and that some balancing of justice claims is necessary.

Similarly, about half of the white groups also tried to balance competing injustice claims. All of the white and interracial groups endorsed the idea that people should be judged as individuals, but half of them avoided a moral conflict by denying the continuing existence of discrimination against blacks. "That was then; this is now" was the vehicle of denial and the basis for claiming exemption from responsibility for discrimination by others in the past. The other half of the white groups and the interracial groups acknowledged that blacks and other minorities continue to operate at a disadvantage, in spite of affirmative action programs.

One might think that the moral complexity and ambiguity of the issue for most groups would inhibit the expression of indignation. Perhaps it does in black groups, since only 53 percent expressed injustice frames on affirmative action compared to 86 percent of the others.[1] But a common pattern seemed to be the expression of double indignation: directed at discrimination against blacks *and* at preferential treatment of individuals on the basis of group membership rather than personal qualifications.

Almost 30 percent of the black groups expressed anger at how affirmative action programs set poor whites and blacks against each other when both groups suffer undeserved hardship; and at the unfairness to everybody – white and black alike – of setting blacks up for failure in positions that they are not adequately trained to handle. The following transcripts show the two contrasting ways in which black groups expressed an injustice frame on the issue. The first group emphasizes the injustice to blacks in an un-ambivalent way; anger is directed against those whites who, in the face of a long and continuing history of discrimination against blacks, shamelessly claim that they are being victimized.

Characters:

Nancy, a homemaker and college student, in her thirties.
Lucy, a human service worker, in her thirties.
Rudy, a musician, in his thirties.
Duane, a machinist, in his thirties.

Nancy: Well, in Memphis – that's where I'm from – I worked in a bank for six years and, um, I worked as a file clerk in the bookkeeping department and in customer service answering the telephone. Well, I know I had the experience for other jobs but there would be – like young white women would come in, you know, no experience at all, except they may know the boss, or know their mother or daughter, and they'd get in another way. I didn't think it was fair and I tried to do something about it, but there wasn't enough co-workers there that was really trying to pull in together. But I didn't think that was fair at all.

  [*later, in response to Cartoon 6 (see Appendix B)*]

Lucy: Where were the white folks yelling "discrimination" when we were enslaved? (pause) I mean, where were they? I didn't see nobody standing in line to wash the white folks' dishes. I didn't see no whites in that line. There were no white folks standing in line when we had to sleep in the barn when they were selling my mama, and her sister and their children, down the road. I didn't see no whites in that same line getting their folks sold down the road. And now they're in the lines talking about we're getting preferential treatment because we're black. All of a sudden, we're beginning to raise our consciousness so that we can fight white America – the prejudiced part of white America that keeps us enslaved – and to say that we ought to have an opportunity to get this job too. And here a couple of white folks try to get in there and say, "Oh, now you're getting preferential treatment." Didn't nobody care about the preferential treatment they've been getting for 300 years.

  [*later*]

Facilitator: You've already said a lot about affirmative action, but just to sum it up, what do you think should be done about affirmative action?

Lucy: I would say there's a multitude of revisions that need to be done. And it's not fair. They paint a very unfair picture of what they're trying to do, and they're trying to give to the blacks.

Rudy: What I think about when I think what could be done to make affirmative action real is let us have some real affirmative actions – none of this affirmative action that we've had in the past. Because it's not affirmative action.

Lucy: Or change the name. It doesn't fit the bill. Affirmative action is not what they're doing. There is nothing affirmative. I think of the word *affirmative* as having a positive connotation.

Rudy: Right.

Lucy: And there's nothing positive about the kind of affirmation that they've given us. I don't see very much that's affirmative.

Duane: I don't see affirmative. If they want to be affirmative –

Lucy: – they're keeping eighty and giving us twenty.

Duane: – with their actions and what they are going to do, I'd say still give me my forty acres and my mule.

Rudy: Speaking of changing the name, what we really need is some *drastic* action.

Lucy: Yeah, I like that.

The next group shows the complex, multifaceted way in which the affirmative action issue sparks double indignation in other black groups where the claims of victimization by whites are taken more seriously. These two patterns of discourse on affirmative action occur with about equal frequency in black groups:

Characters:

Elizabeth, a data processor at an insurance company, in her forties.

Thomas, a transportation worker, in his forties.

Emilie, a billing clerk for an insurance company, in her thirties.

Elizabeth: Well, to give you a good example of – of your quotas, your – your hiring your minorities. There was this girl and I started on this job, same time. Now I don't know if she had office experience from before, but I did. We started same time, doing the same type of work, but because she had a little college background, I don't know if she had any certificate or what-have-you, but because she did go to college, they started her off paying her more than they started me off with. And that wasn't fair, because we were doing the same kind of work.

8. The cartoonist seems to be saying that rich liberals want to give special breaks to blacks at the expense of whites who also need a break. Reprinted with permission.

Thomas: And you're still trying to catch up.
Elizabeth: Right

[*later, near the end of the discussion*]

Thomas: The white male, the ones that have wanted to work, have always been able to get work.
Elizabeth: Yes, those that had a little pull, but you had white poor people just like we categorize ourselves as being poor. They were being pushed out of jobs, and that wasn't fair either. Why take away from the poor white man who was trying to survive and take care of his family? Because he was in the same – to me, he's just as equal as I am. He's out there working, trying to survive, trying to take care of his family. So why take his job away because you had to give it to a black person?
Thomas: It's going back to that Cartoon 8. Why grab over, reach over there and grab his bowl of food when you're sitting in the middle with all of it? Why don't you just say –
Emilie: – Yeah. "We'll share."

Thomas: "Why don't you guys just split mine up and we'll all eat." . . . And it's making the poor whites and the blacks feel this animosity towards each other because we all feel — I feel that if my parents, my father had a had the same chance as this white man's father had when he was coming up, that I would be in a better position right now. But he didn't have that chance. He got out there and do the same work that white man was doing, but he was getting twenty-five cents a day and the white man was getting fifty cents a day. Now, what kind of, what kind of — what is that? I'm not trying to go back a hundred years, but that is a fact.

Injustice frames occurred in 85 percent of the discussions of affirmative action in white and interracial groups. Even in the three white groups without them, at least one person made an explicit injustice claim but had it challenged by others. As with the black groups, there were both single and double indignation discussions, reflecting differences in whether the injustice claims of others are taken seriously or not. The double-indignation pattern appeared in 29 percent of the white groups and in two of the three interracial ones.

The first of the following examples illustrates a white group in which the potential moral complexity is resolved by laying exclusive claim to the victim's role. But note how even in this group, which never overtly acknowledges a black disadvantage, Judy implicitly accepts the argument that equal opportunity hasn't always prevailed in the past by accepting the legitimacy of providing "special things where they go for classes."

Characters:

Linda, a nurse, in her twenties.
Marie, a nurse, in her forties.
Cris, a nurse, in her forties.
Judy, a dental assistant, in her thirties.
Nora, a nurse, in her forties.
Lil, a nurse, in her forties.

Linda: Why should the government pay for a black person to go to school and not me? Now why is he any better than I am? I didn't get any special assistance to go to college. Why should all my friends that are black have special assistance?
Marie: That's right, you had to work your behind off.
Cris: I think, I think they get too much.
Marie: And they — all they do is cry discrimination, and they're in and

we're out – we're the ones being discriminated against, not the
blacks anymore.

Judy: The whole thing with busing and everything. My kids are in parochial
school because of the busing; I never intended to send my kids
to Catholic school, never, because I hated Catholic school when
I was there. So, where are they? The same school I went to.

Cris: I particularly bought my house so my kids could walk to school, and
then they tell me, "No, the black kids are coming to that school
and your kids are going someplace else." That isn't fair; I was
being discriminated against.

Judy: This is a real sore spot that you're hitting here, and if you don't think
it is –

(general laughter)

Judy: It definitely is a sore spot. Everybody is entitled. But you've got a
working-class bunch of people sitting at this table, you know, and
if we're all breaking our backs working, then Joe Shmo should
be out there working, his wife should be out there working, and
as far as – we're not into welfare so I won't even get into that,
but I was gonna say, why not have – if they don't have a job, why
not get them to fill that hole in on Washington Street? Get them
working for a paycheck; give them a little self-respect, and have
them working for a job.

[later]

Cris: When I went – when I went to Boston Latin, the black kids and the
white kids –

Judy: – You had to make the grade.

Cris: – we all had to get the same grade, we all had to pass exams to
get in there. And there was plenty of black kids in there. And we
all busted our ass while we were in there. Now – hey, I left – it
was too hard. There was other black kids that stayed there, you
know? But now it's firemen's exams – there's a level for the black,
there's a level for the white.

Judy: That's not right.

Nora: That's not right.

Lil: I don't feel it's right either. There should be equal opportunity.

Judy: Then they could, you know, maybe set up special things where
they go for classes but not – when the time comes for the exam,
no special treatment! That is a very sore subject. Very sore.

Some white groups acknowledged past or continuing discrimination
against blacks but short-circuited the path to moral indignation by im-

mediately qualifying or undercutting the force of the injustice. But others directed part of their indignation to the treatment of blacks even while they expressed anger at their own unfair treatment. The following group illustrates this double-indignation pattern:

> *Characters:*
>
> *Ida, a bookkeeper, in her late sixties.*
> *Nancy, a secretary, in her forties.*
> *Arlene, a bookkeeper, in her forties.*

Ida: You know, I didn't keep them down. I wasn't even there.

(laughter)

Nancy: See, nobody stopped us. So why should we not encourage?

Ida: I encourage! I absolutely do. I know a couple of instances from really personal experiences that I felt very bad. Early, before you were born, I worked for the State Department in Washington. And one of my best friends, who was an extremely bright gal, was black. And I was leaving. My husband was a student. This was after the Second World War. And they wanted to give me a party. You know, the girls all wanted to get together. And we couldn't have it in a public restaurant, because if we did, we couldn't have invited this girl to join us. Now, *that's wrong!* I mean, that's absolutely – (pause) We had it at somebody's house so she could be included because I wouldn't want a party without her. Now that's very wrong.

Nancy: Oh, sure.

Arlene: Yeah.

Ida: That sort of thing. But today, when a person can't even read or write and they get a better opportunity than someone who has three degrees and is beating their head against the wall trying to get a job opening? Oh, come on!

Nuclear power

The discourse on nuclear power has been indelibly marked by Hiroshima and Nagasaki. Public awareness began with images of sudden, enormous destruction, symbolized by the rising mushroom cloud of a nuclear bomb blast. Even when discourse focuses on the use of nuclear reactors to produce electricity, the afterimage of the bomb is never far from the surface.

Until the 1970s, media discourse on nuclear power was dominated by a dualism about nuclear energy. Boyer (1985, 125) points to the either/or structure of so many post-Hiroshima pronouncements: "Either civilization would vanish in a cataclysmic holocaust, or the atomic future would be unimaginably bright." "We face the prospect either of destruction on a scale which dwarfs anything thus far reported," said the *New York Times* in an editorial a day after Hiroshima, "or of a golden era of social change which would satisfy the most romantic utopian."

As long as the issue was framed as a choice between atoms for war and atoms for peace, it is hard to see who could be against nuclear power development. In effect, there was no significant anti–nuclear power discourse during this era and nuclear power was, in general, a nonissue. "Nuclear power" was an uncontested symbol of technological progress.

By the time of the accident at Three Mile Island (TMI), nuclear power had become a controversial issue. Two years earlier, in our 1977 media sample at the time of the site occupation of the Seabrook, New Hampshire, reactor (see Chapter 4, "Nuclear Power"), many opponents of nuclear power were quoted. But it is striking how little critical framing of nuclear power was ever presented; the opposition itself was the story, not the reasons for it.

Even when comments were quoted that framed the nuclear power issue, opponents rarely suggested an injustice frame and were frequently vague about the human agents involved. CBS, the only network to make any attempt to present the demonstrators' frame, quoted Harvey Wasserman, a spokesman for the Clamshell Alliance: "We are fighting the war that is being waged against the environment and our health." The war metaphor implies an enemy who is waging it, but in using the passive voice, Wasserman left unsaid just who was waging this one.

Newsmagazine coverage quoted many different spokesmen, including Wasserman, Ralph Nader, and representatives from Friends of the Earth, the Sierra Club, and the National Resources Defense Council. But none of the selected quotes suggested a frame on nuclear power; instead, they focused exclusively on the strategy of direct action and whether the demonstrators would succeed. Proponents of nuclear power were treated as mistaken in these quotes, perhaps tragically so, but not as moral offenders.

After the TMI accident, there was an inevitable search for blame, but again it was rarely put in the context of an injustice frame. Accidents are, by definition, unintentional, so one searches for negligence or error but assumes the absence of malice. None of the most prominent frames offered very much of an injustice theme in accounting for the accident.

The most prominent frame after both the TMI and Chernobyl accidents was RUNAWAY (see Gamson and Modigliani, 1989). In it, human agency is blurred. Some reified entity such as society or humankind has chosen to develop nuclear power under the mistaken idea that it can be controlled when it cannot. It has become a force of its own, beyond human agency, a powerful genie that has been summoned and now can not be forced back into its bottle. Genies make poor targets of moral indignation.

The once dominant PROGRESS framing of nuclear power offers a target of indignation in the "coercive utopians" and "neopastoralists" who would retard our economic growth and thereby make us renege on our obligation to the poor and to future generations. But whatever else their sins in this frame, the antinuclear movement can hardly be held responsible, even indirectly, for the accidents at TMI and Chernobyl.

After 1979, PROGRESS became a minority framing in all of the media samples and an increasingly defensive one. *Time,* for example, quoted Alvin Weinberg, introducing him as a nuclear advocate and pronuclear author who believes that the alternatives to this source are "so crummy that we probably should in a cautious way continue this nuclear enterprise" (Apr. 9, 1979, 20). This is not the kind of language that whips up an angry citizenry against those who would deny them their vital energy needs.

The most visible antinuclear framing, PUBLIC ACCOUNTABILITY, has a populist, anticorporate flavor and offers the nuclear industry as a potential target for an injustice frame. Nuclear power companies, in this frame, are frequently dishonest, greedy, and arrogant. Public officials who are supposed to monitor the activities of the industry are all too often captives of it. The nuclear industry has used its political and economic power to undermine the serious exploration of energy alternatives.

After TMI, PUBLIC ACCOUNTABILITY received quite a bit of prominence, but it generally appeared in a weak form. The strong version was typically displayed through one of the following three ideas: (1) profits are emphasized at the expense of public safety, (2) government regulation is ineffective because public officials function as promoters of the industry, or (3) industry interests work against providing full protection and information to the public. The weak version merely suggests some culpability by company managers, with negative consequences for the public or consumers. No analysis of reasons for such culpability is suggested beyond general incompetence, stupidity, laxness, or overconcern with public image. Only the strong form really offers an injustice frame.

By this criterion, only 10 percent of the relevant television utterances after TMI ($N = 99$) offered such an injustice frame and, after Chernobyl, less than 10 percent ($N = 74$) reflected either the strong or the weak version of this package. Very similar figures held for newsmagazine utterances as well.

In sum, media discourse on nuclear power offered very few targets for injustice frames. Although the nuclear power industry was the most likely target offered, even at the high point after TMI, only about 10 percent of the media displays on nuclear power offered it as a candidate for moral indignation. No other actor came remotely close.

Injustice frames in conversations

The example quoted earlier, in which Marjorie expressed indignation about wasting money on nuclear power when people in America are starving and homeless, was a rare event in these groups. Only two other groups had some form of injustice frame on this issue, focusing mainly on how unfair it is that they have so little say about an issue that can affect their personal lives so directly. The dominant emotions evoked by nuclear power are fear and anxiety, not moral indignation.

Arab–Israeli conflict

Israelis and Palestinians make strong and competing claims about deep historical injustices, and these claims appear, of course, in the frames offered by their supporters in the United States. But these are not the dominant frames in American media discourse. Indeed, they must compete with two formidable frames that explicitly downgrade injustice claims, treating them as a distraction and an obstacle to be overcome.

In FEUDING NEIGHBORS, for example, fanaticism and the nurturing of long-standing grievances are the core of the problem. Whether the Hatfields or the McCoys have justice on their side is hardly the issue. The conflict takes on a life of its own, providing new grievances and a continuing sense of injustice to each side as they respond to the latest atrocity by the other. The real victims, in this frame, are the bystanders, not the combatants. They suffer the consequences and, in the case of Arab–Israeli conflict, there is a danger that we may all become such bystanders as the whole world becomes drawn into the conflict. If there is indignation here, it is expressed as a "plague on both your houses." When moments of reconciliation or compromise occur, it is not justice but reasonableness and good sense that appear triumphant.

The official frame, STRATEGIC INTERESTS, understands the issue in geopolitical terms and views the Middle East as a theater of major power

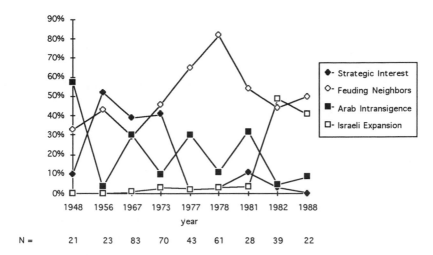

Figure 3.1. Cartoon frames on Arab–Israeli conflict.

competition, a battleground of the cold war. One doesn't ask, in this frame, which of the combatants has justice on its side, but of their value as strategic assets for the superpowers. Injustice claims become relevant only in an instrumental way, because they can be manipulated for advantage. Hence, it was common in this frame during the cold war to suggest that Soviet statements and actions were mischievous in intent, designed to enhance its influence in the Arab world by fanning their grievances and making peaceful resolution more difficult.

We sampled nine critical discourse moments from the Israeli Declaration of Independence in 1948 to a period in 1988 about three months after the *intifada* had begun, at the time of a new U.S. peace initiative (see Appendix A). With one exception, as Figure 3.1 shows for our cartoon sample,[2] the prominence of particular frames depends heavily on the historical context; sometimes they were very prominent in the discourse and sometimes virtually invisible.

The conspicuous exception was the consistent prominence of FEUDING NEIGHBORS, regardless of context. Even at its low point after the Six Day War in 1967, it was reflected in 30 percent of the cartoons. Over the entire forty-year period, it was displayed in half of the 390 cartoons; its major competitors averaged around one-fifth overall.

The other frames all had their moments of prominence, generally competing with FEUDING NEIGHBORS rather than with each other. STRATEGIC INTERESTS had its day from the 1950s through the late 1970s, when many cartoons commented on the flow of oil and the Soviet role. But from the time of Egyptian President Anwar Sadat's 1977 visit to Jerusalem to the present, the STRATEGIC INTERESTS framing has been very muted in media discourse. In effect, the Soviet Union was relegated to the role of minor player and oil anxiety was transferred to the Persian Gulf, reducing its relevance for Arab–Israeli conflict.

ARAB INTRANSIGENCE and ISRAELI EXPANSIONISM did offer competing targets for moral indignation, but it was a strange sort of competition. At any given moment, their competition was not so much with each other as with those frames that played down injustice claims. It is as if only one injustice frame at a time is allowed into this forum of discourse. Until the 1980s, the injustice slot was filled by ARAB INTRANSIGENCE, which even bested FEUDING NEIGHBORS in 1948 to win a majority. But after the Israeli invasion of Lebanon in 1982, this frame surrendered the injustice slot to its rival, ISRAELI EXPANSIONISM, which currently carries on the competition with the nonpartisan FEUDING NEIGHBORS.

In sum, FEUDING NEIGHBORS, the dominant frame in media discourse on this issue, avoids taking sides on the justice claims of the parties in conflict. Until 1977, its main competitor was typically STRATEGIC INTERESTS, a frame that agreed with it in playing down the issue of which side was right or wrong. If these frames offered targets for indignation, it was typically the Soviet Union or fanatics and extremists on both sides. And even the frames that do endorse the injustice claims of the combatants offered no actor within American society toward whom such feelings could be directed.

Injustice frames in conversations

Injustice frames on Arab–Israeli conflict were almost as rare as on nuclear power. It was unusual for any discussion of this issue to take sides between the conflicting parties. Far from deciding where justice lies, most discussions emphasized the irrelevance of the moral concerns of the partisans. Sometimes, as in the discussion of the following interracial group, they distinguish explicitly between foreign policy conflicts in which issues of injustice are relevant and feuds in which the righteousness of the conflicting parties makes compromise and resolution especially difficult and unlikely.

> Characters:
>
> Bob, a human services administrator, white, in his thirties, a college graduate.
> Reggie, coordinator at a health services pool, black, in his forties.

Dot, coordinator at a health services pool, white, in her forties.
Marilyn, a nurse, black, in her thirties.

Bob: It's not like we don't have any other problems to deal with in our own country. So you know, that just adds another problem that we need to be worried about in terms of a couple ideologies fighting it over, as you say, over the Gaza Strip. I mean, if they want to blow themselves into little tiny pieces for the sake of their beliefs, that's fine.

Reggie: I agree. I feel the same.

Bob: I feel the – exactly the same way about the Protestants and the Catholics in Northern Ireland.

Reggie: Um huh.

Bob: I see the same type of conflicts. And, you know, I mean, I got other things to worry about. You know what I mean?

Reggie: Um huh.

Dot: All the people that are getting killed.

Bob: I mean my basement – full of water, right?

Marilyn: You see the same – do you feel the same way about South Africa?

Marjorie: No. Uh uh.

Marilyn: I mean, we're talking about countries at war.

Bob: I see a difference here because we – I see an obvious, um, –

Reggie: – Wrong.

Bob: – wrong being done. Thank you, Reggie. To the black population in South Africa. I don't see necessarily a great wrong being done to the Israelis, nor do I see one to the Arabs. I don't see a great wrong being done to the Catholics versus the Protestants in Northern Ireland.

Marilyn: Um hum.

Bob: So I – I, personally don't share the enthusiasm and the zeal of the participants in this particular conflict, and therefore, I can't sympathize with them.

Conclusion

Explicit outbursts of moral indignation were infrequent in the course of a long conversation. They flared up unexpectedly, coming at unpredictable moments – for example, sometimes at the end of a discussion in which little anger or any other strong emotion had been expressed earlier. Though infrequent, few groups were without them. Overall, more than three-fourths of the groups had conversations on at least one issue in which someone articulated an injustice frame, expressed moral indignation about it, and was supported by others.

There is a strong overall relationship between the prominence of injustice frames in media discourse and in popular discourse. On affirmative action, where the injustice theme is central and highly visible in media discourse, it is equally central and visible in the attempts of working people to make sense of the issue. On nuclear power and Arab–Israeli conflict, where injustice frames have low prominence in media discourse, conversations about these issues rarely express moral indignation.

The causal relationship, however, is complicated and indirect. On troubled industry, for example, in spite of the fact that media discourse frequently offered the Japanese or Third World countries as potential targets of moral indignation, none of these conversations employed such an injustice frame. When the Japanese were discussed, it was typically in an admiring way, for their disciplined and cooperative work habits. When Third World countries came up, as they often did, foreign workers who take American jobs were spared moral indignation because of a presumed lack of choice and desperation that forces them to accept low wages that Americans would not accept.

On the other hand, the targets for indignation that did come up most frequently in conversation were limited to those with visibility in media discourse. On troubled industry, for example, general business practices or specific companies were the most frequent targets of denunciation, as was the double standard of welfare for the rich and neglect for the poor. It was rare to find an injustice frame that went beyond the targets that media discourse made readily available – for example, indignation at American-based multinational corporations that hire Third World workers at substandard wages.

It would be very misleading, however, to conclude that people are parroting what they have taken from the media in developing these injustice frames. When a group expresses indignation at the double standard, it is not because they got the idea from a Herblock cartoon or an Art Buchwald column. They forge the cognitive link themselves by using awareness of an antiwelfare public discourse that deplores poor people's getting government help, combining it with their knowledge of government help for the rich.

The use of injustice frames, it turns out, is a critical catalyst for the appearance of other elements of a collective action frame. In the next chapter, we explore people's sense of collective efficacy and the potential for ordinary people to change the conditions of their daily lives through collective action.

4

Agency

If many intelligent analysts and close observers are right, precious few American working people have any sense of themselves as collective agents of history. Indeed, if I had found such a sense among these Boston area working people, I would immediately have suspected the typicality of the sample and concluded that our methods had produced a deviant group. But if one listens carefully to their conversation, a portrait of passivity and quiescence seems incomplete; there is a rebellious streak as well that flares up in conversations at selected moments. And it expresses a sense of collective agency.

This chapter presents a story of "in spite of." The forces discouraging a sense of agency among working people are overwhelming. Culture and social structure combine to induce collective helplessness. Only individual escape seems possible, typically through some kind of liberating educational experience that strips the scales from one's eyes and opens opportunities. The vast majority seem to remain subject to sociocultural forces that systematically remove from their consciousness any sense that collectively they can alter the conditions and terms of their daily lives.

Most of us, even those with political activist identities, spend most of our time and energy sustaining our daily lives. Flacks (1988, 2) points out that this includes not only meeting material needs but "activity and experience designed to sustain one's self as a human being – to validate or fulfill the meaning of one's life, reinforce or enhance one's sense of self-worth, [and] achieve satisfaction and pleasure." This daily activity typically takes for granted and reinforces the patterned daily life characteristic of a community or society; rarely do people have an opportunity to engage in activity that challenges or tries to change some aspect of this pattern – what Flacks calls "making history."

As long as history making is centralized and hierarchical, with very little opportunity for working people to participate in any of the institutions that set the conditions of their daily lives, they will inevitably feel "that they themselves are objects of historical forces alien to themselves, that they themselves are without power" (Flacks, 1988, 5). Everyday life and history are experienced as separate realms because we have a national political economy that is dominated by centralized, hierarchical, national corporations and a national state.

This structural impediment to collective agency is reinforced by a political culture that operates to produce quiescence and passivity. Merelman (1984, 1) tells us that a "loosely bounded culture prevents Americans from controlling their political and social destinies, for the world which loose boundedness portrays is not the world of political and social structures that actually exists. It is, instead, a shadowland, which gives Americans little real purchase on the massive, hierarchical political and economic structures that dominate their lives." Merelman analyzes the role of television in particular in promoting a loosely bounded culture that backs people away from politics and directs them toward a private vision of the self in the world.

Edelman (1988) points to the powerful social control that is exercised, largely unconsciously, through the manipulation of symbolism used in "constructing the political spectacle." Problems, enemies, crises, and leaders are constantly being constructed and reconstructed to create a series of threats and reassurances. To take it in is to be taken in by it. "For most of the human race," Edelman writes in his conclusion, "political history has been a record of the triumph of mystification over strategies to maximize well-being." Rebellious collective action can even buttress the dominant world view by helping political elites in their construction of a stable enemy or threat that justifies their policies and provides a legitimation for political repression.

Bennett (1988, xii) observes how the structure and culture of news production combine to limit popular participation. "As long as the distribution of power is narrow and decision processes are closed," he argues, "journalists will never be free of their dependence on the small group of public relations experts, official spokespersons, and powerful leaders whose self-serving pronouncements have become firmly established as the bulk of the daily news."

Furthermore, these "advertisements for authority" are surrounded by other reports "that convey fearful images of violent crime, economic insecurity, and nuclear war. Such images reinforce public support for political authorities who promise order, security, and responsive political solutions." Granting that people take it all with a grain of salt, Bennett argues that even minimal acceptance of basic assumptions about political reality is enough to discourage most people from participating actively in the political process.

It is no wonder, Bennett concludes, that few Americans become involved politically and "most cannot imagine how they could make a political difference." One can break out by reading specialized publications with a broader range of discourse, but "those who take the time to do so may find themselves unable to communicate with the majority who remain trapped on the other side of the wall of mass media imagery" (1988, xv).

There is one apparent exception to this cultural discouragement of citizen action – the election campaign. Here one is assured by countless voices that it is important, even a duty, to exercise this right to choose one's leaders. But in fact, elections are presented as a spectator sport in which candidates compete with thirty-second polispots aimed at provoking a response unmediated by conscious thought. The only idea of agency that is promoted in such a culture is individual, reflected in a consumer's private choice of which product to buy.

The consumers, however, are not so passive as this argument suggests. Most occupy a vast middle ground between going along and open rebellion. The powerless have their own ways of expressing opposition – what Scott (1985) calls the "weapons of the weak." These everyday forms of resistance involve evasion, deception, and subtle sabotage rather than rebellious collective action. Scott describes how Malaysian peasants resist the demands of the powerful by those familiar strategies of everyday life: foot dragging, dissimulation, false compliance, pilfering, feigned ignorance, slander, arson, and sabotage.

Although this kind of opposition requires little or no coordination or planning and is carried out by individuals, it has collective aspects. Typically, it is supported by an oppositional subculture. Willis (1977) describes the counter–school culture of British working-class "lads" and how they use the weapons of the weak to evade the demands of teachers and school officials. They find ways to create free space for themselves within a confining environment.

Harding (1981, 57) makes a similar point about the innumerable individual acts of resistance by blacks in their struggle for freedom in America. Behind the acts of collective rebellion that "fired the imagination of blacks and whites alike . . . were the subterranean acts of individual defiance, resistance, creative rebellion, sabotage, and flight." These acts, he argues, helped to create an oppositional subculture that provided a supportive environment for collective action.

Nevertheless, evasion is not collective action. Its primary virtue is that it does not require a sense of collective agency. Those who use it are making lives, not history. Even Scott (1985, 29–30), who clearly respects and admires the weapons of the weak, reminds us not to romanticize them. "They are unlikely to do more than marginally affect the various forms of exploitation that peasants confront." The lads in Willis's school will eventually participate in a similar counter–work culture on the shop floor when they end up in their working-class jobs, reproducing the existing system of class relations.

The result of these sociocultural forces, then, is not a blind acceptance of official portraits of reality but a pervasive cynicism about politics among working people. Halle (1984, 191) comments that in the eyes of almost all of his chemical workers, the view that politicians are duplicitous and corrupt "is one of the most obvious truths about life in America." Furthermore, politicians really do the bidding of powerful corporations and, hence, appear as part of an undifferentiated power bloc of interlocking, selfish interests. Reinarman (1987, 233) describes the public sector and private sector workers he studied as converging "on the notion that 'big business' gets pretty much what it wants from both politicians and thus government in general."

Their practical political wisdom tells them, as Flacks (1988, 88) puts it, that "the authority set-up is more or less stupid and predatory. The best way to deal with it is to try to make your own way, taking what you can, giving back what you must – while always being on the lookout for space and opportunity to enhance your freedom." Gans (1988, 70), reviewing the many reasons for people to avoid political activities, is led to conclude that "it is surprising to find any citizen activity taking place at all."

And yet it does. There are clearly moments when people do take it upon themselves to do more than evade or transcend the terms and conditions of their daily lives and behave as collective agents who can change them. At some level, they harbor a sense of potential agency. Are social scientists, in emphasizing how this culture of quiescence is produced and maintained, themselves promulgating yet another set of reasons for inaction, another discouragement to agency? Where are the cracks where some idea of collective agency stays alive, ready to grow and prosper under the proper conditions, as it did so dramatically and to everyone's surprise in Eastern Europe, for example?

The big truth remains: None of the visible frames on any of the four issues considered here promote or encourage citizen action.[1] Given the dominant political culture, one might expect that grass-roots collective action would never enter the conversations examined here. The facilitator asked nothing that would stimulate such comments. Participants were never asked to consider what they personally or collectively could or should do about these issues. Even the wording of the final question for each issue, "What should be done about the issue of [X]?" avoided the idea of agency. We intended it to be a question on what public policies should be followed, not a question on what they should do about it as citizens; and they interpreted it in this way. Nevertheless, citizen action spontaneously enters the conversation on at least one issue in 81 percent of the groups. Almost 25 percent of the groups had people who either described their own experience or personally knew someone who had participated in a strike, demonstration, or act of civil disobedience.[2]

On rare occasions, the discussion of existing citizen action even led a group to ponder the personal relevance of such action. The following example involves a group we encountered earlier, discussing affirmative action (Chapter 3) and their overall response to participating in the research (Chapter 2). This segment on nuclear power includes additional participants who did not speak earlier. Ida is alone among the group in supporting nuclear power, but she has accommodated her position to the others by conceding that safety measures need to be carefully monitored.

Characters:

Maggie, an office worker, in her fifties.
Nancy, a secretary, in her forties.
Ruth, an office supervisor, in her fifties
Ida, a bookkeeper, in her late sixties.
Arlene, a bookkeeper, in her forties.

(They are responding to the facilitator's question on what should be done about nuclear power):

Maggie: I wish they could come up with another way. Let's organize a group to find another way [laughs]. There's money again. We have to pay these people for their time and thinking.

Nancy: Concerned citizens.

Maggie: Well, fine, *free* concerned citizens! Well, if I'm one, it will take me a while, honey.

Ruth: I'm not aware of all the dangers involved. But I'm sure that all these people that are demonstrating, that don't want the power plants in their home town, know a lot more about it than I do, and maybe if everybody knew just what the dangers were. I don't know if that would help any at all.

Ida: Are you sure they know? Maybe some of them do —

Ruth: If they're out there demonstrating that they don't want their children

growing up in this neighborhood with the power plants there, they
    must know –
Ida: They'd probably be very happy if those same power plants were
    providing the power in someone else's neighborhood.
Ruth: Probably, yeah. I drove behind cars that had "No Nukes" stickers.
    I didn't know what the hell they were talking about. I'm not really
    informed as to all the dangers, but yet I don't want to stand in
    the way of progress.
Ida: It's a tough question. We just have to have faith in our leaders, I
    guess, and hope they'll do the right thing for us, that's all.
Arlene: I'm glad people are against it. I really am.
Ida: Keeps them on their feet –
Arlene: You bet your life. I'm glad that people have the nerve and the
    guts to go up there and fight it and everything, because if they
    didn't they would do exactly as they please.
[Murmurs of agreement]
Ruth: So why aren't we out there demonstrating?
Arlene: Because you can't. I don't feel that strongly about it, but now that
    I'm getting going here –
Nancy: You can't do everything.
Ruth: After tonight, I'm sure that when we read anything about it, we're
    going to read it differently.
Arlene: Yeah, this has an effect on us, just talking, because you don't
    even, you don't think about it until you're *asked* about something.
Ruth: Yeah.
Arlene: This thing has always bothered me. This thing has.

The general pattern that media discourse downplays and discourages
citizen action remains, but when one looks closely at each issue in turn,
the monolith looks more like a mosaic with complex patterns.

Troubled industry

Media discourse on this issue was overwhelmingly framed as a debate
between those who favor an unfettered free market and those who favor
various degrees of state planning or partnership in the process – some form
of industrial policy. To the extent that working people appeared at all as
an agent in these visible frames, it was as organized labor, with union
leaders as their spokespersons. They appeared, of course, in their role as
individual sellers of their labor power and as consumers, but they were
given no role as collective contributors to policy on troubled industry.

It turns out, though, that one of the critical discourse moments that we sampled on this issue occurred at a moment of significant citizen action – a community effort by workers and other citizens in the Mahoning Valley area in Ohio to buy and run the Youngstown Sheet and Tube Company. Sheet and Tube had been acquired in 1969 by a New Orleans–based conglomerate, the Lykes Corporation, which had used it as a cash cow. Rather than modernizing the plant, Lykes used its cash flow to service the debt it had assumed in buying Sheet and Tube and to finance other new acquisitions.

In 1977, it tried to sell the depleted company but found no buyers among other foreign and domestic steel companies; in September, it announced that it would permanently close its largest mill in the area, laying off 4,100 employees. An estimated 3,600 additional jobs would be lost through effects on local suppliers and retail businesses. Meanwhile, the United Steelworkers of America, its primary weapon, the strike, rendered largely useless by changes in the worldwide steel industry, tried desperately to hold on to the gains it had won in the past, but seemed incapable of any initiative.

In response, a broad group of religious leaders formed the Ecumenical Coalition of the Mahoning Valley to search for a solution to the crisis. At the suggestion of local steelworkers, they began exploring the possibility of a combined worker–community buyout. Alperovitz and Faux (1982, 355) describe it as embodying "concerns for jobs rather than welfare, for self-help and widespread participation rather than dependence on absentee decision-makers."

The new company was to be known as Community Steel, directed by a fifteen-member board with six members elected by the company's workers, six by stock-holders, and three by a broadly based community corporation. Thousands of residents pledged savings to a fund that would purchase the factory, and the coalition received a grant from the Department of Housing and Urban Development (HUD) to conduct a feasibility study. Eventually, the plan faltered when the Carter administration failed to support the needed loan guarantees, but the two-year Youngstown effort was clearly the largest and most significant attempt to convert a plant to worker–community ownership.

Was it visible in national media discourse? When covering a continuing issue such as the decline of the troubled steel industry, journalists look for a topical peg on which to hang their stories. The Carter administration provided one when it offered a six-point plan to deal with the problems of the steel industry late in the fall of 1977. If there was a story in the Youngstown effort begun a couple of months earlier, this was an excellent opportunity to include it. It was receiving extensive coverage in local media. Grass-roots efforts of this sort are novel enough, and it was too soon to know what the outcome would be. HUD Secretary Patricia Harris was calling for "new models of community involvement to solve these problems" (Alperovitz and Faux, 1982, 355). One might expect that the normal assumption in this discourse that citizen action is irrelevant might well be suspended in such an instance.

We chose a two-week period after the announcement of the administration's plan for aiding the steel industry to sample media commentary. Our sample yielded six opinion columns, five cartoons, and three newsmagazine stories on the steel industry, but no network television coverage. We searched in vain for *any* reference to citizen action in the Mahoning Valley in the heart of the steel industry.

Four of the five cartoons had figures representing workers, generally signified by a lunch box, worker's cap, or hard hat. These workers were worried but always passive; never the subject of what is happening, always its unfortunate object.

With one exception, the newsmagazine coverage also presented workers exclusively in their role as victims or beneficiaries of others' actions. Officials or industry spokesmen expressed their plans to keep or recover jobs for steelworkers or complained about how Japanese imports were forcing steelworkers out of jobs. *Time*'s coverage was full of Japan bashing but did contain at least a small hint that workers can be agents. It included a photo of a group of mostly middle-aged white men, many of them wearing sports jackets with shirts open at the collar, standing in front of the White House fence, facing the camera. One of them holds a picket sign reading "Save the Steel Valley." The picture was captioned "U.S. steelworkers picketing White House: Wistful plea for 'just about anything.' " The accompanying story mentioned a coalition of industry executives, "union men," and congressmen from steel producing areas who "have brought heavy pressure on the Carter Administration to do something."[3]

Steelworkers appeared in all six opinion columns but never as agents. There were numerous references to workers as victims, losing their jobs. But James Reston thought they partly brought it on themselves, chiding American workers who "increasingly condemn the integrity of work and reject the authority of their managers" and quoting approvingly from a former Nixon administration Labor Department official who claimed that workers "no longer think that hard work pays off" and "increasingly resist authority in their companies, communities, churches, or governments."[4]

Nicolas von Hoffman alluded to Youngstown Sheet and Tube but referred only to the merger talks between Lykes, its parent company, and another conglomerate, the LTV Corporation, which had earlier swallowed Jones and Laughlin Steel.[5] As for citizen action around Sheet and Tube, von Hoffman either considered it irrelevant or did not know about it.

Worker action did appear allegorically in an Art Buchwald column in the form of a "delegation of elves" confronting Santa Claus about the lack of work in Santa's toy factory.[6] Santa explains that "it's out of my hands," since he has sold out to a conglomerate that only cares about the bottom line. One elf "demands" to know why he sold out in the first place, and Santa explains how he needed capital and couldn't compete. "You know how I feel about you little fellows," Santa tells the elves. "I've worked with you all my life. But what can I do when the Japanese start dumping Farrah Fawcett dolls down every chimney at a quarter of the price that we can make them for up here?" The elves sadly accept a Christmas of unemployment as Santa tells them, "I'm sorry, but that's the way the beach ball bounces." So much for collective action.

Agency in conversations

In spite of its absence in media discourse, 43 percent of the conversations on troubled industry spontaneously referred to collective action by workers. Not all of it was sympathetic by any means. In four groups, all of them white, comments were directed against the ability of unions to protect sloppy or unmotivated workers by threatening to strike if the company tries to fire them. In another three, disparaging comments were made about the ineffectiveness of strikes or unions more generally.

Sympathetic references, however, occurred in 30 percent of the groups and tended to recur more often in later discussion. Sometimes they occurred in the same discussion that contained belittling ones, as in the following example:

> *Characters:*
>
> *Carol, a bookkeeper in her thirties.*
> *Cissy, a bus driver, in her forties.*
> *Constance, a clerk at an insurance company, in her thirties.*
> *Sally, a clerk at an insurance company, in her twenties.*

Facilitator: Would you say that anything that has happened on the issue of troubled industry has affected you personally, or anyone in your family, or friends?
Carol: Friends.
Facilitator: Can you say more about what happened to them?

Carol: Well, they did – they went out, they picketed, they fought for what
they wanted. They didn't get a result. The company was shut
down in the end. And now they're unemployed.

[later]

Facilitator: We've talked about ourselves and the other people that we
know. Can you think of larger groups in this country that might
stand to gain or lose on what policies are set on troubled industry,
what's done on troubled industry?

Sally: How about, like with nurses. Like who've picketed for more – like
the people at Carney Hospital. They've picketed till they get what
they want. Like that?

Cissy: It worked.

Sally: It worked, really, 'cause they got what they want, right? They didn't
fire them. They're still working. So they got what they want.

Facilitator: Anyone else?

Constance: Like the big unions. People will see if they could get more
money. Like the insurance company could have like a union. And
they picketed until the union tried to get them more money, and
they go back to the work.

[Later, in response to Cartoon 4.]

Constance: This cartoon's saying that this company got what they want,
right?

Facilitator: What do you think?

Constance: It says – well, I got what I want so you can – bye, I don't
need you anymore, you know. Got what I want, really want, out
of you. So. I'm going somewhere else.

Sally: Like I was saying earlier, like the insurance company that we work for,
they gave us lower wages but, hey, we give them what they want.
"Give them this salary that we want to give them. Forget it. They
don't want it, they can walk out." Some union people, like who have
a union, they have to fight for it, okay? They have to give us what *we*
want. And like this guy here laying flat. That means he's going to be
laying flat – he have to take what they give him.

Cissy: Yup. Run right over.

There was no evidence in any of the 30 percent of the groups with
supportive discussion of collective action on troubled industry that public
discourse was the source of their sympathy. They must necessarily look
beyond it to their own experiential knowledge and popular wisdom to find
the resources to sustain it. In fact, a substantial minority do this.

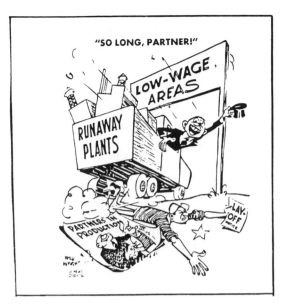

4. Fred Wright. Copyright, United Electrical, Radio and Machine Workers of America (UE). The cartoonist seems to be saying that companies are ready to forget all about their partnership with workers and to take off for areas where they can pay lower wages whenever it suits their interests.

Affirmative action

The story of agency in media discourse on affirmative action is much more complicated; citizen action once had a prominent place but faded rapidly in the 1980s. The three most recent critical discourse moments we sampled all focused on Supreme Court decisions, not an obvious venue for emphasizing the relevance of citizen action. Even with the type of stimulus event held constant, there is a dramatic shift in the centrality of the civil rights movement from the Bakke decision of 1978 to the Memphis Fire-fighters decision of 1984.

One can see this change most dramatically in the way the story was treated on television. Visually, affirmative action was linked to the civil rights movement and to contemporary expressions that implied its continuing relevance. In 1978, all three networks showed footage of a demonstration by women and minorities in San Francisco protesting the Bakke decision. There were shots of pickets and marchers, of signs and banners saying "Fight Racism, Overturn Bakke" and "Abajo con Bakke" [Down with Bakke]. Heroes and heroines of the civil rights movement such as

Julian Bond, Jesse Jackson, and Coretta Scott King were interviewed, along with spokespersons for the NAACP, the Urban League, the Southern Christian Leadership Conference (SCLC), and the Congressional Black Caucus. They were, of course, identified in print as well as orally. ABC showed shots of Martin Luther King at a White House ceremony with President Lyndon Johnson for the signing of the Civil Rights Act.

By the next year, at the time of the Weber decision, this same visual message was still there but had become more muted. Two of the networks showed the NAACP convention in Louisville, and ABC included audience shots of black men and women singing, clapping their hands, and swaying to music. CBS did not cover the convention but used numerous spokesmen for civil rights groups.

This positive imagery of the civil rights movement in the late 1970s certainly did not put media coverage of affirmative action at odds with official discourse. Eleanor Holmes Norton, a black woman, headed the Equal Employment Opportunity Commission (EEOC) and was the Carter administration's principal spokesperson on the issue. As a young attorney just out of Yale Law School, Norton had helped to write the brief for the Mississippi Freedom Democratic Party's 1964 challenge to the seating of the all-white Mississippi delegation to the National Democratic Convention. She had a long history of participation in both the civil rights and women's movements. Norton responded to the Bakke decision by making it clear that the EEOC would continue its affirmative action efforts. "My reading of the decision," she said, "is that we are not compelled to do anything differently from the way we've done things in the past, and we are not going to."[7]

After the Weber decision, Norton expressed the satisfaction of the Carter administration that "the court appears to have done away with the reverse discrimination issue in employment discrimination law. As a result of the Weber decision, employers and unions no longer need fear that conscientious efforts to open job opportunities will be subject to legal challenge."[8] The inclination of journalists to adopt official views of the world worked in this instance to support a sympathetic view of the civil rights movement and citizen action associated with it.

By 1984, official discourse on affirmative action had undergone a shift. In the early years of the Reagan administration, affirmative action had low priority but there was little adoption of the rhetoric of opposition. The Labor Department relaxed the rules for federal contractors and the requirements for remedial action, but Secretary of Labor Raymond J. Donovan explained it as merely a way of reducing the amount of paperwork. "This regulatory package keeps the necessary safeguards for protected groups, while cutting down the paperwork burden for employers."[9]

Internal differences within the Reagan administration apparently prevented full backing of the efforts led by Assistant Attorney General William Bradford Reynolds to ban all "color-conscious programs." Other administration officials at the EEOC, Labor Department, and Civil Rights Commission defended some forms of affirmative action.

By 1984, when the Supreme Court confronted the conflict between affirmative action and seniority in deciding who should be fired first in the Memphis firefighters' case, the Reynolds group had won the internal battle in the Reagan administration. The Justice Department filed briefs in this and other cases, arguing that all race-conscious programs were illegal, even when adopted in response to undeniable past discrimination against blacks. When the Supreme Court upheld the primacy of seniority even though it might mean that most of those laid off were minorities who were recently hired under an affirmative action agreement, Reynolds called the decision "exhilarating" and Solicitor General Rex Lee said, "It's a slam dunk."[10]

In contrast to the coverage of earlier decisions, the civil rights movement had virtually disappeared from the visual coverage of the issue and appeared in ways that obscured or denied its relevance. No pickets, marchers, or any other symbol of social movement activity appeared on any of the television news programs, nor did any icons of the civil rights movement. The NAACP was the only civil rights organization represented by spokespersons. Furthermore, on two of the three networks, Reagan administration officials hailed the decision against the Memphis affirmative action program as pro–civil rights. Clarence Pendleton, chairman of the Civil Rights Commission (and black), applauded the decision as "a mighty blow for civil rights, not a mighty blow against civil rights."[11]

In sum, national media discourse on affirmative action did portray citizen action as part of the story, even when the news peg rested on Supreme Court decisions that are supposedly insulated from popular pressure. The civil rights movement is a story about ordinary people making history; it legitimizes, albeit retrospectively, collective action as a positive force for change. On this issue, then, media discourse does not uniformly discourage a sense of collective agency among the citizenry; in some contexts, it can even be seen to support it.

But every silver lining has a cloud. This piece of the story was present only during the period in which official discourse supported the goals of civil rights activists. When official discourse shifted from sympathetic to unsympathetic, the affirmative action story shifted as well; the civil rights movement lost its visibility, and citizen action lost its relevance in media discourse on the issue.

Agency in conversation

Spontaneous discussion of collective action occurred in 38 percent of the conversations on affirmative action, and in three-fourths of these, the depictions were positive and supportive. The stories people told were about an earlier time – the 1960s or the 1970s – and included both the civil rights movement and antibusing actions during the bitter conflict over desegregation of the Boston public school system. Considering the time lapse, the continued salience and conversational presence of these episodes suggest a special vividness in memory, as in the following examples:

> *Characters:*
>
> *Gertrude, a secretary, black, in her thirties.*
> *Robert, a lifeguard, black, in his late twenties.*
> *Danny, a customer service representative for a rental car company, black, in his early twenties.*

Gertrude: I wonder how much difference affirmative action would make. I'm sure it helps a lot as far as job placement. If they didn't have it, a lot of companies wouldn't hire blacks.

Danny: Okay.

Gertrude: And some other minorities. But a lot of these other minorities are together so much that they say, bump them. They open up their own business anyway.

Danny: Here in Massachusetts.

Gertrude: And those kids come out cum laude in school. So what's wrong with black folks and black kids?

Danny: Uh huh. Nothing. They're just spoiled or they're in the norm.

Gertrude: They're not in the norm. That's just it.

Robert: You know what it is? They have not struggled. They have not dealt with a whole lot of things that – I mean, you're too young [*addressing Danny*] but you're around for some of this stuff, right. I wanted to go to the – march with them –

Danny: – Demonstration?

Robert: Yeah, with Martin Luther King. I wanted to go. I was thirteen years old at that time. I was into black history, and I would read up on these lynchings that they used to do down there. And I guess I got a little hostility in myself. I was here on Blue Hill Ave. during the riots of 1967. You know what I'm saying? And heard about Watts and heard about this, that, and the other.

The second example is from a group in South Boston, a center of white opposition to the court-ordered school desegregation plan:

> *Characters:*
>
> *Peter, a cook, in his twenties.*
> *Gabriele, a nurse's aid, in her early twenties.*
> *Tim, a car shuttler, in his twenties.*
> *Bill, a telephone maintenance worker, in his twenties.*
>
> *(They are in the midst of discussing the facilitator's question on whether they have been affected personally by anything that has happened on affirmative action.)*

Peter: I missed a year of school because of busing. My mother would just not send me. I lived next to Southie High, right, and I couldn't go to that school. You know, when the busing started, and my mother wasn't about just to send me over there, because no one else was going, you know. There was a bunch of songs like, "We're not going to go."

Gabriele: Why did they have to bus them? I mean, why do they have to mix them? If they're happy the way they are, leave them. There was so much trouble because of the busing. You know?

Tim: I know. Look at how many people dropped out and stuff because of busing. People got stabbed, killed, and stuff.

[*Later, in discussing what should be done about affirmative action.*]

Peter: I don't want to see busing all over again. I've seen people get their – I lived right next to the high school, right? I used to come home from lunch from the gate and walk a block down from about the street here and I seen people get bats, I've seen a baby carriage without a baby in it, a horse. [Police] at night chased people in my hallways 'cause people used to, you know, terrorize the school. [Police] used to come out of the school at night time – "Let's chase everybody." I'll never forget that. Never. Never in my life. I live right next to the school. I've seen it all out my window. Guy come right – they call, "Get acey-doucey," [*laughs*] right? There was his name when I was about seven, eight, nine, – seen his whole teeth bashed in from a billy bat. Came into my house, my mother took him in, you know, no teeth at all, and he'd get out.

Tim: Slip some dentures on him and send him back out.

Bill: That says the whole thing.

Although these experiences of collective action are rare, they remain especially alive in memory and available as a resource in discussing the issue. The references frequently express ambivalence; collective action experiences are sometimes associated with anxiety and fear but also with a sense of the excitement of making history. People bring them into the conversation without prompting, even though the relevant incidents may have occurred many years ago.

Only on the issue of affirmative action did significant racial differences appear. Almost half of the black groups but only 6 percent of the white groups had predominantly supportive discussions of citizen action ($p <$ .01). The black groups drew on the civil rights movement and the black struggle generally. The white groups were less likely to bring any collective action into their conversation on the issue, were more likely to focus on the antibusing movement rather than the civil rights movement when they did, and made mostly negative comments about antibusing collective action regardless of their views on affirmative action.

Clearly, sympathetic discussion of collective action has a great deal to do with sympathy for the goals of such action, and this varies from issue to issue. Many black groups framed affirmative action as the latest chapter in a long, unfinished story of the black struggle for inclusion, and the civil rights movement appeared as an earlier and successful chapter in that effort. But this framing was rarely present in white discussions of the issue. Hence, given this difference in the overall framing of the issue, it is not surprising that the civil rights movement rarely played much of a role in conversations on this issue among whites.

Nuclear power

The nuclear power discourse also contains a story about citizen action. In the late 1950s and early 1960s, a movement against the atmospheric testing of nuclear weapons called public attention to the long-range dangers of radiation. Milk, "nature's most nearly perfect food," as the dairy industry advertised it, was found to contain strontium–90. A famous ad, sponsored by the Committee for a Sane Nuclear Policy (SANE), warned the public that "Dr. Spock is worried."

Some of this increased public awareness about radiation dangers spilled over into concern about nuclear power. Local controversies developed over the licensing of a few reactors. But after passage of the Limited Test Ban Treaty of 1963, concerns about radiation receded from media discourse.

Citizen action became part of the nuclear power story with the rise of the anti–nuclear power movement in the 1970s. One of its major accomplishments was to trigger particular media practices that opened the discourse – but in restricted ways. Before the 1970s, journalists did not apply the balance norm to nuclear power; its application is triggered by controversy. Operationally, this requires either extensive or dramatic citizen action by challengers or public opposition to nuclear power policies by powerful elites – neither of which occurred until the early 1970s.

The norm of providing balance on controversial issues is vague, but it tends to be interpreted in certain specific ways. In news accounts, balance is provided by quoting spokespersons with competing views. To simplify the task, there is a tendency to reduce controversy to two competing positions – an official one and an alternative sponsored by the most vested member of the polity. In many cases, the critics may share the same underlying frame and taken-for-granted assumptions as officials, differing only on narrow grounds.

The anti–nuclear power movement, like many movements, consisted of a broad coalition of movement organizations with different frames on nuclear power and different strategies for changing nuclear policy. A study of network television coverage for the ten years prior to the accident at Three Mile Island (TMI) showed a sharp rise in overall coverage of the nuclear power issue beginning in 1975; by the first three months of 1979, before TMI, the networks had run twenty-six stories related to nuclear power.[12]

The anti–nuclear power movement was most likely to be represented by spokespersons for the Union of Concerned Scientists (UCS), with Ralph Nader in second place. Spokespersons for direct action groups such as the Clamshell Alliance were rare, although their actions – especially the 1977 site occupation of the Seabrook, New Hampshire, nuclear reactor – sometimes drew extensive coverage.

We sampled media discourse in a two-week period in the spring of 1977, covering both the Seabrook action and an effort by President Jimmy Carter to gain international support for controlling the spread of nuclear technology. This sample produced fifteen television segments, two newsmagazine accounts, six cartoons, and five opinion columns.

Television coverage focused exclusively on the visually rich collective action at Seabrook and its aftermath, driving the Carter initiative out of the picture. A strong supporter of the Seabrook reactor, Governor Meldrim Thomson of New Hampshire, inadvertently helped to turn what might have been another barely visible citizen action into a major continuing story. The 1,414 demonstrators who were arrested were not, as the "Clam" had expected, released on their own recognizance. Instead, they were charged with criminal trespass and asked to post bail ranging from $100 to \$500. Most refused, and they were then held in five National Guard armories for twelve days, while camera crews and network and print journalists came to town. Each of the networks ran segments on five different days, although sometimes merely a short update.

The television story was about a dyadic conflict between Governor Thomson and his allies and the Clamshell Alliance over whether or not the Seabrook reactor would be completed. The central question addressed was who will win and, hence, there was very little direct commentary about nuclear power as such. But the coverage did present images of citizen action on nuclear power as it implicitly addressed the question: What kind of people are against nuclear power?

For a deaf television viewer, the answer would seem to be people who wear backpacks and play frisbee. All three networks featured these images in more than one segment. One saw beards and long hair, bandanas, "No Nukes" buttons, and people playing guitars and doing needlepoint. Outside the courthouse, after the demonstrators had been released, viewers saw happy family reunions, with many children.

These visual images do not have a fixed meaning. One who believes that the experts know best might see frivolous flower children and environmental extremists who look as if they will not be happy until they turn the White House into a bird sanctuary. A more sympathetic viewer might see loving, caring, earthy young people who are socially integrated and concerned about our shared environment.

There were network differences in the words accompanying these images. The CBS and NBC coverage left the interpretive work to the viewer, but ABC offered its own interpretation. Viewers were told that these are the same kind of people who were involved in antiwar demonstrations, "demonstrators in search of a cause." The network allowed two members of the Clam to speak for themselves, quoting their determination to win ("We have to stop it at any cost") while omitting any quotations dealing with their reasons for acting.

The demonstrators were presented relatively sympathetically in newsmagazine coverage. Both *Time* and *Newsweek* mentioned their commitment to nonviolence, and *Newsweek* added their exclusion of drugs, weapons, and fighting. The accompanying photographs reinforced the television images of backpackers; *Newsweek* called them "scruffy" and mentioned playing frisbee, playing guitars, and reading Thoreau. *Time* also quoted the publisher of the *Manchester Union Leader,* William Loeb, who likened the Clam to "Nazi storm troopers under Hitler," but characterized him in a discrediting way as an "abrasive conservative."

The cartoons and columns, with one exception, ignored the antinuclear movement in their commentary on the issue. Only Jeremiah Murphy brought in antinuclear protesters, linking them with 1960s images of antiwar protesters – scruffy beards, longish hair, and braless women. Some of them, he wrote, "really don't know what they are protesting and – far worse – don't care."[13]

After 1977, whether it was treated sympathetically or not, the anti-nuclear power movement had become a visible, established part of media discourse on the issue. When we sampled media coverage after the Chernobyl accident, we found all three networks showing American or European antinuclear protestors, with a total of eight separate instances. The protestors' signs reminded viewers that "Chernobyl can happen here" or "Chernobyl is everywhere."

Unlike affirmative action, no national administration has ever promoted or supported citizen action on nuclear power. Media attentiveness, in this case, occurred in spite of official discouragement. And even though no collective action since 1977 has come close to the national visibility of the Seabrook occupation, the antinuclear movement has succeeded in keeping citizen action visible in the issue discourse. Again, the generalization that media discourse uniformly suppresses any sense of collective agency seems seriously incomplete for nuclear power and perhaps even misleading.

Agency in conversations

The prominence of citizen action in media discourse is reflected in conversations as well, with spontaneous discussion of the anti–nuclear power movement in more than half (54 percent) of the groups. However, positive and negative references are more or less balanced, with only 29 percent of the groups having predominantly sympathetic discussions.

In one group that was divided on the merits of nuclear power, a pro-nuclear participant complained about Seabrook's being unable to open after all of the money spent on it. "The place is built, is ready to open," he asserted. "But they're not letting them open it. The demonstrators are not letting them open it."

Negative comments, however, were much more likely to belittle collective action than to deplore its effectiveness. One participant referred to "all of that protesting. Some crazy people laying out holding hands, don't want to let people through to do whatever has to be done over there." But discussions of ineffectiveness frequently imply regret that collective action isn't more meaningful, as in the example following of an interracial group we encountered earlier (see Chapter 3, "Arab–Israeli conflict"):

Characters:

Reggie, coordinator at a health services pool, black, in his forties.
Marilyn, a nurse, black, in her thirties.
Marjorie, an office manager, white, in her forties.
Susie, a receptionist at a nursing agency, white, in her early twenties.

(They are responding to the facilitator's question about what larger groups in the country are affected by what happens on the nuclear power issue.)

Reggie: The human race! The human race. Everybody's worried about it; that's what I wrote on my little thing there [the questionnaire]. Everybody! The entire human race.

Marilyn: The entire human race.

Marjorie: What's that they say? "One nuclear bomb can ruin your whole day."

(laughter)

Marjorie: You know what I wonder, though? If *all* the people − well, not all the people − a good majority of the people feel that way [against nuclear power], how come the government keeps doing − I mean, don't we have any power?

Susie: 'Cause they're making money on it.

Marjorie: I mean, you go and you march and you carry your little poster and you sign your little thing −

Reggie: − What's that gonna do? That's not gonna do anything at all. I mean, it makes people aware.

Marjorie: − and the government keeps −

Susie: The majority of the people are against it, I think.

Marjorie: Majority? Psshhh!

Susie: The majority, but the government isn't doing anything about it.

Marjorie: If I was a crazy woman, I'd have a drink.

In three of the white groups, someone described friends or relatives who engaged in acts of civil disobedience. Such collective action seems to earn grudging respect even when the person discussing them is generally sympathetic to nuclear power.

Characters:

Mike, a custodial supervisor, in his forties.
Bob, an administrator at a college, in his thirties.

(Earlier, Mike asserted, "Nuclear power is definitely the way the country is going." The group is responding to the facilitator's

> *question on whether anything that has happened on this issue*
> *has affected the group members personally.)*

Mike: I had a cousin that got locked up in Seabrook.

(*laughter*)

Mike: And I ended up getting in an awful argument with him. He was telling me his views of why he was standing there, and I told him why he got locked up. And I still feel as though he was in the wrong. But if a person believes in it and that's what they want to do, then that's his prerogative. Twenty-five dollars later, we shook hands.

(*laughter*)

Bob: Did you bail him out?

Mike: Nope.

> *[Later in the conversation, near the end.]*

Mike: I'm not close to a nuclear power plant. Ah, people – I have a cousin in Seabrook – it's in his backyard, so I can't really feel the same as they do.

Bob: Yeah.

Mike: As far as I'm concerned, *I* think it's the way the country's gonna go. They've been probably a little more involved in it because it's been in their backyard. They probably know a little more about it. They probably have more fliers on it. They seen some of the more radical people than I would 'cause these are the people that *go* outside of these plants and protest and picket, stand in the rain. I look at it, I believe in the peoples' conviction, if that's what they want to do, if that's what they feel strong in, fine. But they have to prove it to me.

Arab–Israeli conflict

Domestic citizen action by Americans with ties to the old country is a routine part of the reporting of foreign conflicts. Rallies and demonstrations by ethnic groups are expected, and are duly reported and typically scrutinized for their electoral relevance, that is, for the behavior of a voting bloc. It becomes especially newsworthy when any large ethnic group is upset with elected officials belonging to a party that the group has supported in the past. The general message here implicitly encourages citizen action: If domestic ethnic groups are substantial in size and cohesive – and, hence, have significant electoral leverage – collective action is important.

Coverage of citizen action on Arab–Israeli conflict fits this general picture, but with some complications. Collective action by people in other countries has frequently been a central part of the story, but domestic citizen action has been strictly a routine ethnic sidebar. From 1948 to the mid-1970s, rallies by American Jewish groups in support of Israel during its various wars were a standard part of the coverage. During the October 1973 war, for example, *Time* wrote, "Rallies, marches and meetings are being held everywhere." The article described events in Los Angeles and Chicago while showing a picture of a large group of demonstrators with signs and Israeli flags, with the caption "New Yorkers gathered at City Hall to demonstrate their support of Israel in Middle East War."[14] Smaller demonstrations by Arab-Americans in support of the Arab protagonists in the war were also noted in passing.

By 1982, domestic citizen action was still an ethnic story, but with a new twist. We sampled media discourse during the Israeli invasion of Lebanon and shortly after the massacres at the Sabra and Shatilla refugee camps by Lebanese Christian forces under Israeli control. *Newsweek* contrasted the flurry of "muted" protests by American Jews compared to the more vocal critics in Israel itself. The caption accompanying two pictures of demonstrations used a quote, "There is a need to speak out," and labeled them "Anti-Begin protests in Boston and San Francisco."

Within the American Jewish community, especially since 1982, there has been increasing public criticism of Israeli government policy, and occasionally, this has included criticism of U.S. inaction or passivity as well. But concerns about U.S. Mideast policy are typically expressed in various forums of public discourse or in more private conversations and meetings, not through grass-roots citizen action.

It is difficult to find in this coverage any overall tendency in media discourse to render citizen action invisible. When it occurs, it is given its due as part of the story. But it is invariably framed as part of the ethnic politics of the Jewish and, to a lesser extent, the Arab-American community. The subtext is that citizen action on the Arab–Israeli issue is relevant only insofar as it expresses the concerns and identities of these two particular ethnic groups. For the working people in our sample, 99 percent of whom have no strong ties with either group, citizen action on Arab–Israeli conflict is implicitly defined as irrelevant in media discourse.

Agency in conversations

The conversations fully reflect the subtext. Domestic citizen action of any kind on Arab–Israeli conflict is never brought into the conversation. Foreign collective action – in particular, terrorism – is often part of the discussion, but the speakers always assume the role of potential innocent victims.

Conclusion

I make no claim that this close analysis of media discourse on the four issues studied here forces us to abandon the generalization that American political culture systematically discourages the idea that ordinary citizens can alter the conditions and terms of their daily lives through their own actions. But this message comes through more equivocally on some issues than on others, and in some special contexts, a sense of collective agency is even nurtured.

The generalization seems strongest for discourse on troubled industry. Significant citizen action in the steel industry, undertaken with a degree of official encouragement, nevertheless remained invisible in national media discourse. On affirmative action, citizen action was visible when an administration sympathetic to the civil rights movement was in power and became largely invisible when official discourse turned unsympathetic. Official sympathy for citizen action, then, may alter its normal disparagement or invisibility and encourage journalists to treat such collective actors as relevant players in the policy arena.

On nuclear power, citizen action became and remained visible in spite of an official discourse that belittled it and attempted to diminish its importance. Apparently, there are circumstances in which media discourse will portray a movement as a significant actor even without official encouragement. Finally, although citizen action by Americans is present and is treated sympathetically in the discourse on Arab–Israeli conflict, it is only relevant and encouraged for Jewish Americans and Arab-Americans as a legitimate expression of ethnic politics. By implication, citizen action by others or in anything except an ethnic context is rendered irrelevant.

The media role in portraying collective agency seems, to a substantial degree, issue specific and variable rather than constant. In considering working people's sense of collective agency, then, it seems more useful to differentiate media discourse by issue domain. If their sense of collective agency differs from one issue to another, perhaps it reflects some of these differences in the political culture of the specific issue.

The conversations examined here provide abundant evidence of cynicism about politics and government, belief in its domination by big business, and the impossibility of working people like the group members to alter the terms of their daily lives. All of these themes that existing studies of American workers have emphasized are replicated here. I have not presented evidence on these points from the conversations but have simply accepted this as the starting point for analysis.

The cynicism, however, is partly situational. The interaction situation, as I argued in Chapter 2, encourages cynical chic. People are frequently less cynical privately than their public stance would indicate and, in any event, they are not consistently cynical. Every time a Solidarity movement in Poland or a "Velvet Revolution" in Czechoslovakia happens, we are reminded that this portrait of helplessness and resignation is incomplete.

Part of the incompleteness is fostered by an overemphasis on how media discourse contributes to social control. It clearly does in many respects on many issues, but there is enormous variability among issues. Media coverage frequently and inadvertently keeps alive and helps transmit images of group protest.

On nuclear power, in particular, a strong case could be made that media discourse has been more of a help than a hindrance to the antinuclear movement. It serves no official agenda to have antinuke protestors taken so seriously that they provide potential models for the next community where one might wish to construct a nuclear reactor. Indeed, nuclear officials in industry and government who might consider commissioning a new reactor must certainly be deterred by the likely prospect of prolonged local protest with extensive media coverage.

Media-amplified images of successful citizen action on one issue can generalize and transfer to other issues. The repertoire of collective action presented on a broad range of political issues in media discourse – of boycotts, strikes, and demonstrations, for example – can easily be divorced from the particular context in which it is presented and adapted to other issues. Despite the differences in media discourse, sympathetic discussions of collective action occur at least as often on troubled industry as they do on nuclear power. But it is also true that such discussion focuses on strikes rather than on community–worker buyouts of companies, a possibility that media neglect has kept out of people's consciousness.

Even where national media discourse renders citizen action irrelevant, local media and experiential knowledge often provide awareness of its potential relevance. It only takes one person to introduce the topic through his or her personal knowledge to stimulate others to bring in examples that they have heard or read about. The result is that a majority of the groups (57 percent) had a sympathetic discussion of collective action on at least one issue, and most (81 percent) brought such matters into the conversation in some form. Although the meaning given to such action varied from issue to issue, the overall tendency to discuss collective action sympathetically was equally great in black and white groups.

Sympathetic discussion of collective action, however, is still a far cry from a full-fledged collective action frame. My claim is only that models of successful collective action are a common part of how these working people negotiate meaning on three of the four issues. The potential collective agency that this implies can be activated when it is integrated with the other components of collective action frames. But before we get to this part of the story, we need to take a closer look at the final component: collective identity.

5

Identity

Being a collective agent implies being part of a "we" who can do something. The identity component of collective action frames is about the process of defining this "we," typically in opposition to some "they" who have different interests or values. As Melucci (1989) suggests, social movements elaborate and negotiate this meaning over time, and some even make the question of "who we are" an important part of their internal discourse.

It is useful to think of collective identities as three embedded layers: *organizational, movement,* and *solidary group.* The organizational layer refers to identities built around movement carriers – the union maid or the party loyalist, for example. This layer may or may not be embedded in a movement layer that is broader than any particular organization. The identity of peace activists, for example, rarely rests on one organization; people support different efforts at different moments while subordinating all organizations to their broader movement identity. Finally, the movement layer may or may not be embedded in a larger solidary group identity constructed around people's social location – for example, as workers or as black women.

Sometimes these different layers are so closely integrated that they become a single amalgam: A movement arises out of a particular solidary group with widespread support from it, and one particular organization comes to embody the movement. Often, however, the different layers are separate. Many working-class Americans, for example, identify with working people but have no identification with their union and think of the labor movement as something that happened fifty years ago.

This chapter focuses on the solidary group level. More specifically, it examines the extent to which people use their social location in framing the four issues and the extent to which media discourse encourages such framing. To what extent are categories of class, race, and gender important in their understanding of politics, and to what extent do they see issues as embodying a we and a they?[1]

A collective action frame must be adversarial. Some groups attempt to mobilize their constituents with an all-inclusive we. We are the world, humankind, or, in the case of domestic issues, all good citizens. Such an *aggregate* frame turns the we into a pool of individuals rather than a potential collective actor. The call for action in such frames is personal – for example, to make peace, hunger, or the environment your own responsibility.[2]

There is no clear they in such aggregate frames. The targets are not actors but abstractions – hunger, pollution, war, poverty, disease. These abstractions do not point to an external target whose actions or policies must be changed. If pollution is the problem and we are all polluters, then we are the target of action. We are the they in such frames, and neither agent nor target is a collective actor.

Collective action frames, in contrast, are adversarial; we stand in opposition to or conflict with some they. They are responsible for some objectionable situation and have the power to change it by acting differently in some fashion. We and they are differentiated rather than conflated.

A blurry they, by itself, does not imply an aggregate frame. It is quite possible to have a clear and collective we, while the they remains vague because it is so elusive. This is especially likely to be true when the main targets of change are cultural more than political and economic. If one is attacking, for example, the dominant cultural code of what is normal, the decisions of governments and powerful corporate actors may be secondary. In the pursuit of cultural change, the target is often diffused throughout the whole civil society and the they being pursued is structurally elusive.[3]

In such a situation, the mass media are likely to become the ambivalent target of action. To the extent that they reflect the cultural code that the group is challenging, they are necessarily an adversary. But since they also are capable of amplifying the challenge and expanding its audience, helping it to reach the many settings in which cultural codes operate, they are necessarily a potential ally as well. Hence the characteristic ambivalence with which so many movement organizations approach the mass media.

In sum, frames with a clear we and an elusive they are quite capable of being fully collective and adversarial; unlike aggregate frames, agent and target of action are not conflated. These frames, then, are simply a more complicated type of adversarial frame.

Individualism

The same sociocultural forces that discourage a sense of collective agency also discourage thinking about issues in collective terms. Gans (1979, 51) describes individualism as an enduring value in the news. Individuals, acting on their own terms rather than collectively, are continually presented as "a source of economic, social, and cultural productivity" and "a means of achieving cultural variety." Not just news but also entertainment and advertising are heavily implicated in the process. The "loosely bounded culture" promoted by television directs people toward a private vision of the self in the world.

The pervasive culture of individualism is reflected in the language of working people as well. Gans (1988, ix), calling it "middle American individualism," describes it as "first and foremost a mixture of cultural and moral values for dealing with everyday life and of goals for guiding self-development and familial improvement." People's hearts, Gans argues, are in their microsocial lives, where they are concerned with seeking control, security, comfort, and convenience for themselves and their families. "For all practical purposes," he writes (1988, x), "Washington, New York, and the other centers of American society are, for many people much of the time, on other planets."

Gans never directly examines political talk, but others do. Carbaugh (1988) takes as his text the audience discussion of issues on a popular television talk show, *Donahue*. His rich and subtle analysis focuses heavily on what he calls the "equivocal enactment of individuality and community." One needs to understand this idea to appreciate the obstacles to thinking about political issues collectively.

This equivocal enactment is seen most clearly in discourse on the symbol of the person as an "individual." This symbol, Carbaugh writes, allows speakers to transcend the differences that are implied when people are discussed as members of social groups – as men and women, blacks and whites, working people and paper pushers, or other collective categories. "By defining persons as individuals, speakers can state what is common among all persons and groups." With this symbol, one asserts simultaneously that we are both all alike and each unique in being individuals. Through its use, "a definition of persons is constructed which enables meanings of both a common humanity and a separate humanness" (1988, 23).

In this discourse, persons as individuals have rights; social groups and institutions are moved to the rear. Although the term *equal rights,* for example, could apply to the claims of a group as well as to those of an individual, the discourse privileges the rights of individuals and makes the articulation of collective claims problematic. The assertion of injustices based on social inequalities, for example, must contend with a culturally normative response that asserts that we are all individuals, and implicitly denies the relevance of social location and group differences.

This denial is further strengthened by a closely related discourse that distinguishes the *self* as a unique person from the *social role.* In this sample of American talk from *Donahue,* the self is independent, aware, and expressive; its polemic counterpart, the social role, is dependent, less personally aware, and closed. "The self," Carbaugh writes (1988, 98), "is given a voice through a rhetoric of individual freedom, voluntary choice, and self-assertion; social role is given a voice through a rhetoric of slavery, obligatory choice, and accommodation. . . . Where self radiates the preferred unique humanness of the individual, social role glimmers a dispreferred quality of commonality."

This discourse on the person as an individual transcends ethnic, racial, and gender differences among working people. To use Carbaugh's phrase, they all "talk American." This does not preclude them from using adversarial frames on some issues as well, but such talk remains continually problematic and vulnerable to challenge.

Troubled industry

Media discourse on troubled industry is remarkably free of adversarial frames. The most prominent frame is PARTNERSHIP: We are all in the same leaky lifeboat, and everybody needs to row and bail to keep us afloat. Collective categories such as business, labor, and government are part of the analysis, but the central issue is cooperation among them. Adversarial relations are hangovers from the past and part of the problem that needs to be overcome. Cartoon 1 (Appendix B) expresses it.

There are important variations of this frame. One version makes government the senior partner, directing an industrial policy, and another makes business the senior partner, with government as facilitator. Both variations make labor the junior partner, and neither is adversarial.

The major competitor to the PARTNERSHIP frame, FREE ENTERPRISE, challenges the cooperation idea without introducing an adversarial component. It emphasizes the self-correcting character of the market system, in which the weak and inefficient lose out to the strong and efficient. One must allow this market mechanism to operate without messing things up with government intervention. Some versions of this frame have a strong antilabor component, but they are not really adversarial. They depict powerful unions as working against the real interests of working people by making American products no longer competitive. Wage restraint, in this frame, is in the collective interest of workers and management alike.

A CAPITAL FLIGHT frame, which is adversarial, is part of a broader public discourse.[4] The root of the problem, in this frame, is the investment decisions made by private multinational corporations in search of a docile, unorganized, or cowed labor force. Within the United States, this means moving from unionized to nonunionized regions; outside of the United States, it means investing in countries with authoritarian governments that suppress working-class organization, frequently with violence. But this adversarial frame is invisible in the national media discourse on troubled industry.[5]

Adversarial frames in conversations

A central theme in the enormous literature about the lack of class consciousness among American workers is what Williams (1950) calls the "selective tradition." Workers think and talk about social class differently when they are at work and when they are at home in their communities. This subjective division, Katznelson (1981, 6) argues, is even true of blue-collar workers who live in immediate proximity to their factories:

In South Chicago . . . mammoth steel mills loom over the surrounding communities that house their workers. In the mills, these workers see themselves as labor (in opposition to the steel companies and, on occasion, to capital more generally); and as labor they are quite militant. The ordinary idiom of plant life is that of class. . . . Yet as soon as these workers pack up and go home, they cease to see themselves primarily as workers. On the East Side and Hegewisch, in Irondale and Slag Valley, they are Croatians, Mexicans, Poles.

Halle's fine study (1984) of industrial workers in a New Jersey chemical plant suggests three overlapping ways in which class appears in their discourse.

1. Life at Work. The focus is on their position in the system of production and centers on the symbol of the "working man." "Blue collar [male] workers in America," Halle writes (1984, 204), "refer to themselves as 'working men' but rarely as 'working class.' "

Halle asked them, in interviews, to explain what they meant by the term and elicited one or more of the following cluster of ideas: Working men do physical work, dangerous or dirty work, boring and routine work, factory work, and/or closely supervised work. It is, in their minds, not simply a descriptive category but a moral one; they do "real" work compared to those who push paper and "just sit on their butts all day" or are grossly overpaid for clean and pleasant work.

Clearly, there are class-conscious elements in such a symbol. It links the job features of blue-collar work with the idea of productive labor, implying that only those whose work involves such features are really productive. Managers and, in general, upper and lower white-collar sectors are not. The idea reflects a more general solidarity with blue-collar workers that transcends their particular location in a chemical plant. One can find in this idea a lay version of the labor theory of value.

If class consciousness of this sort is widespread, it is also quite limited, as Halle points out. As many of these workers use it, it implies as much hostility toward the poor as toward big business; furthermore, *poor* becomes a surrogate for blacks and Hispanics who are not working men and working women but people on welfare who are unwilling to work. It also contains a more ambivalent sexism, implying "that blue-collar work is for men, not women, and a related implication that lower white collar work is less than productive" (1984, 219). This hinders the building of alliances between blue-collar workers and lower white-collar workers.

Finally, although the symbol of working man implies a critical view of the system of production, it is not coupled with any belief in or sense of possibility of an alternative organization. Working people don't receive their just reward compared to less productive managers, but this implies a need to increase the relative reward, not to change the system.

2. Life Outside of Work. When Halle's chemical workers used the term *class,* they focused on their life outside of the workplace – especially where they live, their standard of living, and their lifestyle. Their occupation or relation to the means of production is largely irrelevant here. They live in neighborhoods with other people of similar income, only a minority of whom are blue-collar workers. Outside of work, they are not working men but "middle class" or "lower middle class."

This discourse distinguishes them from the rich and the poor but blurs the middle range. For those who see the poor as mostly blacks and Hispanics, any racism contained in their identity as working men carries over. The tacit sexism, however, is removed; their class identity here is family based and not gender specific.

3. Populism. Working people sometimes employ a third set of class images centered on such symbols as the *little person,* the *ordinary person,* the *common people,* or simply *the people.* This broad category is used in contrast to the *rich and powerful,* the *government, big business,* and the

like. Government and big business become combined through images of power in which corporate economic interests subvert and dominate political policies and decisions. The distinction between life at work and outside becomes irrelevant in these images of class.

This form of class consciousness can be mobilized for right-wing as well as progressive causes. Nationalist and nativist movements have used it to support mobilization against new immigrants and minorities. But as Halle observes (1984, 302), it contains opportunities as well for a politics based on the struggle for "the dignity of the worker, for fair and safe working conditions, for a vigorous trade union movement, for equal treatment of working men and working women and whites and blacks."

The people whose conversations we are analyzing in this book differ from Halle's sample in three significant ways. The people he studied were all male, almost all white, and from the relatively well-paid industrial sector. Our working people are varied in race and gender and are more heavily drawn from the less well-paid service sector. There are some major differences in their discourse, especially in the ways that race and class combine in it and in the absence of the sexism included in the concept of the working man. But his overall distinction among the three types of class discourse remains highly useful for understanding how these Boston area working people make sense of political issues.

Halle's work suggests that the particular class discourse that people use, if they use any at all, depends on the nature of the issue. They respond as working people, he hypothesizes, on unemployment, occupational safety, plant closings, and import quotas. On many other issues, however, they respond as middle-class people or as populists or with some combination of these class identities. Troubled industry is clearly an issue that ought to engage any class identity rooted in the workplace.

A caution is in order in interpreting the conversations here. Adversarial class frames sometimes entered the discussion without prompting of any sort, but our design did include two specific efforts to stimulate such discourse. The first prompt was a broad one, merely inviting the group to consider the relevance of larger social cleavages. The facilitator said, "Let's talk about whether any larger groups of people might be affected. That is, what groups in this country might stand to gain or lose by what policies are followed on troubled industry?" Note that nothing in this question suggests any particular content about the relevant categories. Hence, the choice of class categories, rather than some other set or none at all, is not the result of facilitator prompting.

However, we also used a much more specific prompt on troubled industry, a CAPITAL FLIGHT cartoon with a class conflict theme (see Cartoon 4, Appendix B). In presenting the cartoon, the facilitator told participants that "the cartoonist seems to be saying that companies are ready to forget all about their partnership with workers and to take off for areas where they can pay lower wages whenever it suits their interest. What do you think about this?"

Given the increasing specificity of the prompts, the point at which class discourse first appears tells us something important about the salience of class cleavages for the group's understanding of troubled industry. And if it fails to appear even under the prompting of a cartoon that explicitly suggests it, it seems safe to conclude that class discourse is irrelevant for their understanding of troubled industry.

The analysis here distinguishes weak and strong forms of class discourse. The weak form includes any use of class categories to understand the issue under discussion, be they populist, work based, or consumption based, regardless of whether an adversarial relationship is implied. The strong form includes two additional elements that make it adversarial: implied or explicit opposition, tension, or conflict between social categories and the collective identification implied in the use of we–they language.[6]

Almost two-thirds of the groups (65 percent) made some use of class categories in discussing troubled industry. However, it arose spontaneously in only 19 percent of them and in only 41 percent before the strong stimulus of the CAPITAL FLIGHT cartoon. When it occurred, its use was modest and sporadic. It was not a category of first resort for most groups and arose only after prompting in most of the groups where it appeared. Slightly more than a third of the groups (35 percent) used adversarial class frames at some point in their conversation on troubled industry.

People were not consistent in the type of categories they used, moving back and forth among populist, consumption, and work-based versions. Frequently a single person would begin using one term – say, *working people* – and would switch in the next sentence to the *little guy* or *poor people*. Half of the groups that used class categories used some combination of terms.

The most common language of class discourse, however, was populist, illustrated by the symbols of "people with money" and "little people" in the following example. Michael, who had earlier criticized unions and expressed a business-led PARTNERSHIP frame to which no one else responded, appears to go along initially but quickly softens and undermines the adversarial tone with a joke.

Characters:

Sally, a clerk at a dry cleaners, in her twenties.
Marie, a cashier in a supermarket, in her twenties.
Michael, an office manager in a computer company, in his thirties.

(They are responding to the PARTNERSHIP cartoon in Appendix B):

Sally: It's a cartoon.

(laughter)

Facilitator: What do you mean by that?

Sally: I don't think it can happen. I don't think it will happen because there's too many crooked people out there. Granted, you would like to see the industries go up and everything, but I still think someone's getting something somewhere.

Marie: It's great to put people to work and build and what not, but I don't know, to do that, I guess you have to know someone and be there, I guess.

Sally: I think the majority of people with money *are* crooked. I'm sure some of them had to fight their way to get where they are, but I think most of them cheat and stole from the country and didn't think of the little people underneath them to get where they are.

Michael: Well, I'm going to agree with that. Some people with money, it breeds greed, you know.

Sally: *Most* of the people.

Michael: Well, look at me, I'm rich. I'm not greedy, am I?

(laughter)

Class discourse, using production-based class categories, did occur but rarely. The group in the following example is the same one we encountered earlier discussing nuclear power (Chapter 3) in which Marjorie denounced a value system ("it sucks") that can find places to build nuclear plants but won't deal with homelessness.

Characters:

Daniel, a mover, in his thirties.
Marjorie, a waitress, in her forties.
Cliff, a mechanic, in his thirties.
Betty Ann, a tax auditor, in her thirties.
Paul, a tire changer, in his thirties.

Facilitator: What larger groups in this country might stand to gain or lose by what policies are followed on troubled industry?

Daniel: Well, all the labor unions lose.

Facilitator: Okay, in what ways?

Daniel: All the labor unions − 'cause they're all losing their power; they're all losing their membership. Look at all the people get thrown out of work and all the labor unions are having to give back. All the gains they've made over the years. Industries are shipping all their jobs overseas. So they have a lot more leverage over the worker. And all the big businessmen will be making all the more money 'cause it's cheaper to make a car overseas.

Facilitator: Um hum.

Daniel: But they forget where they made their money in the first place. They made it on the backs of all the workers here.

(*Later, discussing the closing of the Quincy shipyard by General Dynamics in the context of earlier government help to the Chrysler Corporation.*)

Marjorie: Did [General Dynamics] asked to be helped?

Cliff: No, Dynamics was robbing them anyways, blind. They just ship the jobs overseas.

Betty Ann: General Dynamics was ripping them off. They were all government contracts, and they were just ripping them off.

Paul: Yeah, $1,000 for a coffee pot. That's a big contract, General Dynamics. They're not hurting; they just didn't − Quincy Shipyard wasn't profitable enough or something.

Daniel: And it didn't hurt General Dynamics − to close Quincy. They did it for their own benefit. The only people who were hurt were the workers.

Paul: They've got shipyards all over the place.

This type of adversarial, work-based class discourse is a rare exception, not a common occurrence. The distinctions Halle observed seem to blur in application to particular issues; or, put another way, when issues such as troubled industry do produce class discourse, it is both work based and consumption based at the same time. Plant closings not only stimulate some people's collective identity as working people but conjure up images of falling from middle class to poor as well.

Racially based frames. Black and white groups were equally likely to include adversarial class frames in their discussion of troubled industry, but almost 60 percent of the black groups used racial categories as well.[7] It was common in these discussions to conflate race and class through a discourse in which black means poor and white means rich. About two-thirds of the conversations using race or combined race–class categories were adversarial. In a majority of them, it came up completely spontaneously, before even the gentle prompt about larger groups that stand to gain or lose; none of the cartoons prompt the use of racial categories.

The result of using both race and class categories among black groups was a significantly higher overall rate of adversarial framing on troubled industry. Whereas only 24 percent of the white groups used some form of adversarial frame on this issue, 65 percent of the black groups employed it ($p < .05$).

Affirmative action

In contrast to troubled industry, media discourse on affirmative action heavily emphasizes adversarial frames. Visually, it is a story about a conflict between black and white workers. In the early years especially, white construction workers in hard hats symbolized the opposition to the demands of black workers for inclusion. The Conrad cartoon (Cartoon 5.1) expresses this dominant framing.

Television visuals told a similar story. In 1972, only ABC went beyond a thirty-second "tell-story" during our sample period, and its four-minute segment showed two scenes with construction workers in hard hats and another of steelworkers in coveralls. In 1978 and 1979, hard hats appeared on all three networks. In 1984, at the time of the Memphis firefighters' decision, hard hats were replaced by fire hats and police caps, but the visual message remained the same. Columnists and newsmagazine coverage frequently quoted white union leaders or rank-and-file workers in opposition to black civil rights leaders.

In the later years, the dominant REMEDIAL ACTION frame was strongly challenged by different versions of NO PREFERENTIAL TREATMENT. The source of the adversarial situation is different for these rivals. Where REMEDIAL ACTION locates it in acts or structures of discrimination and the exclusion of blacks from many parts of the labor market, NO PREFERENTIAL TREATMENT places the blame on the programs developed as a remedy. In this framing, it is the use of racial criteria and the lack of color blindness rather than discrimination that creates an adversarial situation.

Adversarial frames in conversations

Affirmative action was the only issue that stimulated a discourse on the person as an individual, but it did so almost universally. It was present in

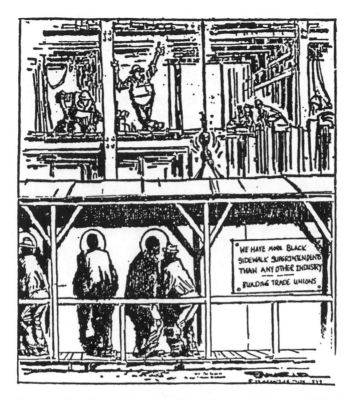

Cartoon 5.1. Remedial action. (Paul Conrad. Copyright, 1969, Los Angeles Times. Reprinted by permission.)

every white and interracial group and in almost 60 percent of the black groups as well. Since affirmative action conversations are so racially dependent, we must examine the content by type of group.

White groups. In white groups, it is typical for people to claim that everyone should be judged as an individual. People with purple skin will be especially gratified to learn that many groups emphasize the irrelevance of their color, as in "I don't care whether a person is black, white, or purple." The following excerpts illustrate how this discourse functions in discussions of affirmative action. Note how, in the second example, Ruth's attempts to make a negative generalization about blacks are emphatically denied by using this discourse on the person as individual.

Characters:

Debbie, a bus driver, in her thirties.
Billie, a delivery van driver, in her fifties.

(During the initial, open-ended discussion.)

Debbie: I remember hearing on the news not too long ago that there was a big conflict over the fact that they promoted a black — maybe it was a policeman. They promoted him, and there was a lot of squawk because they said he wasn't the man the most qualified for the job and he was promoted because he was black. And that's just as absurd as *not* promoting him for the job because he's black. You know, if somebody gets a job just because of their race — whether they're minorities or not — it's not right.

Billie: I wish they did right from the beginning — right when they first got into school. Each one has a right to have an education regardless of what they are, who they are — if they're purple. They have as much right as anybody else does.

Characters: (Note that this group appeared earlier in Chapters
2, 3, and 4.)

Arlene, a bookkeeper, in her forties.
Ruth, an office supervisor, in her fifties.
Ida, a bookkeeper, in her late sixties.

(During the initial, open-ended discussion.)

Arlene: I think education is very important.
Ruth: Do you think they have that drive?
Ida: Some do and some don't!
Arlene: Just like anyone else.
Ruth: I'm not talking about the few that might have it, I'm talking about the whole group.
Arlene: Listen, if you took twenty-five kids in my classroom that were all of Polish descent. Now we're talking all one nationality. What, do you think we're all the *same*? Naah. One was lazy, the other one did not talk; the other was a genius; the other one never shut up. There was all different types and we were all Polish, all one nationality, you know what I mean? All in the same thing.
Ida: That applies for everybody.
Arlene: For everybody.

A particular life-stage model is implicit in this discourse. There is a time during which one is growing up and preparing for life, and a time when one is an adult, out there living in a tough world. Equal opportunity means giving all people a fair chance to learn and develop their unique individual capacities, regardless of race. Education becomes central in this discourse as the symbol of equal opportunity. The slogan of the United Negro College Fund, "A mind is a terrible thing to waste," captures this belief perfectly in a phrase.

Most white working people would like to live in a world in which race is irrelevant during the growing-up period. Then, in adulthood, each person could be judged on his or her individual merit and accomplishment. But in about half of the white groups (47 percent), there was an explicit acknowledgment that blacks are disadvantaged as a group and that some form of racial discrimination remains. This leaves people uncomfortable with a completely color-blind policy and searching for some middle ground. There is a solution that resolves this dilemma for them: programs to give those who come from disadvantaged family environments a fair chance to compete on equal terms as they are growing up, coupled with complete color blindness once the job race has begun at age eighteen or so.

Interracial groups. The symbol of the person as an individual is integrative through its emphasis on a common humanity; this was especially apparent in the three interracial groups. Black and white members reaffirmed it together, thereby providing a strong shield of protection against the potential divisiveness of their racial differences.

Discussing affirmative action in interracial groups is a delicate matter. The participants must find a path through a mine field. Two of the three groups were work based, and should someone make an insensitive remark, the wounds could linger and affect the atmosphere of the workplace. Special group dynamics operate in such a discussion. In the following group, Lance is the only black member. From the outset, Eileen is outspoken against affirmative action and George stakes out an equally strong position of support for such programs, allowing Lance to become something of a mediator.

Characters:

Eileen, a bus driver, white, in her twenties.
Lance, a bus driver, black, in his twenties.
Pete, a bus driver, white, in his twenties.
Carol, a bus driver, white, in her thirties.
George, a bus driver, white, in his thirties.

(In response to the initial, open-ended question.)

Eileen: I think it's a bunch of bullshit.

Lance: I agree, I agree.

Eileen: I do.

Lance: I agree.

Eileen: I don't think that whether I'm black or white, that I should get a job if I can't do it.

Lance: – or a woman.

Pete: – or male or female.

Carol: Right. Right.

[Later, still during the open-ended discussion]

George: The black man's always been a minority, he's always been cheated, he's always been stepped on.

Eileen: Yeah, but now *we're* the minority, George, if you open your eyes.

Carol: But doesn't he have the same – the same opportunity for education?

George: How can he when he has *never* had the education of a white man?

[after a further sharp disagreement between Eileen and George on whether blacks get an equal education.]

George: We have deprived the minorities. Yeah.

Lance: George, it's all right, it's all right.

(All talking at once. Something unintelligible said followed by laughter.)

Lance: George, you're all right.

Eileen: Lance, he likes you.

(laughter)

[Later, near the end of the discussion]

George: Lance, if it wasn't for affirmative action, you wouldn't be here.

Lance: So what? I'd be doing something else.

Eileen: *[addressing George]* No, he probably would be.

Carol: He might be because he is a fighter and he has goals.

Eileen: *[addressing Lance]* You moved right up on that list.

Pete: If they didn't have affirmative action, you'd be working someplace half decent. You got that personality, and you're a good driver.

Lance: Damn right I would.

The shared assertion of Lance's individuality and qualifications got the group safely through the mine field. George and Eileen could sharply disagree, leading the group to joke about their stepping outside and settling this dispute in the parking lot, without creating a racial cleavage. The enactment of the person as an individual united even these antagonists.

In the context of affirmative action, black members – a minority in all three interracial groups – asserted their qualifications for the work they do, against any unspoken suspicion that they hadn't earned the right, through their own individual efforts, to be where they are.

> *Characters:*
>
> *Rick, a plumber's apprentice, black, in his twenties.*
> *Thomas, a mounted ranger, black, in his twenties.*
> *Four other men, with varying jobs, white, in their twenties.*
>
> *(During the open-ended discussion at the beginning.)*
>
> Rick: Every job that I've ever had, I've been praised for what I've done, not for what I am or for what they want me for. I don't care if I'm hired for one reason, okay, as long as I can do a good job and I know I'm earning my paycheck. I'm not just there – "Well, we'll just have you sit in the office, just chill out, watch *The Three Stooges* all day, and we'll still pay you." You know what I mean?
>
> *(later in the discussion)*
>
> Thomas: I cut it every day. You don't cut it, hey, they – like I said, civil service test – there's a lot of more guys waiting for your job. They tell you to be at eight, you're supposed to be here. They ain't gonna call you up and say, "Hey, get out of bed. You're supposed to be at work."
>
> *(laughter)*

Black groups. The symbolism of the person as an individual is an American discourse, as much a part of African-American culture as it is of other groups. Even in the 40 percent of the groups where this discourse did not occur, it seems safe to assume that it would be enthusiastically affirmed if the facilitator had raised it. There is less need in black groups for this affirmation of common humanity, since they often assert their shared experience as blacks and no potential racial cleavage threatens.

The continued existence of racial inequality was a taken-for-granted assumption in almost all black groups; no one denied the centrality of race in affecting their economic opportunities. However, the 60 percent of the black groups that included discourse on the person as an individual faced an additional complication in using it to understand affirmative action. In talking about affirmative action, they had to integrate it with their belief that some form of continuing discrimination remains a fact of life.

Characters:

Charles, a city maintenance worker, in his forties.
Roland, a sales clerk in a department store, twenty years old.
Lucinda, an office worker, in her forties.
William, a truck driver, in his forties.

Facilitator: Would you say that anything that has happened on the issue of affirmative action has affected you personally, or any of your friends or relatives?

Charles: Well, affirmative action is just depending on how you look at it because – concerning we minority, they look at us that everything is affirmative when we make some mistake. You know? There ain't no slack about it – affirmative, you did wrong and that was it, you know.

Roland: One thing I don't want to happen to me when I grow up is to get hired for a job just because I'm black.

Lucinda: You want to get hired for the job because you're good at it or –

Roland: – because I'm qualified for it.

Lucinda: Yeah, sure.

Roland: Not because I'm black. I don't want to fit no quota system or something like that.

William: Right now, it is – as long as you're black, you don't – you don't fit, you're not qualified.

Roland: Right. But I'm glad we do have this affirmative action 'cause if we didn't, I wouldn't get even – even take my application.

Lucinda: You wouldn't get in the door, in other words.

Roland: Right. Yeah.

Characters:

Ellie, an office worker in a hospital, in her forties.
Connie, a family planning counselor, in her twenties.

(Responding to the final question on what should be done about affirmative action.)

Ellie: If it's the only – I feel like if it's the only way that blacks and minority are going to have to, you know, get their – they're never gonna get their just due. But I feel like affirmative action is necessary; it's a needed vehicle to ensure that people – that blacks and minorities *do have* some type of opening where they can get into these – But as far as I'm concerned, I feel like affirmative action is just another prop. You know, another way to get around the real issue that blacks are equal, minorities are equal, everybody's equal, and they should be able to do whatever they want to do, get whatever jobs and education, as long as they, themselves, feel good about theirselves and go for and do what they want. Like, they should have a free hand to do that without anybody even stand in a doorway and saying, "Well, you're black; I need you in here 'cause you're a number, and I need that number."

Connie: That's right.

Ellie: And never mind about you're a person, or you're a human, or you're qualified; forget that.

They achieved integration by repudiating the idea of affirmative action as preferential treatment or undeserved advantage and affirming it as, in theory, a way of providing equal opportunity for individuals who have been denied it. As it is practiced, many are skeptical that it succeeds in overcoming continuing racial inequality, and some doubt that it was ever intended to succeed in this way.

For black groups that doubt the effectiveness of affirmative action, it becomes the worst of both worlds and creates a no-win situation. It fails to provide equal opportunity and, at the same time, it stigmatizes blacks and causes understandable resentment among whites. Even as black groups recognize the continuing relevance of race for economic opportunity, they assert their preference for a society in which one is judged as an individual and not as a group member. Racial discrimination obviously violates this norm, but they make clear how hurtful it is even when well-meaning others deny their unique personhood by treating them as part of a social category. The following excerpt provides an especially poignant example of this reaction:

Characters:

Waverly, a nurse's aide, in her twenties.
Robert, a cook, in his thirties.
Tessie, a child-care worker, in her thirties.

(Responding to the question of whether they have been affected personally.)

Waverly: I was laid off a job. They just lost all the works in one day, and then they had a meeting that afternoon. And we all lost our jobs. I felt cheated, but there wasn't anything I could really say. My boss told me and my boss's wife – and I'm not prejudiced either

– but she told me, "I'm gonna always have a job. It's 'you people' I'm worried about."

Robert: What'd she mean by "you people?"

Waverly: So when she said "you people," I knew she was prejudiced, so when I lost the job, I didn't really care after that.

Tessie: So when you at your job, you feeling like they were always looking at you like "you people?"

Waverly: Yeah, all the time.

Tessie: It did something to you mentally.

Waverly: I was shocked when she said that. You know, 'cause I worked with them before this job. I worked with them.

Robert: You ain't got to feel defeated, though.

Waverly: Before she said that, she always, you know, when she moved up in another nursing home and she asked me to come work for her, called me and asked me, and I told her I couldn't do it. So she asked me why, and I didn't tell her *that* was the reason, but that's what I felt. She always looked down on me.

In spite of the power of this discourse on the person as an individual, adversarial frames occurred in 78 percent of the conversations on affirmative action. In almost half of the white groups (47 percent), the adversarial frames mixed class and racial categories – and in half of these, it came up spontaneously. In the other half, it was stimulated by the DIVIDE AND CONQUER cartoon (Appendix B), which shows a white-collar, white person, who is eating a fancy steak dinner, taking a bowl from a white worker and giving it to a black worker. The facilitator told them that "the cartoonist seems to be saying that rich liberals want to give special breaks to blacks at the expense of whites who also need a break." This particular framing of affirmative action is invisible in media discourse except for occasions when it is displayed derisively.

The exchange in the following white group is typical of conversations that weave race and class together in adversarial frames that incorporate both elements. This is the same group whose earlier discourse on troubled industry illustrated a populist class discourse.

Characters:

Marie, a cashier in a supermarket, in her twenties.
Sally, a clerk at a dry cleaners, in her twenties.

(Discussing the initial, open-ended question on affirmative action.)

Marie: I think it's right. I think everybody should have the opportunity to go out and do what they feel is their thing, no matter what color or what race or whatever. They're human beings, after all.

Sally: Now I'm not prejudiced, but I took it as they were going to help out the blacks and the Hispanics and minorities. What do they think, all the white people around here are poor little rich boys or something? They don't want to help us out, here? Just the black person?

Marie: Yeah, yeah, that's true.

Sally: I mean, they have got a bad shake throughout the years, the black people and everything, from stereotyped people. "And you drink out of this fountain, you go to the back of the bus" and everything. But things have changed now, I think. You're always hearing, "Give to the United Negro College," which I'm sure a hundred people do. (laughter) I'm not prejudiced at all, but I think there's a lot of white people out here too, that are being – that should, like she said, equal for everybody, get every type of schooling they want.

(*later, in response to the DIVIDE AND CONQUER cartoon*)

Sally: I agree. *Strongly*. I think blacks do need a break, and I think that they –

Marie: – Everybody needs a break.

Sally: A lot of times, it's like people don't like you because they're stereotyping if you're a black person. You could come from a good family background and everything, but they're prejudiced whether they admit it or not, and they're not going to hire. They'll hire the white person over you. But I don't think they should give everything to the blacks. There's many – a lot of white people out here who need help just as much as the black.

It is more common in black groups to conflate race and class through a discourse in which black means poor and white means rich. The following example illustrates this fairly common race–class combination:

Characters:

Reba, a mental retardation supervisor, in her forties.
Gladys, a property manager, in her forties.

(*Discussing the final question on what should be done about affirmative action*)

Reba: Let's look at it this way. If you've always had, like say a little piece of land or something. And you had that land you ain't did nothing with it. You don't even care about this little land. It been left for you to fifty million generations. And all of a sudden somebody comes along and say, "Hey, this land could be made housing for about five thousand people" or something. You know what I'm saying? The thought is, they know it's theirs, they don't want to do anything with it, but just to keep you from getting it. They will hold on to it and hold on to it. Once you have it, it's hard to lose. It's like a rich person being poor. We're poor people, so we're used to being poor. Okay? We can adjust, we survive. But you think about somebody being rich and all of a sudden they wake up the next morning and they are poor. They kill themselves. They go right out and shoot themselves.

Gladys: Commit suicide.

Reba: They can't cope. We have learned through hardships and things to be able to cope. White people are very selfish, and they are not going to give up what they've got. Or they spent forty thousand years in their home, it's passed down from their grandmother. Buy this house and its doubled, because now you go there and you're black, you know. You know these people are gonna fight you tooth and nail.

In sum, the presence of the privileged discourse on the person as an individual complicates but does not prevent the presence of adversarial frames on affirmative action based on race, class, or a combination of the two. These occurred in 88 percent of the black groups and in 76 percent of the white groups. Although most of these employed racial categories, 27 percent of the groups used adversarial frames based on class or some combination of race and class.

Nuclear power

There are elements of adversarial class frames in media discourse on nuclear power, with pro- and antinuclear sponsors competing directly for the loyalties of working people. Class enters the picture in the pronuclear PROGRESS frame through linking nuclear power to economic growth and development. Technological progress, which nuclear power symbolizes, is the engine of economic growth; growth promises jobs and a higher standard of living for poor and working people.

The adversarial element enters when opponents of nuclear power are depicted in class terms – as indulged children of the affluent who have everything they need. They have secure professional jobs in hand or awaiting them and can afford to ignore the imperatives of economic growth.

These "coercive utopians" (McCracken, 1977, 1979) are intent on imposing their anti-growth vision on others at the expense of the real interests of working people. This frame invites the viewer to see the backpacking, guitar-playing, frisbee-tossing, scruffy-looking Seabrook demonstrators in these adversarial class terms (see Chapter 4). Opponents of nuclear power oppose the class interests of working people.

One antinuclear frame, PUBLIC ACCOUNTABILITY, offers a competing class discourse on nuclear power. "If Exxon owned the sun, would we have solar energy?" it asks. The root of the problem is the organization of nuclear production by profit-making corporations, which minimizes accountability and control by the public. Company officials are depicted as dishonest, greedy, and arrogant; one cannot rely on what they say. Public officials, who are supposed to monitor the activities of the industry, are all too often captives of it.

In the hands of a movement organization such as Critical Mass, there is a clear adversarial framing, although it seems more populist than production based. As it appeared in the media, however, even this populist form became watered down. As a case of "the people versus the interests," no specific identity as working people was engaged. Class identity was blurred by clustering working people and middle-class professionals into an amorphous "public." The Herblock cartoon (Appendix B, Cartoon 10) is typical of the way this framing appeared. If there is still a trace of adversarial class discourse here, it certainly has an attenuated form.

In sum, there was a pinch of adversarial class framing in media discourse on nuclear power, but it did not provide the dominant flavor. The message for working people is mixed and confusing, since a pronuclear PROGRESS frame suggests that nuclear power is in the interests of working people and PUBLIC ACCOUNTABILITY suggests that it is in the interests of powerful elites. Furthermore, although both of these framings are continually visible in media discourse, RUNAWAY, the most prominent media frame since 1979, has no adversarial flavor at all.

Adversarial frames in conversations

Adversarial frames on nuclear power appeared in only 14 percent of the conversations, and even these few took different forms and appeared sporadically. Less than 10 percent used adversarial class frames, and none took up the version offered by PROGRESS. Opponents of nuclear power were not always depicted positively, but no one ever presented them as class adversaries in any discussion. The class discourse that occasionally occurred was all of the populist type, directed against corporate greed.

   Race-based adversarial frames appeared in slightly less than one-fifth of the black groups. Nuclear power was presented as a white technology, not in the interests of black people. As one woman put it in response to the facilitator's question on whether they knew people who were affected personally by what happens on nuclear power: "[People] here in the ghetto don't get involved with that, okay? He want to live. He don't want to die right now. And if he's going to die, it's sure not from that. He's going to die from his pleasure, not from the white man's experimental stuff that they has over there, you know." But more typically, the relevance of race was explicitly denied, and overall, there were very few differences between white and black groups in the framing of nuclear power.

Arab–Israeli conflict

The only collective identity invoked by media discourse on this issue is a national identity as Americans. The ethnic angle is framed in interest group rather than adversarial terms. Arab and Jewish Americans are recognized as having partisan identifications and a special interest in the conflict; they are observers who root for one side or the other but are not significant players. Any adversarial relationship between these ethnic groups is very low in salience and, in any event, they represent a small minority of the population. No domestic social cleavages of class or race are treated as relevant in media discourse.

Adversarial frames in conversations

Adversarial frames never occurred in white or interracial groups, but racially based ones did occur in 24 percent of the black groups. These were not based on any suggestion of racial solidarity between blacks and Arabs as people of color; only a single person in one group suggested this, and no one else supported her or accepted the relevance. The occasional uses that occurred emphasized the disproportionate sacrifice that blacks and other people of color suffer in the human cost of foreign intervention. The following example involves the same group that we encountered earlier discussing affirmative action, but this time Charles is alone in developing the frame.

> *Characters:*
>
> *Charles, a city maintenance worker, in his forties.*
>
> *(The facilitator presents the STRATEGIC INTEREST Cartoon 13, Appendix B)*

Facilitator: The cartoonist seems to be saying that the Arab–Israeli conflict is part of a big Middle East chess game between the Russians and the United States in which each is trying to use its allies to gain an advantage over the other. What do you think about this?

Charles: Well, like you said, the two superpowers, they're negotiating the war. *But,* unfortunately, in the world they're negotiating, we blacks getting caught in the middle. We have experience; we have seen it.

Facilitator: Um hum.

Charles: About six months ago, we see what happened in Berlin with the bombing of a discotechque. A black man died. Came out in *Time* magazine on the *front* page. An American, they didn't say a black man, they said an American. Our president, our actual president, Ronald Reagan – I'm saying he's behind a rule against black people. When I say that our president put a black man in *Time* magazine, front page, right? Then, he went and bombed Libya. The black people. I don't care what it said, terrorist or whatever. Blacks. We bombed Grenada, they're blacks. There's a lot of people, and black people, don't know about it.

Facilitator: Um hum.

Charles: That people that got killed over there was black people. You hear about Cuba. Everybody said, "Oh, Cuba got killed. Cuba got –" They are black. Mostly island, most West Indian island, mostly *every* island is Afro. Afro-Puerto Rican, Afro-Jamaican, Afro-Barbados, Afro-everything. And we got killed in that move.

Facilitator: Um hum.

Charles: It wasn't white people that got killed.

These occasional adversarial frames are nonpartisan with respect to Arab–Israeli conflict. They support a FEUDING NEIGHBORS frame in which the innocent bystanders who get hurt are disproportionately people of color.

Conclusion

The foremost concerns of working people are with their immediate, everyday lives, but this does not mean that they think only as individuals and family members in making sense of political issues. Nor does the fact that they strongly affirm every person as a unique individual who should be judged as such preclude them from thinking collectively. A variety of larger collective identities are, in fact, brought into play as they talk about politics.

Perhaps the most striking finding is that some 86 percent of the groups used an adversarial frame on at least one issue. They did not necessarily use it consistently throughout the discussion, and sometimes it did not occur until the facilitator's question or a cartoon helped to stimulate it. Nevertheless, it occurred with enough regularity in a broad range of groups to conclude that this element of collective action frames was present in their thinking and was widely shared.

On some issues, adversarial frames seemed present in spite of rather than because of their prominence in media discourse. Troubled industry and Arab–Israeli conflict were almost never framed in adversarial terms.[8] For nuclear power, the picture is more complicated, with competing adversarial class frames offered but generally in weak or equivocal form. Only on affirmative action was media discourse heavily adversarial.

Adversarial frames in conversations are an imperfect match. As in media discourse, they appeared most frequently on affirmative action but are complicated by the presence of a privileged discourse on the person as an individual that transcends racial differences. On troubled industry, they appeared in close to half of the conversations in spite of their absence in media discourse. On nuclear power and Arab–Israeli conflict, they were as muted in conversation as they are in the media and, in the nuclear power case, perhaps more so.

Certain aspects of the situation make adversarial frames more likely to appear. With the exception of three interracial groups, the others were homogeneous in both race and class – the two social cleavages examined here. Sharing a common social location made it easier for them to invoke a shared collective identity. An adversarial frame does not introduce a cleavage into the group but calls attention to a common bond.

One can see this effect most clearly in the three interracial groups, where a racially based adversarial frame never occurred, even on the affirmative action issue, where it is so common in black and white groups. The presence of an external social cleavage within the group suppresses the expression of an adversarial frame and promotes either a substitute adversarial frame based on class or a discourse that emphasizes the person as an individual and denies the relevance of social location.

Overall, black groups made significantly more use of adversarial frames than did the others, averaging 1.94 issue conversations that include them compared to 1.05 in the remainder ($p < .05$). This greater use seems easy to understand. Being black is a pervasive collective identity in American society, and it comes into play in many groups on issues other than affirmative action. There is no comparable collective identity in being white, and the introduction of a racially based adversarial frame on issues such as troubled industry or nuclear power would undoubtedly seem bizarre and racist in most white groups. But black groups also use more adversarial frames based on *class,* suggesting that adversarial framing may generalize to include more than one collective identity.

The different elements of collective action frames – identity, agency, and injustice – do not exist in isolation but frequently support each other. The next chapter explores the relationship among them and the connection with political consciousness as expressed in talk and action.

6

Talk and action

Talking about politics with friends in someone's living room, at the behest of academic researchers, is many steps removed from action. Imagine that these conversations on nuclear power, for example, were occurring in a community where an application was currently pending for the construction of a new nuclear reactor. Imagine further that there were active antinuclear groups who were demonstrating against it and threatening to occupy the site. Action contexts of this sort dramatically change the salience of collective action frames by making them immediately and personally relevant.

Political consciousness, as many students of social movements have observed, is forged in the process of collective action. Fantasia (1988), for example, shows how "cultures of solidarity" are constructed by workers while interacting with each other over time in concrete action settings. Ideas emerge and change, and are subjected to scrutiny and negotiation as events and conditions are interpreted and reinterpreted. He contrasts this with "the belief of many academics and radical activists that it is necessary for people to have an intellectual grasp or 'correct line' on society before they can change it." Similarly, Marshall (1983, 272) challenges "the widely held belief among academic observers that it is somehow necessary for men and women to encompass society intellectually before they can attempt to change it."

The view that consciousness precedes and causes action may be implicit in much writing on working-class consciousness, but few if any observers of social movements would accept it. The emphasis in most of the social movement literature of the past fifteen years has been on consciousness, commitment, solidarity, and collective identity as processes that develop simultaneously, mutually influencing and reinforcing each other. No one should expect working people to use collective action frames extensively when they talk about political issues divorced from any meaningful action context.

The appropriate context brings nascent elements to life if they are there.

The most likely action context is a threat to the pattern of people's daily lives – a plant closing, the siting of a nuclear plant or toxic waste facility, a call-up of military reserves, and the like. There is nothing automatic or certain about how people will respond to such events. Any threat or deprivation can be interpreted in different ways. The ease with which fully developed and integrated collective action frames are constructed depends on the extent to which people already share the elements of these frames.

It is difficult to construct them from scratch. If people already share a sense of moral indignation and injustice, think of themselves as a we in opposition to some they, and have shared models of people like themselves acting to change conditions, the raw materials are in place. If one or more of these factors is absent, the process will take longer and is more likely to be aborted at some point.

Collective action frames are not merely aggregations of individual attitudes and perceptions but also the outcome of negotiating shared meaning. Examining their elements as they are constructed in talk does not bring us closer to an action context, but conversations are a *collective* product. The dynamics of opinion leadership and the normative pressures that arise in groups are not distractions from what people really think but are a natural part of the collective process in which political consciousness is negotiated.

Clearly, the elements of collective action frames were more in place for some groups than for others and on some issues far more than on others. However, full-fledged collective action frames that integrated all three elements were rare indeed. To be more precise, this happened in 22 percent of the conversations on affirmative action, 5 percent on troubled industry, and not at all on nuclear power or Arab–Israeli conflict. Combining these elements is part of the business of constructing collective action frames over time. Although it rarely happened in these conversations so divorced from action, we can learn more by analyzing how the three elements that have so far been treated separately were joined by some groups on some issues.

Injustice as the key

Injustice and adversarial frames

There is no logical necessity that an injustice frame also be an adversarial frame. People can be treated badly through stupidity or lack of awareness by those pursuing their own selfish interests or by institutions and programs that reflect misplaced priorities. The injustice may include a clearly defined

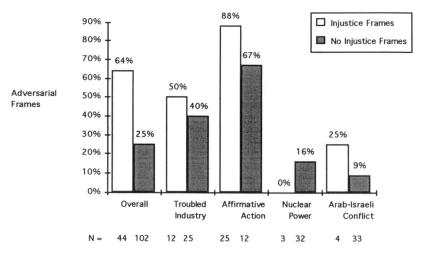

Figure 6.1.   Injustice and adversarial frames.

they who are perpetrating the injustice at our expense – or it may not. Nor does an adversarial frame necessarily imply an injustice. The adversaries may have competing interests that bring them into conflict without acting in ways that arouse moral indignation.

Nevertheless, there are good theoretical reasons for expecting groups that use an injustice frame in understanding an issue to include adversarial elements in the package as well. An injustice frame makes the injured party collective, not individual. What one has suffered personally is shared by some implied we. Righteous indignation without a they at which to direct it is difficult to sustain. It is frustrating and confusing to be angry and not know whom to be angry at. An adversarial frame helps to resolve this tension by interpreting and directing the emotional component of an injustice frame. Hence, we should expect them to be correlated.

As Figure 6.1 shows, there is a strong overall relationship. When injustice frames appeared in issue conversations, almost two-thirds (64 percent) used an adversarial frame as well; this figure dropped to 25 percent in the issue conversations that lacked injustice frames ($p < .001$). On issues such as nuclear power and Arab–Israeli conflict, in which injustice frames were rare, adversarial frames were equally rare; on affirmative action, where injustice frames were widespread, so were adversarial frames. And even when the issue is controlled, adversarial frames tended to be more common in those discussions of affirmative action and troubled industry that also used injustice frames.

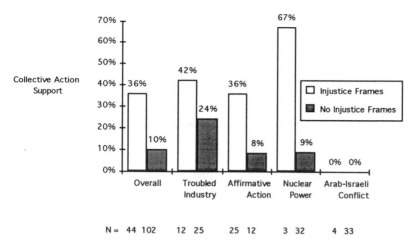

Figure 6.2. Injustice and collective action support.

Injustice and support for citizen action

Again, there is no necessary reason why the adoption of an injustice frame requires sympathetic discussion of citizen action on these issues or vice versa. One may feel an injustice while being unaware of grass-roots efforts at change or, if aware, may think them misguided or futile. One may be sympathetic to antinuclear protesters because they keep authorities on their toes without postulating any unfairness or working up any righteous anger.

But again, there are good theoretical reasons for expecting a connection. If an unfair situation is regarded as immutable, it is not likely to lead to moral indignation; an injustice frame implies the possibility of change. Collective action by ordinary citizens may not be the best way of achieving it, but at least such people are making an effort. Indignation exerts a push toward action and predisposes a sympathetic response to those who attempt it.

As Figure 6.2 shows, the hypothesized relationship is clearly there. More than a third of the conversations with injustice frames contained some sympathetic discussion of collective action on the issue; only 10 percent of the groups without an injustice frame included such positive attention ($p < .001$). One should not make much of the differences on nuclear power, since there were only three instances of injustice frames, but on affirmative action and troubled industry as well, groups with injustice frames were substantially more likely to include supportive discussions of collective action.

Adversarial frames and support for citizen action

The use of adversarial frames to understand an issue was completely independent of sympathetic discussion of citizen action in these conversations. Only five groups never used an adversarial frame on any issue, but three of these five had supportive discussions of collective action on some issue. Of the fifteen groups that used adversarial frames on two or more issues, an identical 60 percent had sympathetic discussions. On troubled industry and nuclear power, there were twenty-one discussions in which collective action was supported, but only three of these also used adversarial frames; furthermore, one of these three failed to link the two ideas in a common package.

Only on affirmative action discussions in black groups was a common link made between adversarial frames and support for collective action. Almost half of the conversations (47 percent) integrated sympathetic discussion of black civil rights efforts and an adversarial frame in a common package that approximates the model of a full-fledged collective action frame.

Conclusion

The injustice component of a collective action frame facilitates adoption of the other elements. It increases attentiveness to social movements that attempt to rectify the injustice and encourages sympathy toward their efforts at collective action even when people are not ready to join. It promotes personal identification with whatever collectivity is being wronged and the search for targets who are responsible for the undeserved hardships that members of the recipient group suffer. Hence, it is the key to integrating the three elements of collective action frames.

II

How people negotiate meaning

The process of negotiating meaning about public issues is broader than that of constructing collective action frames. I focused on the elements of these frames in Part I because of my interest in the kind of political consciousness that is most relevant for social movements. Part II steps back from this immediate concern to address more general questions about how people make sense of the news.

Chapter 7 explores the resource strategies they use. To what extent do they use media discourse as a primary resource versus the knowledge they have gained from their personal experiences and popular cultural wisdom? To what extent do they integrate these different resources into a shared frame on different issues?

Chapter 8 explores the importance of cultural resonances in enabling people to integrate different resources. To what extent do resonances between issues frames and broad cultural themes and counterthemes contribute to their ability to use multiple resources in making sense of an issue?

Chapter 9 explores the complicated connection between how interested and engaged people are in an issue and how it affects their everyday lives. To what extent can issue engagement be stimulated by media discourse independently of any direct experience of the consequences? To what extent does the intensity of people's interest in an issue affect the resource strategies they use and their success in integrating different resources?

Part II is an attempt to understand the general process of how people construct meaning about public issues. The answers ultimately have important implications for the presence or absence of collective action frames. Chapter 10, the concluding chapter, brings the two parts together, showing how frames that successfully integrate different resources in the process of constructing meaning are more likely to be injustice frames.

7

Media, popular wisdom, and experience

Think of each issue as a forest through which people must find their way. These are not, of course, virgin forests. The various frames in media discourse provide maps indicating useful points of entry, provide signposts at various crossroads, highlight the significant landmarks, and warn of the perils of other paths. However, many people do not stick to the pathways provided, frequently wandering off and making paths of their own.

From the standpoint of the wanderers, media discourse is a cultural resource to use in understanding and talking about an issue, but it is only one of several available. Nor is it necessarily the most important one on some issues, compared, for example, with their own experience and that of significant others in their lives. Frequently, they find their way through the forest with a combination of resources, including those they carry with them.

Conversational resources

When people state an opinion, they usually explain to others the basis for their conclusion. Sprinkled throughout the conversations quoted in earlier chapters are numerous examples of claims about the world that frame the issue in a particular way and serve to justify this framing. I focus on three types of conversational resources: *media discourse, experiential knowledge,* and *popular wisdom.*

Media discourse

Every group on every issue showed some awareness that there is a public discourse around them, even if they made minimal use of it and frequently apologized for not having better command of it. In fact, most groups drew on it in some fashion, even if they failed to integrate it with other resources. On some issues – and in some groups on most issues – it was the main or even the exclusive resource they used in constructing meaning. Other resources appeared only sporadically on matters that are tangential to their framing of the issue.

The public discourse that people draw on is much broader than the news and takes many forms. In discussing affirmative action, for example, several groups quoted the advertising slogan of the United Negro College Fund that "A mind is a terrible thing to waste." A variety of movies and television programs were brought in more than once, including *Silkwood* and *The China Syndrome* in discussions of nuclear power.

Nor do people confine the media discourse on which they draw to the immediate issue under discussion. Frequently, they attempt to understand one issue by comparing it to other related issues. On nuclear power, more than one-third of the groups discussed the explosion of the space shuttle *Challenger,* which had occurred earlier in the same year (1986). About one-fourth of them introduced the conflict in Northern Ireland in discussing Arab–Israeli conflict. When we sampled media discourse, we put boundaries around which materials were included, but conversations spilled over such neatly contained definitions of relevance.

Often it is difficult to know for certain whether a remark draws on media discourse because people do not identify the source of their knowledge. Those who followed media discourse on the troubled steel industry, for example, would know the story of U.S. Steel. Buttressed by low-interest government loans, the company chose not to reinvest in modernizing their plant facilities to produce steel competitively; instead, they embarked on a policy of diversification, acquiring the Marathon Oil Company in the process. Eventually, they even dropped steel from the company name, becoming the USX Corporation.

It would appear, in the following conversation, that Bob is aware of this part of the public discourse and is drawing on it as a resource.

> *Characters:*
>
> *Madelyn, a worker in a candy factory, in her fifties.*
> *Bob, an assistant manager at a car wash, in his thirties.*
> *Daniel, a printer, in his twenties.*

(Discussing the initial, open-ended question on troubled industry.)
Madelyn: These people have a hard time to find another job. Some of
        them are older people, and then they have to relocate, and not
        even live in the community they were brought up in.
Bob: That's true.
Madelyn: And then business suffers too, you know, because the thing

shuts down, these people have to move it, they don't have the money to spend.

Bob: Like in the steel industry in the Midwest. The steel industry is just about gone in the United States. Although, probably, we have the most knowledge about it and the best people to do it. There's no money in it for the businessmen, so they don't put it out.

Madelyn: Yeah, and in Maine there's a paper mill that's in big trouble. They were on strike because they don't want them to have seniority. They're trying to make slaves out of them, you know. So, if the company won't back down, he says they won't give them what they want. So you know what they're going to do? They're going to shut down, and they're going out to Minneapolis or somewhere like that. And they tell them, like, "you come if you want," and there's about 1,200 people working there, and that's all there is, is that paper mill.

Daniel: You want to buy a house up in Maine —

Madelyn: You can get them cheap.

Daniel: You can. A house —

Madelyn: — $18,000.

Daniel: Yeah, $18,000, but then, there's no work up there. But there's work in certain mills, but the guys are on strike and who wants to be a scab and cross the picket line, especially since that guy's been putting his blood, sweat, and whatever into it and you're going to go across the line and they're going to start trouble, and they're going to threaten your families and stuff.

Madelyn: They follow them home, see where they live. And they threaten to burn their house down —

Daniel: The government — President Reagan should do something. He's out for himself. He's not for the poor people. That's my feeling about him. You know, they should get somebody else in office.

Madelyn: Like Nancy.

(laughter)

Bob does not flag his source of knowledge by saying, "I saw *a program on television* about the steel industry" or "I *read an article* that the steel industry is just about gone in the United States." However, the content implies awareness of the U.S. Steel story or others like it. Fortunately, most uses of media discourse in our groups are not as subtle and inferential as this one but are quite explicit. More than 95 percent of the usages that we coded fell into one of the following categories:

Spotlighted facts.   The advantage of media frames for journalists is that they serve as guidelines in helping to select what information to spotlight and what to ignore. Facts take on their meaning by being framed in some fashion. Many facts are spotlighted by certain frames and ignored or discounted by others.

People bring in a variety of these informational elements from media discourse to support the frames that spotlight them. Their information may or may not be veridical, and sometimes it is challenged and corrected by others, but accuracy is not the issue. As used here, the words *fact* and *knowledge* always include implicit quotation marks that beg the question of their truth and treat them all as factual claims.

To illustrate how spotlighted facts support particular frames, take the explosion of a nuclear plant at Chernobyl in the Soviet Union, an accident that occurred only a few months before these conversations took place. Chernobyl entered the conversation in some form in 86 percent of the groups. Of course, not everyone got the name exactly right, but we included such variations as *Chernova, Grenoble,* or just *Russia.* The context makes it clear enough what they are talking about.

The mere mention does not indicate what about Chernobyl is relevant, but this becomes clear as the conversation continues. The most frequent point is that Chernobyl illustrates the dangers of nuclear accidents; people can get killed immediately or experience delayed injury through radiation effects. No frame in media discourse challenges this fact, but it is certainly not emphasized by supporters of nuclear power. Instead, they spotlight another fact: Soviet nuclear reactors are designed less safely than U.S. reactors. By implication, the U.S. nuclear industry has this potentially dangerous technology under control.

About 17 percent of the groups explicitly introduced this fact, as in the following examples. The first group is one we have quoted frequently before.[1]

Characters:

Ida, a bookkeeper, in her late sixties.
Ruth, an office supervisor, in her fifties.

Ida: You see, our plants are built better than that one as it is. There's
         something – (*pause*) they're supposed to have here.
Ruth: I was just wondering how long it had been in operation before they
         had this accident. (*pause*) It certainly wasn't a new plant.
Ida: No, it wasn't. But it didn't have the safety features that our plants
         already have.

Characters:

Joe, a firefighter, in his fifties.

Joe: Look at Chernobyl. They're comparing it to the nuclear power plants in the United States. They can't do that! Chernobyl happened with stuff that the United States did in nuclear power forty years ago. That plant's antiquated. Know what I mean?

Drawing on this spotlighted fact in the conversation always occurred in the service of a pronuclear frame that discounts the significance of the Chernobyl accident for the future of nuclear power in the United States. Ida is a minority of one on nuclear power in her group, and no one else helps her to construct her preferred frame. No one, for example, supplies her with the term *containment structure* when she searches for details on why U.S. plants are safer. The alternative package that the others were developing does not spotlight the fact that the Chernobyl plant had a different and inferior containment structure. Hence, it was not a relevant resource for their purposes, and the conversation quickly moved on to other aspects of the issue.

Public figures. Conversations frequently bring in public figures who are seen as significant actors on the issue. In 1986, Ronald Reagan made the most appearances, entering the conversation on every issue, although infrequently on certain ones. On troubled industry, he sometimes entered as a symbol of union busting, and reference was made to the breaking of the air traffic controllers union. On affirmative action, he came up in many black groups as the ringleader of the effort to take away "all the things that we have fought for" (Vanessa, Chapter 1).

Many other public figures made their appearance more selectively on a given issue. Lee Iacocca made frequent appearances in discussions of troubled industry and, perhaps more surprisingly, Khadaffi appeared in almost one-third of the discussions of Arab–Israeli conflict. The U.S. bombing of Libya was another recent event, and the threat of terrorism against Americans was quite salient in some groups.

As with Chernobyl, different uses can be made of the public figures invoked. Iacocca was typically presented in a hero's robes as the savior of the moribund Chrysler Corporation. But occasionally, a group used the enormous compensation Iacocca received to draw a different lesson from the Chrysler story. Similarly, Khadaffi was typically cast as a fanatic and villain, but again, oppositional readings occasionally occurred. "I like Khadaffi because he's flashy" said a woman in one group.

The use of public figures in a conversation is counted as a resource only if it is used to develop and support a shared framing of the issue. Celebrity gossip that does not make a relevant point does not count. The remark about Khadaffi's personal style, for example, was not used to support any particular frame and would not qualify as an example of using media discourse.

Catch phrases.   People signal the use of media discourse by using particular catch phrases that are a prominent part of it. On affirmative action, for example, about one-third of the groups used the phrase *reverse discrimination.* To allow us to infer the use of this resource, they had to use the actual language of public discourse and not merely a paraphrase that expressed the idea. It was not enough, for example, that they claimed that whites are being discriminated against if they did not use the phrase *reverse discrimination.*

Other slogans came up much less frequently, including "A mind is a terrible thing to waste" and "Last hired, first fired" on affirmative action. On troubled industry, people occasionally spoke of the "foreign trade deficit" and "buy American"; on nuclear power, "no nukes" and "split wood, not atoms" were invoked a few times. However, no catch phrase from the public discourse on Arab–Israeli conflict appeared in more than one group.

Experiential knowledge

People frequently make their points in these conversations by telling a story. Sometimes these stories are about someone they read about or heard on a radio talk show, but the majority of them are anecdotes about themselves or someone they know personally. These stories have a point to make, and if the speakers are uncertain about whether the point is clear, they make the lesson explicit.

Although every story has its unique features, they also form generic types related to the framing of an issue. Comments about the "hard time" involved when people are laid off their jobs may stimulate either a supporting *hardship* story or a discounting *readjustment* story. A hardship story typically emphasizes the impact on people's self-esteem and the devastating effect on their families, as well as the economic difficulties involved; a readjustment story typically emphasizes the importance of personal motivation in overcoming life's inevitable adversities. Such generic stories recur on every issue and contribute to framing it in particular ways; the choice of one rather than another is crucial to the construction of a shared meaning on the issue.

These personal anecdotes are one of the primary mechanisms in using experiential knowledge as a conversational resource. Such knowledge has a privileged place; it says, "I know because I saw it myself, firsthand." One does not contradict or deny other people's experience, although it may be discounted as an exception or countered with one's own experiential knowledge to support an alternative framing. More typically, people add their own stories of the same genre, further buttressing a collective frame.

Experiential knowledge may be direct or vicarious in varying degrees. Sometimes the story is not about oneself but about one's spouse, partner, or child. At the other extreme, people tell stories about friends of friends or about someone they once knew at work. It is difficult to know exactly where to draw the line at which experiential knowledge is so vicarious that it hardly seems personal at all.

Empathy allows people to transcend their personal experience and to imagine how they would feel in another person's situation. Madelyn is able to experience vicariously what it must be like for older workers with families to leave "the community they were brought up in" and move to "Minneapolis or somewhere like that." But being able to make this empathic leap is not the same as using one's own experience as a conversational resource. It does not claim the privilege of something witnessed or experienced directly. Hence, we coded as experiential knowledge only those claims that were based on personal experiences and those of immediate family or household members.

Popular wisdom

People bring to bear many popular beliefs that transcend the specific issue in question. Frequently, they flag their references to this resource by using such phrases as "That's the way life is," "In my experience," "It's human nature," "As everyone knows" and the like. When they tell a story, they often begin or end it by a general rule of thumb that relates the experience to some popular maxim that it illustrates. Or, conversely, a statement of some proverb will stimulate the introduction of experiential knowledge to make the same point concretely.

Popular wisdom as a resource depends on shared knowledge of what "everyone" knows. Although everyone's experiential knowledge is in some respects unique, popular wisdom depends on the common elements. Hence, the greater the degree of homogeneity of life experience among a group of people, the greater the popular wisdom available to them as a resource. Popular wisdom frequently is part of a particular subculture, rather than part of a broader national culture. Vanessa's rhetorical question (Chapter 1), "How in the world can something be reversed when we've been discriminated against all our lives?", draws on what every black person is presumed to know. In these groups, the popular wisdom expressed is often oppositional.

The two major devices by which popular wisdom enters these conversations are (1) rules of thumb and (2) analogies to everyday life situations. The rules of thumb include proverbs, maxims, and biblical sayings. In the following example, Tom implies such a rule and Luke makes it explicit.

> *Characters:*
>
> *Tom, a sales clerk in a stereo store, in his early twenties.*
> *Luke, a sales clerk in a department store, in his early twenties.*
>
> *(Discussing the initial, open-ended question on nuclear power.)*

Tom: I don't feel that the federal government can really guarantee the safety of nuclear power. I know they have got pretty strict regulations. There's no guarantee that any time a leak could erupt and cause a very, very disastrous situation.

Luke: Any time a human being is in control of it, anything can happen.

There are many paraphrases of this same generalization in other groups – for example, "You can't avoid human error" or "It's human nature to cut corners." Competing maxims are used to frame the nuclear power issue in a different way. "Everything in life has risks" or "You can get killed crossing a street," for example, use popular wisdom to debunk the special dangers of nuclear power.

Popular wisdom is also introduced through analogies between the issue and familiar situations from everyday experience. In the following example, Evelyn offers a rule of thumb about how to handle intractable fights, and Thomas likens Arab–Israeli conflict to a family feud.

> *Characters:*
>
> *Evelyn, a nurse, in her thirties.*
> *Lucas, a worker in a shelter for the homeless, in his twenties.*
> *Thomas, a tailor, in his thirties.*
>
> *(The group is discussing Arab–Israeli conflict and responding to Cartoon 15, Appendix B.)*

Evelyn: I think that when you have two sides fighting, if you can't stop the fight after numerous attempts, walk away and leave them. The United States does not have to live over there in Palestine or Israel; they've got the United States. Come home; let 'em fight it out until it's over. Because you wouldn't go leave your home to go and witness some fight with somebody a thousand miles away. Why? It makes no sense to me.

(*Later, responding to Cartoon 16, Appendix B.*)

Lucas: They have to have, both of them have to, ah, acknowledge each other's right to exist somewhere.

Thomas: You know, the war between these two – it, it's a lot deeper than just – it's not money or, or power or – it's just a, ah, like a family feud. (*laughs*)

Lucas: Yeah, a family feud.

Comparing resources

Any single resource has its limits. By using a combination of different types of resources to construct a shared frame, a group gives it a solid foundation. To see why, I compare the types of resources on two dimensions.

Personal versus cultural

Let me concede at the outset that none of these resources is purely personal or cultural. Even our personal experience is filtered through a culturally created lens. "Big Brother is you, watching" in Miller's (1988) clever phrase. We walk around with hyperreal images from movies and television and use them to code our own experiences. Media discourse is not something out there but something inside our heads.

I recall a friend who described a critical formative episode from his childhood that had influenced his development in important ways. He once discussed the episode in the presence of his parents who insisted that it had never happened. He, in turn, was utterly convinced that they had simply forgotten or repressed it. Later, much abashed, he confessed to me that while watching late night television, he had discovered that his cherished personal experience was really a scene from an old movie.

At the other extreme, people bring their own experiences and personal associations to their readings of cultural texts. Media images have no fixed meaning but involve a negotiation with a heterogeneous audience that may provide them with meanings quite different from the preferred reading. Khadaffi's sartorial style may signal craziness to the photojournalist or editor who spotlights it, but it signals style and flashiness to some viewers. Media images, then, are not purely cultural but are infused with personal meanings as well.

Nevertheless, the mix of cultural and personal varies dramatically among the three types of resources. Our experiences may have cultural elements but they are overwhelmingly our own private resources, not fully shared by others. People distinguish between knowing something from having experienced it and knowing something secondhand or more abstractly, and they generally give a privileged place to their own experiential knowledge. Experiential knowledge is valued precisely because it is so direct and relatively unmediated. Although there is plenty of selectivity in the memory of experiences, it is our own selectivity, not someone else's.

Media discourse, at the other extreme, is a useful resource precisely because it is public. In spite of personal elements, it is possible to talk about the accident at Chernobyl on the basis of assumed common images and factual knowledge. If everyone may not know the particular element of media discourse referred to, it is nonetheless public knowledge, available to anyone who wants to know. Unlike personal experience, you can look it up. Media discourse, then, is predominantly a cultural resource.

Popular wisdom is in the middle, an amalgam of personal and cultural. On the one hand, it embodies the lessons of personal experience. One's experiences take on meaning by being linked to these rules of thumb. They help to transform the unique experience of different individuals into a bit of popular wisdom that invokes others' similar experiences. By bridging the personal and cultural, popular wisdom helps to make experiential knowledge relevant to framing the issue under discussion.

Popular wisdom is also part of the media discourse on these issues. Analogies to everyday life and popular maxims are often invoked to make abstract frames more immediate and concrete. Popular wisdom is not only a conversational resource but a resource for sponsors of different media frames and for journalists as they interpret events. By linking media discourse to popular wisdom, it is thus brought closer to experiential knowledge.

Issue versus metaissue level

Media resources refer to a particular issue domain. Even when other related issues are introduced, this media discourse is still issue specific. When people talk about the *Challenger* explosion in discussions of nuclear power, for example, they are borrowing from one issue domain to make sense of another, but they are still operating at the level of issues.

Popular wisdom and experiential knowledge are not bounded or defined by issue domains. A vast array of personal experiences and popular wisdom may become relevant in the course of a conversation, and any of them may be a resource for a large array of different issues. The popular wisdom that one should walk away from a fight if one cannot stop it could be applied to many other conflicts besides the Arab–Israeli one. Personal experiences at work or in other aspects of one's personal life may be relevant for many different domains.

Iyengar and Kinder (1987) offer experimental evidence of the special impact of integrating the personal and cultural. First, they review a large number of studies that show that Americans sharply distinguish the quality of their personal lives and their judgments about public issues. For example, crime victims do not regard crime as a more serious problem for society as a whole than do those personally untouched by crime; people's assessments of economic conditions are largely unrelated to the economic setbacks and gains in their own lives; and the war in Vietnam was not rated as a more important problem among those who had close relatives serving there than among Americans without such personal connections to the war.

Iyengar and Kinder then designed a series of experiments to test more subtle connections between media coverage and personal effects. One experiment concentrated on three issues – civil rights, unemployment, and social security. Their procedures involved showing edited television news broadcasts to their subjects, varying the amount of coverage of these issues systematically. (Stories on a variety of other issues were included as well.) In different conditions, subjects saw either no coverage, intermediate coverage, or extensive coverage by varying the total number of stories on each of the three issues.

Subjects varied on whether they were in a category that was personally affected. Blacks were contrasted with whites on civil rights, those out of work with those currently working on the unemployment issue, and the elderly with the young on social security. At the end, all subjects were asked to name the most important problems that the country faced.

The authors found that on two of the three issues – civil rights and social security – members of the personally affected group were especially influenced by the amount of television coverage they watched. On the unemployment issue, they found no differences between the employed and unemployed. Only this last result is consistent with the earlier studies showing the lack of relationship between people's personal lives and their views on public issues.

Iyengar and Kinder interpret their results in ways that suggest the integration of personal and cultural resources. "We suspect," they write, "that the key feature distinguishing civil rights and social security is that they are experienced psychologically both as personal predicaments and as *group* predicaments." Although they do not use the term, *collective identity* processes come into play that do not operate on unemployment. It is not merely that I am affected but that we are affected. And people are especially sensitive and responsive to media coverage that suggests that "our" problem is an important problem for the country.

In sum, by failing to use all three resources in constructing a frame, a group is unable to bridge the personal and cultural and to anchor their understanding in both. By failing to link their understanding of an issue with popular wisdom and experiential knowledge, their issue understanding is ad hoc and isolated from their more general understanding of the world. Hence, there is a special robustness to frames that are held together with a full combination of resources.

Resource strategies

Groups were not asked to reach a consensus and, hence, were under no external pressure to come up with a shared meaning. However, the demands of conversation include their own built-in pressure. When there is disagreement, participants frequently search for points on which they can all agree. More important, it is difficult to carry on a conversation if they cannot even agree on what the issue is and what is at stake. Hence, there is a group dynamic that pushes participants toward a common framing, even when they disagree about solutions.

Nevertheless, not all groups succeeded in constructing a shared frame on every issue. I treated them as having such a shared frame if either of the following conditions was met: (1) At least two participants contributed to the elaboration and construction of the frame, and no one challenged or attacked it directly, or (2) Someone was explicitly critical and offered an alternative, but no one else contributed to constructing the alternative and the group defined the person as offering a minority view.[2]

Overall, more than 80 percent of the issue discussions resulted in a shared frame, but each issue presented its own separate challenge. As Figure 7.1 shows, groups were overwhelmingly likely to come up with a shared frame

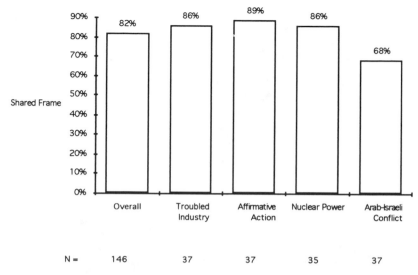

Figure 7.1. Shared frames by issue.

on troubled industry, affirmative action, and nuclear power but less likely on Arab–Israeli conflict where only about two-thirds of the groups (68 percent) did so.

When groups do develop shared frames, their resource strategy varies from issue to issue. Since popular wisdom is almost always used at some point, the critical variable is the extent to which they integrate both experiential knowledge and media discourse in developing their frame. In particular, I distinguished three resource strategies:

1. Cultural. These discussions rely on media discourse and popular wisdom in framing the issue but do not integrate experiential knowledge in support of it.
2. Personal. These discussions rely on experiential knowledge and popular wisdom in framing the issue but do not integrate media discourse in support of it.
3. Integrated. These discussions rely on a full combination of resources, bringing together media discourse and experiential knowledge.

Resource strategy, as Figure 7.2 shows, is heavily issue dependent. Although some groups made slightly more use of media discourse than others,

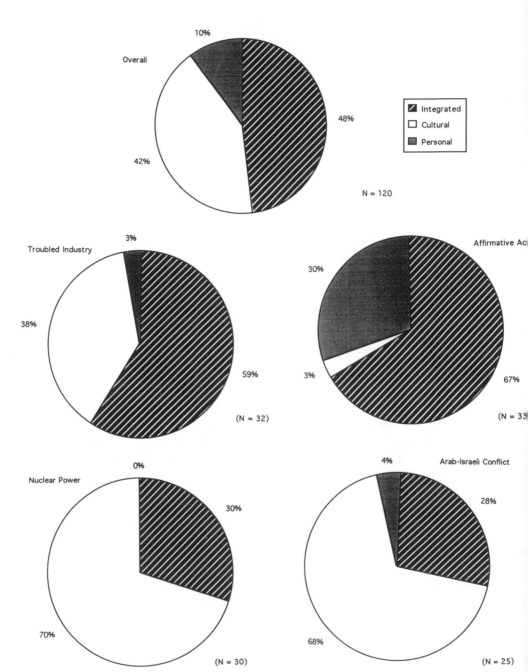

Figure 7.2. Resource strategy by issue.

such differences were overwhelmed by issue differences. Integrated resource strategies were quite likely on affirmative action and troubled industry but much less so on nuclear power and Arab–Israeli conflict, where less than a third of the groups used the full array.

With respect to resource strategies, nuclear power and Arab–Israeli conflict are very similar issues. The conversations overwhelmingly began with media discourse; in contrast, less than half the groups began with this resource on troubled industry and less than one-third on affirmative action. A substantial minority also drew on some relevant personal experience on these issues as well, but the predominant strategy was cultural.

Initially, I thought that the issues of nuclear power and Arab–Israeli conflict were so far removed from people's daily lives that it surprised me to find such a substantial minority introducing experiential knowledge in support of their shared frame. The following example illustrates the variety of experiences that people bring to bear on such issues as the enforcement of safety regulations and the realism of evacuation plans. It involves the same group we quoted earlier to illustrate the use of popular wisdom on nuclear power.

Characters:

Luke, a clerk in a department store, in his early twenties.
Pat, a clerk in a department store, in his early twenties.
Tom, a clerk in a stereo store, in his early twenties.
Rich, a photographer's apprentice, in his early twenties.

(They are discussing the initial, open-ended question on nuclear power.)

Luke: One time this guy told me about – I was on the Hudson on this boat and we passed by this nuclear power plant. And he said, "Yeah, well, they were – there was this thing about how they're not running it safely and –

Pat: – That's the one the Mafia were running?

(laughter)

Pat: True. There was one.

Rich: Our power plants? Uranium smuggled in from Columbia.

Luke: No. They were supposed to be showing these safety films. They were say – well, something like the government said, "You have to show safety films to all the workers." And it turned out that they got the safety films and put 'em like in a drawer, and they ordered porno flicks – and they sat around and watched porno movies instead of watching what they were supposed to. So, that is what scares me.

Rich: From my window at school, I could see the Yankee – No, what was it? What was the one in Vermont? Vernon, the Vernon power plant.

Pat: You could see that?

Rich: Yeah.

Pat: You could see the lights of the plant?

Rich: You can see the lights – about eighteen miles down the river. And they were *busted* every three or four months for venting off the steam, which is really illegal. You're supposed to cool it with the water tanks and everything. But it cost a lot of money, and they didn't care. I mean, they're run so lax.

Tom: There's a place in Charlestown – I used to work on these boats, and there's a dock out there with a sign that says "Radiation Hazard – No Swimming." Turns out the nuclear submarines used to dock there and pump out the coolant water into the water in Charlestown.

Luke: They did a thing at our school. The power plant in Vermont that he was talking about. We used to have every Wednesday and Saturday, they had this safety whistle that would like – drills. They'd just test the whistle.

Rich: Yeah. How do you know what to do, though?

Luke: Well, see, the thing was – the plan was that buses from Northampton or Amherst – like the public transportation buses were supposed to drive up there and get all the people and bring 'em down. There's two things, two problems: First of all, if there was actually a meltdown or something, there's no way you can get – we're so close, and we're down river – there's no way you can get away in time. And also, do you think that a bus driver in Northampton who's farther south is actually gonna drive up towards the nuclear power plant to get people?

(laughter)

Integrated resource strategies were quite common on affirmative action and troubled industry, but the two issues show an important difference. Affirmative action is the only issue on which personal strategies are more common than cultural strategies, and the first resource utilized is more

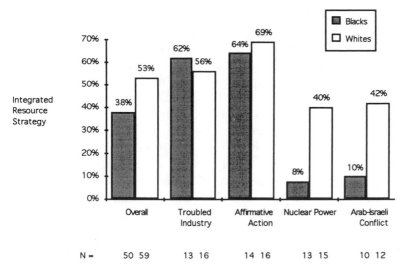

Figure 7.3.   Resource strategy by race.

likely to be experiential knowledge than media discourse. Personal strategies outnumbered cultural ones by a ratio of 10:1 on affirmative action but, on the other three issues combined, cultural strategies outnumbered personal ones by a ratio of 50:2 ($p < .001$).

In many respects, black and white groups followed similar resource strategies. They were almost identical in the resource they used first, and the pattern of their resource strategies was the same over the four issues. For whites and blacks alike, affirmative action was the highest in integrated strategies, followed closely by troubled industry, with nuclear power and Arab–Israeli conflict well back. But as Figure 7.3 shows, there were some overall differences.

Whites used an integrated resource strategy in 53 percent of their issue conversations with a shared frame compared to 38 percent in the black groups (p = n.s.). A look at the individual issues reveals that it is primarily the media discourse issues of nuclear power and Arab–Israeli conflict that account for the difference. White groups were more likely to draw on experiential knowledge as well in constructing a frame on these issues, but this was rare in black groups. On affirmative action and troubled industry, there was little or no difference.

Conclusion

Resource strategies among working people are heavily issue specific. They use a combination of experiential knowledge, popular wisdom, and media discourse in framing issues, but the particular mix varies. For some issues, media discourse and popular wisdom are the primary resources, and they generally do not integrate experiential knowledge in the framing process. For other issues, they generally begin with experiential knowledge and popular wisdom. Sometimes they also bring in media discourse in support of the same frame, but sometimes they ignore this resource. Nuclear power and Arab–Israeli conflict exemplify the former kind of issue, and affirmative action exemplifies the latter; troubled industry falls somewhere in between, but it is rare for people to ignore media discourse in framing it.

There are theoretical reasons for expecting that frames based on the integration of all three types of resources will be more robust. They enable people to bridge the personal and cultural and to link issue frames to broader cultural themes. If this is true, then we should expect the framings of affirmative action and troubled industry to be especially robust, since the majority of groups follow an integrated strategy in constructing them. Nuclear power and Arab–Israeli conflict, where the majority of groups use media discourse and popular wisdom but not experiential knowledge, should be more subject to fluctuations in the prominence of different frames in media discourse.

Are college-educated people different in their resource strategies? Probably they are more likely to attend to the media spectacle and to rely on it more heavily as a primary resource. Perhaps they are also less likely to draw on popular wisdom and experiential knowledge and, therefore, to use integrated resource strategies in the framing process. If so, this suggests the intriguing hypothesis that they are more likely than working people to be affected by shifts in the dominant media frames on an issue. But this is a topic for another study.

I have said relatively little about the nature of the popular wisdom that people use in understanding these issues. What they choose to emphasize is especially important because of its ability to tie issue frames to broader cultural themes. Issue frames gain plausibility and seem more natural to the extent that they resonate with enduring themes that transcend specific issue domains. As we see in the next chapter, the popular wisdom used on these issues has a strong adversarial and oppositional character, giving it a special relevance for collective action frames.

8

Cultural resonances

Not all symbols are equally potent. Some metaphors soar, others fall flat; some visual images linger in the mind, others are quickly forgotten. Some frames have a natural advantage because their ideas and language resonate with a broader political culture. Resonances increase the appeal of a frame by making it appear natural and familiar. Those who respond to the larger cultural theme will find it easier to respond to a frame with the same sonorities. Snow and Benford (1988, 210) make a similar point in discussing the "narrative fidelity" of a frame. Some frames, they write, "resonate with cultural narrations, that is, with stories, myths, and folk tales that are part and parcel of one's cultural heritage."

The resonance concept focuses on the relationship between the discourse on a particular issue and the broader political culture of which it is a part. Both media discourse and popular wisdom have such resonances. Through their link to the same cultural themes, they are brought together in support of a shared frame and promote an integrated discourse strategy.

Themes and counterthemes

I prefer the term *themes* to the more commonly used *values* for a particular reason. My argument emphasizes the dialectic nature of themes: There is no theme without a countertheme. Themes are safe, conventional, and normative; one can invoke them as pieties on ceremonial occasions with the assumption of general social approval, albeit some private cynicism. Counterthemes typically share many of the same taken-for-granted assumptions but challenge some specific aspect of the mainstream culture; they are adversarial, contentious, oppositional. Themes and counterthemes are paired with each other so that whenever one is invoked, the other is always present in latent form, ready to be activated with the proper cue. In referring to the challenging member of this pair, *countertheme* seems a clearer term than *countervalue*.[1]

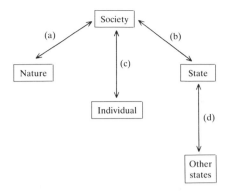

Figure 8.1.   Dimensions of cultural themes: (a) technology, (b) power, (c) dependence, (d) nationalism.

The analysis here focuses on the four dimensions of cultural themes indicated in Figure 8.1.[2] The technology dimension focuses on the relationship between society and nature; the power dimension on society and state; the dependence dimension on individual and society; and the nationalism dimension on the relationship between one's own state and other states. Each dimension becomes engaged in media discourse on a variety of issues, and each has a central theme and a countertheme with deep historical roots in American culture.

1. Technology themes: Progress through technology versus *harmony with nature*. Few would question the appeal of a "technofix" for a wide variety of problems in American society. "American emphasis upon efficiency has consistently impressed outside observers," Williams (1960, 428) comments in his discussion of American values. " 'Efficient' is a word of high praise in a society that has long emphasized adaptability, technological innovation, economic expansion, up-to-dateness, practicality, expediency, 'getting things done.' " The inventor is a cultural hero: Benjamin Franklin, Thomas Edison. Mastery over nature is the way to progress, know-how, problem solving.

This theme is reflected in a view of politics that treats issues as problems that are susceptible to technical solution. How can we solve the problem, how much is it going to cost, and is it worth it? "There isn't a Republican and a Democratic way to clean streets," argued the Progressive era advocates of nonpartisan municipal government. Overtly nonideological, this theme presents itself as pragmatic, willing to try whatever is needed to do the job. Issues present technical problems to be solved, and one ought to get the best expertise available to help overcome the problems that the country faces.

Alongside this theme, a countertheme exists that is more skeptical of, or even hostile to, technology. Harmony with nature rather than mastery over nature is emphasized. Schumacher (1973) writes of "technology with a human face." "In the excitement over the unfolding of his scientific and technical powers, modern man has built a system of production that ravishes nature" (293). Our technology must be appropriate and in proper scale. There is an ecological balance to maintain.

To quote Emerson, "Things are in the saddle and ride mankind." The more we try to control nature through our technology, the more we disrupt its natural order and threaten the quality of our lives. Lovins (1977) argues for "soft energy paths" that "respect the limits that are always with us on a little planet, the delicate fragility of life. . . . We need, like Faust, to refashion hubris into humility; to learn and accept our own limits as a fragile and tenuous experiment in an unhospitable universe" (1977, 218 and 170). Illich (1973, 84) calls for a technology of responsibly limited tools since "a tool can grow out of man's control, first to become his master and finally to become his executioner." Ellul (1964, 14) warns us that "technique has become autonomous; it has fashioned an omnivorous world which obeys its own laws and which has renounced all tradition." Goodman (1970, 193) points to the absurdity of "desperately relying on technological means to solve problems caused by previous technological means."

Winner (1977) calls this countertheme *autonomous technology* and traces its long roots in political thought. He underlines its challenging nature by describing the defensive overreaction he received from many scientists, engineers, and managers with whom he raised apparently innocuous questions implying possible negative effects of technology. "You're just using technology as a whipping boy," he was told. "You just want to stop progress and send us back to the Middle Ages with peasants dancing on the green."

Much of popular culture reflects the countertheme: Chaplin's *Modern Times*, Huxley's *Brave New World*, Kubrick's *2001*, and countless other films and books about mad scientists and technology gone wild, out of control, a Frankenstein's monster turning on its creator. All of this nature-ravishing technology carried on in the name of "progress" – with quotation marks to indicate the irony. In the words of the Joni Mitchell song, "Paved paradise, put up a parking lot."

2. Power themes: Interest group liberalism versus *popular democracy.* *Interest group liberalism* is Lowi's (1967) term for the American public's philosophy by which the decisions of government are guided and justified. I prefer it to *pluralism* because it sharpens the contrast with the countertheme and is less vague, focusing on political rather than a broader social pluralism. In this view of the American polity, "the most important difference between liberals and conservatives, Republicans and Democrats . . . is to be found in the interest groups they identify with. Congressmen are guided in their votes, presidents in their programs, and administrators in their discretion, by whatever organized interests they have taken for themselves as the most legitimate; and that is the measure of the legitimacy of demands" (Lowi, 1971).

The elaborate bargaining game among interest groups supposedly provides a variety of benefits. With a sufficiently large number of competing groups, no one group can dominate. Coalitions are fluid and impermanent, formed more or less de novo for each issue. Furthermore, issues divide groups in different ways so that many groups not in a present coalition are potential coalition partners on subsequent issues. "Because one center of power is set against another," Dahl (1967, 24) writes, "power itself will be tamed, civilized, controlled, and limited to decent human purposes, while coercion, the most evil form of power, will be reduced to a minimum."

Interest group liberalism encourages a political culture of self-restraint and moderation. In popular wisdom, half a loaf is better than none. The polity will "generate politicians who learn how to deal gently with opponents, who struggle endlessly in building and holding coalitions together, who doubt the possibilities of great change, who seek compromises" (Dahl, 1967, 329).

Abuse of power by an autocratic state is only one of the demons that interest group liberalism hopes to exorcise. Drawing inspiration from de Tocqueville, it promises protection from the "tyranny of the majority" by keeping political participation by the masses indirect. "At least since de Tocqueville," Wolfe (1977, 305) writes, "intermediate associations have fascinated political observers, who view them as central to the stability of democratic society. In theory, mediating mechanisms work to the degree that they temper the excessive demands on the citizen and the authoritarian needs of the state, producing the happy compromise known as pluralism."

Interest group liberalism is distrustful of direct participation, opting for the controlled negotiation among leaders of interest groups with a stake in decisions. "How could a mass democracy work if all the people were deeply involved in politics?" Berelson, Lazarsfeld, and McPhee (1954) wonder. "Lack of interest by some people is not without its benefits. . . . Extreme interest goes with extreme partisanship and might culminate in rigid fanaticism that could destroy democratic processes if generalized throughout the community." Dahl (1967) heralds it as a compromise "between the political equality of all adult citizens on one side, and the desire to limit their sovereignty on the other. As a political system, the compromise, except for one important interlude [the civil war], has proved to be durable. What is more, Americans seem to like it."

Just how much they like it, of course, is challenged by the countertheme of *popular democracy,* which emphasizes direct participation. Many writers recognize the tension between theme and countertheme and make it central to their analysis. "The history of politics in capitalist societies," Wolfe (1977, 9) writes, "is the history of the tension between liberal and democratic conceptions of the state." Weaver (1981, 281) sees their collision reflected throughout newspaper and television journalism in America – a collision between "the populist notion that the people should rule directly in their own felt interests, and the republican notion that established institutions should rule in behalf of the public interest under the scrutiny of the electorate."

The countertheme emphasizes the elitist nature of the American political system and its departure from a more egalitarian ideal. Pole (1978, ix) traces the idea of equality in American history, making a strong case for its challenging position: "Only at comparatively rare – and then generally stormy – intervals has the idea of equality dominated American debates on major questions of policy. Equality is normally the language of the underdog."

A good contemporary expression of the countertheme is found in Wolin's (1981, 2) editorial in the founding issue of the journal *Democracy: A Journal of Political Renewal and Radical Change:*

Every one of the country's primary institutions – the business corporation, the government bureaucracy, the trade union, the research and education industries, the mass propaganda and entertainment media, and the health and welfare system – is antidemocratic in spirit, design, and operation. Each is hierarchical in structure, authority oriented, opposed in principle to equal participation, unaccountable to the citizenry, elitist and managerial, and disposed to concentrate increasing power in the hands of the few and to reduce political life to administration.

The countertheme emphasizes how little elections change anything, since, regardless of who is elected, the rules of American politics favor the rich and powerful few at the expense of the many. It is the people versus the interests, the power elite, the ruling class, the military–industrial complex. Or as the populist governor of Kansas, L. D. Lewelling, put it in an earlier era, "the plutocrats, the aristocrats, and all the other rats" (quoted in Canovan, 1981, 51).

3. Dependence themes: Self-reliance versus *mutuality.* "The 'success story' and the respect accorded to the self-made man are distinctly American, if anything is," writes Williams (1960). "The ideal individual struggles successfully against adversity and overcomes more powerful forces. . . . 'Self-made' men and women remain attractive, as do people who overcome poverty or bureaucracy," writes Gans (1979, 50) about values in the news.

In this theme, the best thing we can teach children is how to stand on their own two feet. The people to admire are those who start at the bottom and work hard to get ahead, relying on their own judgment and resources rather than on others. Striving, risk taking, achieving, independence. To try hard and overcome difficult obstacles is creditable. To fail because of lack of effort when success is possible is reprehensible. Calculated risk taking is frequently necessary to overcome obstacles and, indeed, is part of striving. One cannot expect everything to go one's way, and bad luck is simply an obstacle that one must overcome – not something to whine about.

Starting out poor is a special case of bad luck. The truly admirable are those who, by striving, are able to overcome the obstacles of humble birth and go on to achieve fame and fortune. The self-made man or woman embodies all of these ideals – a person who has pluck and resourcefulness, tries hard, makes use of the opportunities that come along, is not thrown off or demoralized by the bad luck or evil encountered, learns by mistakes and improves, until material success is finally achieved.

The nineteenth-century popular novelist Horatio Alger parlayed this formula into his own wordly success. He used some variation of it in about 120 novels, estimated to have sold at least 17 million copies. He was, to quote Fink (1962, 30), "a major pump station on the pipe line that carried the American dream."

Alger's heroes were not selfish individualists, who believed in every man for himself and the devil take the hindmost. They had character traits that kept them on the path of righteousness and made them deserving of their success. Typically, they found a rich patron to help them along. His villains were also lucky and shrewd, but their character flaws ultimately led to their downfall. The Alger hero, "Ragged Dick," thinks of his best friend as he watches his bootblacking days disappearing behind him: " 'I wish Fosdick was as well off as I am,' he thought generously. But he determined to help his less fortunate friend, and assist him up the ladder as he advanced himself" (Alger 1962, 215). There is no tension, then, between the idea of charity toward the less fortunate, or noblesse oblige, and the *self-reliance* theme.

It is independence, not selfishness, that is challenged in the *mutuality* countertheme. Mutuality assumes more reciprocity and equality of status than is implied by charity. The central issue is whether we recognize our interdependence and mutual need for others and treat them accordingly, or use other people as a means to personal advancement.

In the countertheme, striving for individual success is an ego trip. One achieves self-actualization not through individual achievement but by creating a decent and humane society in which people are sensitive to the needs of others and mutually supportive. The best thing we can teach children is to need and care about other people. The people to admire are those who are more concerned about being true to their friends and the welfare of the group than about getting ahead. The beloved community. The Woodstock nation.

"It's easy to produce examples," Slater (1970) observes, "of the many ways in which Americans try to minimize, circumvent, or deny the interdependence upon which all human societies are based. We seek a private house, a private laundry, self-service stores, and do-it-yourself skills of every kind. An enormous technology seems to have set itself the task of making it unnecessary for one human being ever to ask anything of another in the course of going about his or her daily business." In the words of the poet Donne, "No man is an island, entire of itself; every man is a piece of the continent, a part of the main."

4. Nationalism themes: Global responsibility versus *America first.* World War II produced a reversal in the status of theme and countertheme. *Global responsibility,* until then a countertheme in public discourse, became official doctrine, embraced by both major political parties as political elites found consensus in the repudiation of a discredited isolationism.

America first, even during its years as a dominant theme, always represented a limited form of isolationism: It meant separation from the conflict among European powers and the avoidance of specifically political entanglements. Active involvement in the affairs of other countries in the Western Hemisphere and in international commerce were taken for granted. George Washington's Farewell Address not only declared "It is our true policy to steer clear of permanent alliances with any portion of the foreign world" but also exhorted the nation to "Cultivate peace and harmony with all." Thomas Jefferson's inaugural address called for "Peace, commerce, and honest friendship with all nations – entangling alliances with none."

This kind of isolationism was never incompatible with expansionism in what was regarded as U.S. turf. The Monroe Doctrine, in telling European powers to stay out of this hemisphere, managed to affirm both a pan-American isolationism *and* U.S. expansionism. The (then) countertheme of global responsibility was reflected in the idea of America's international mission as a light unto nations. "Behold a republic . . . which shakes thrones and dissolves aristocracies by its silent example," intoned William Jennings Bryan in 1900.

As long as America's international mission was a matter of setting an example and its expansionism was limited to the Western Hemisphere, there was no real challenge to the dominant theme. It was only with the expansionism of the late nineteenth century that global responsibility emerged in political discourse as a genuine countertheme. The most influential voice was that of the naval historian Alfred Thayer Mahan, who advocated an expanded navy that would enable the United States to become a true global power and not merely a regional one. Gunboat diplomacy, for Mahan, was not a matter of pursuing selfish national interests but a more active way of achieving America's international mission. The expansion of American influence in the world would bring enlightenment to backward peoples and confer upon them the bounties of Christianity and American political genius.

With the advent of World War II and the cold war, public discourse fully embraced the global responsibility theme. American withdrawal from the world after World War I and its failure to support the League of Nations were treated as tragic errors, to be contrasted with support for the United Nations and the idea of collective security after World War II. The concept of no entangling alliances with European powers was defined as a historical anachronism, inappropriate for the modern world. A bipartisan consensus embraced a dominant U.S. role in the creation of political–military alliances, not only in Europe but in other regions as well. No more Fortress America: one world. Think globally. What Franklin Delano Roosevelt had declared in 1937 in a contested discourse now seemed an obvious truism: "The U.S. must, for the sake of their own future, give thought to the rest of the world."

Neither theme nor countertheme has a monopoly on nationalist and patriotic symbolism. The global responsibility theme can be invoked without using such symbolism as it is in ideas of common security and ecological interdependence among nations. But the United States as the leader of the free world, as fulfilling its international mission of defending and spreading political liberty and free markets to the benighted, allows for plenty of flag waving.

Popular wisdom and cultural resonances

Popular wisdom, as I argued earlier, is simultaneously a cultural and per-sonal resource. On the one hand, it encapsulates the lessons of commonly shared life experiences and has a concrete reference point in people's direct or vicarious experiential knowledge. On the other hand, these maxims and analogies to everyday life events frequently resonate with broad cultural themes.

Not every bit of popular wisdom is tied to some larger theme. Much of it is situational. "He who hesitates is lost" and "There will always be human error" suggest no larger theme in the abstract, but put in the context of an issue, they may invoke cultural resonances. "He who hesitates is lost" can be used to suggest that failure to proceed with nuclear power now will cost a future generation the energy it needs for continued economic growth. Put in this context, it invokes the progress through technology theme. Similarly, "There will always be human error," put in the context of the dangers of nuclear power, invokes the autonomous technology component of the countertheme.

The rules of thumb and analogies to everyday life in popular wisdom are specific devices for expressing cultural themes. They concretize and condense the themes in the same way that a particular metaphor or catch phrase expresses a frame on an issue. Media human interest stories of people who respond to plant closings by trying harder and taking initiative instead of giving up invoke the self-reliance theme in the same way that readjustment stories in conversations do. Each forum has its own ways of tapping cultural resonances in framing an issue.

When the resonances of widely used popular wisdom on an issue are the same resonances invoked by a media frame, it is easy for people to make a connection between this frame and popular wisdom. If the same popular wisdom can then be linked to experiential knowledge on an issue, this becomes integrated into the frame as well. Hence, common cultural resonances are a key mechanism for linking resources in an integrated resource strategy.

All four of the issues considered here engage at least one of the themes. Sometimes the most prominent resonances in media discourse correspond to those invoked by popular wisdom, but this varies from issue to issue, as does the dialectic between theme and countertheme. Again, to understand how the general process operates, it is useful to examine each issue in detail.

Troubled industry

Media discourse on this issue engages both power and dependence themes. Self-reliance enters the discourse in a complicated way. Two of our critical discourse moments centered on large corporations seeking government help to avoid bankruptcy. As described in Chapter 3, many commentators were intrigued by the central irony that apostles of free enterprise were seeking government handouts. "Socialism for the rich and capitalism for the poor" conveyed it in a catch phrase. Implicitly, the government bailouts of Lockheed and Chrysler were framed in the context of a broader discourse on welfare.

The resonances of the self-reliance theme on this issue function mainly to embarrass and discredit the proponents of the loan who are politically allied with opponents of the welfare state. The proponents of the loan would decouple this issue from the self-reliance theme by framing it as irrelevant. No double standard is involved because one is talking about apples and oranges. In the various versions of the PARTNERSHIP frame, the issue is the relationship of state and market, not individual and society. The relationship between government and business has nothing to do with people being able to stand on their own two feet. Hence, the self-reliance theme is viewed as a red herring.

In contrast, the FREE ENTERPRISE frame calls attention to the central irony. There are not apples and oranges here, but two varieties of apple. Individuals compete in a labor market, whereas companies compete in a commodity market, but in either case, it is the natural forces of the market that weed out the weak from the strong. Harsh as these forces are, they reward the virtues emphasized by the self-reliance theme.

FREE ENTERPRISE is not the only frame that appreciates the central irony. One can be critical of the double standard but favor a welfare state or a more radical reorganization of the economy. The CAPITAL FLIGHT frame invites the government to intervene, not to guarantee loans to Lockheed or Chrysler, but to encourage employee ownership and involve the workers and communities affected in decisions about the flow of capital. However, this frame was invisible in the media discourse at these moments.

The net result is that even though the commentator who invokes the central irony of "welfare for the rich" may not advocate the FREE ENTERPRISE frame, this is the frame that gets a boost. The combination of its strong resonances with the self-reliance theme and its much greater visibility compared to CAPITAL FLIGHT make it the major beneficiary of invoking the central irony.

If the PARTNERSHIP frame is hurt by the self-reliance theme, it has other cultural resonances working in its favor. Regardless of whether government or industry is the senior partner, this frame resonates with the interest group liberalism theme. Business, government, and labor are the organized interests involved in the bargaining game. The agreements that emerge from this negotiation among public, industry, and union officials represent compromises that should provide the broad base of support that enables them to work. Guaranteed loans to Lockheed and Chrysler are part of the bargaining game, a chip that the government offers in return for concessions from the other players. They cannot be judged outside of the context of this larger game. Opposition to compromise, in this frame, comes from zealots who do not accept the power sharing that is part of our pluralist system.

Finally, the America first countertheme is invoked by a FOREIGN IN-VASION frame that is prominent at some critical discourse moments. Its symbolism suggests a continuation of the World War II military conflict with Japan, and the countertheme is invoked by the catch phrase "Buy American." The MacNelly cartoon (Appendix B, Cartoon 3) expresses it well.

Chapter 3 described the strong tendency of media discourse to blame the Japanese for the problems of the steel industry. Of twenty-seven blaming attributions, some 63 percent focused on Japan or other countries as the primary culprits. But this FOREIGN INVASION frame had very low prominence during other critical discourse moments.

In sum, prominent packages in media discourse resonate with the self-reliance and interest group liberalism themes and, in some periods, with the America first countertheme. Another countertheme, popular democracy, resonates with a CAPITAL FLIGHT frame, but since this frame is invisible in media discourse, so is the resonant countertheme.

Resonances in conversations

There is a recurrent bit of popular wisdom that came up in more than half of the groups discussing troubled industry. Although it is put in somewhat different words in different groups, the essence of it is that whatever happens, the rich somehow manage to get richer and the poor people are hurt. Overall, some version of this sentiment was expressed on this issue in more than half of the total groups and in more than 70 percent of the black groups. Its characteristic use is illustrated in the following two examples.[3]

> Characters:
>
> Lil, a nurse, in her forties.
> Chris, a nurse, in her forties.
> Linda, a nurse, in her twenties.
> Nora, a nurse, in her forties.
> Judy, a dental assistant, in her thirties.
> Marie, a nurse, in her forties.

[Responding to the facilitator's question of whether the issue of troubled industry has affected anyone personally.]

Lil: Well, my father worked down at Quincy Shipyard for many years, so I can identify with that; I was born and brought up in Quincy for quite a number of years, and I know how much the city relies on the shipyard.

[Later, in response to the facilitator's question of whether larger groups stand to gain or lose.]

Cris: All right, the Quincy Shipyard, now. *[Real estate developer]* Flatley's gonna take that over. It's like everybody – it's almost like it was planned. Ya know, all of a sudden it's closed, and all of a sudden Flatley is right there to make his millions, you know. He'll build his condos and his hotels and, ya know –

Linda: – so he'll gain while other people lose.

Cris: Yeah.

Nora: The bigger, bigger industries will gain. . . .

Judy: Yeah, money goes to money. It always seems to follow suit that money goes to money, and the poor guy that's honest and goes in there and he does his job –

Marie: It always affects the working class.

Lil: – the lower-income and the working-class families.

Characters:

Duane, a machinist, in his thirties.
Barbara, a teacher in an after-school program, in her thirties.
Lucy, a human service worker, in her thirties.

[They are responding to the PARTNERSHIP cartoon, no. 1, Appendix B.]

Duane: I think that this cartoon is full of it.

Lucy: I think this cartoon is a cartoon.

Facilitator: Can you say more?

Duane: The government really don't care too much about its part because it's going to get his. And the businessman, I can take him or leave him. It's the labor person, in the long run, that's gonna be left out.

Barbara: That's the one that's the most poor, and he's not getting anywhere.

[Later, in response to the FOREIGN INVASION cartoon, no. 3, Appendix B.]

Lucy: The United States has put itself in a predicament – I mean, they have caused poverty to be happening in this country. The rich are getting richer and the poor are getting poorer. They don't see to it that the poor are fed. This is supposed to be the land of the free and the home of the brave and the land of opportunity, equal opportunity. But I don't see anything equal about it. When there are rich folks over here, across the way from me, who have more than what they need, and right around the corner there are places like Rosie's Place [*a shelter for the homeless*]. And they don't have enough to eat or folks sleeping on the streets.

[*Later, in response to the CAPITAL FLIGHT cartoon, no. 4, Appendix B.*]

Duane: [They say] that we all need to pull together as one in order to keep this company above water. And then going back in the office, sitting up there calling somebody out there in California, saying, "Well, hey, you know I just told a man, 'Hey, we all pull together, everything is going to be all right.' But I'm telling you, man, hey, we're going to move out. We're going to shut down this department, and that department, and we're going to ship the things down to Haiti. Because all we've got to do is pay them people thirty-seven cents an hour where I'm paying somebody up here ten dollars an hour to run the same machine." And they leave us, and what do they do? They leave the worker standing still.

The only other resonances embodied in popular wisdom on the troubled industry issue invoke the self-reliance theme, but this occurred in only 14 percent of the groups. It took the form of emphasizing a loss of job as one of the facts of life; being able to bounce back from such misfortune instead of falling apart is a measure of one's character. The event itself is treated, in such discussions, as the result of natural market forces beyond human agency. This bit of popular wisdom shares the cultural resonances of the FREE ENTERPRISE frame.

None of the other themes invoked by media frames received any visibility in the discussions of troubled industry. The interest group liberalism theme was, if anything, repudiated in frequent assertions that the partnership idea is fraudulent, since labor inevitably gets the short end of the stick. Nor did the America first theme receive more than token support through the occasional invocation of the "buy American" slogan. Expressions of anti-Japanese sentiment were rare, with the Japanese typically given credit for the discipline of their work force and their spirit of cooperation, in invidious comparison to American workers and companies. Nor are Third World workers blamed for their willingness to accept lower wages, since they are widely regarded as too desperate to have a choice. The frames that invoke these themes fail to connect with any popular wisdom that shares the same resonances.

I argued earlier that the use of popular wisdom that shares resonances with media frames helps to promote an integrated resource strategy. There is some support for this hypothesis in the troubled industry conversations. More than two-thirds of the groups that utilized popular wisdom resonating with the popular democracy countertheme also were successful in using an integrated resource strategy; only one-third of the groups that omitted such popular wisdom used an integrated strategy ($p < .05$). Furthermore, three of the five groups that used popular wisdom invoking the self-reliance theme also achieved an integrated resource strategy in constructing a shared frame.

The predominance of the popular democracy theme in these conversations stands in sharp contrast to its virtual invisibility in media discourse. The result is that the CAPITAL FLIGHT frame, in some version, is the dominant one in these conversations among working people in spite of being so rarely displayed in national media discourse. Duane's parable of the boss who privately tells his confederate that the company is moving to Haiti is all the more remarkable for this absence. Whatever its source, Duane's understanding and use of the CAPITAL FLIGHT frame cannot rest on this idea's having been relentlessly pounded home in media discourse.

The driving force in these discussions is not the media but an experientially based popular wisdom that resonates with the popular democracy countertheme – in spite of its lack of prominence in media discourse. Nor is the prominence of the self-reliance theme in media discourse reflected in a similar prominence in these discussions, coming up in only 14 percent. For the overwhelming majority of the groups in this sample, the policy debate between advocates of PARTNERSHIP and FREE ENTERPRISE frames was largely irrelevant. And the PARTNERSHIP frame, in particular, seemed to find no resonances for its interest group liberalism theme among these working people.

In sum, the popular wisdom of working people in discussing this issue leads to a very different set of resonances than the ones invoked by the dominant media frames. The countertheme of popular democracy is all but invisible in media discourse but is clearly the most important theme in popular discourse. The version of CAPITAL FLIGHT that appears in these conversations lacks the coherence and developed argumentation of the version in public discourse. With little or no help from the media, people on their own produce a less sophisticated populist version, sharing the same underlying frame and cultural resonances. One can only speculate about the prominence of the CAPITAL FLIGHT frame in these conversations, given a media discourse that made it more culturally available.

Affirmative action

On this issue, rival frames compete with each other for the resonances of the self-reliance theme. The battleground centers on the symbol of equal opportunity: All packages lay claim to it. The self-reliance theme assumes equality of opportunity. With resourcefulness and a few breaks, even a poor bootblack can become a millionaire, but only if he is given a fighting chance to succeed.

For the REMEDIAL ACTION frame, affirmative action programs are necessary to achieve true equality of opportunity. "In order to get beyond racism, we must first take into account race," wrote Justice Harry Blackmun in his opinion on the Bakke case in 1978. "And in order to treat some persons equally, we must treat them differently." Institutional racism is not a thing of the past but a present reality.

NO PREFERENTIAL TREATMENT frames are equally adamant in their invocation of equality of opportunity. The core concept of justice poses equal opportunity for all individuals against statistical parity for government-approved groups. "A quota is a divider of society, a creator of castes, and it is all the worse for its racial basis, especially in a society desperately striving for an equality that will make race irrelevant" (Bickel 1975, 133).

During the 1960s, demonstrators for civil rights frequently carried signs reading "Equal Rights for All Americans." In the contest over affirmative action, this catch phrase no longer differentiated among competing frames, as all sought the cultural resonances invoked by equal opportunity. No other cultural themes are engaged by the media discourse on this issue.

Resonances in conversations

Racial differences in the framing of affirmative action overwhelm any easy generalizations to be made about cultural resonances on this issue. Black and white groups differ radically in what they take for granted and in the starting point for their discussion. Everyone is in favor of self-reliance and the equal opportunity it implies, but alternative ways of framing the issue make this theme relevant in different ways.

As I argued in Chapter 5, blacks and whites alike partake in what Carbaugh (1988) describes as a discourse on the person as an individual. Persons as individuals have rights, and social groups are moved to the back of this discourse. Although the term *equal opportunity* could apply to the claims of a group as well as those of an individual, the discourse privileges the rights of individuals and makes the articulation of collective claims problematic.

In white and interracial groups, it is universal in discussions of affirmative action for one or more people to claim that everyone should be judged as an individual, but the same assertion is made in the majority of black groups as well. This belief is as much a part of African-American culture as it is of the culture of other groups. Black groups, then, must contend with the formidable appeal of an anti–affirmative action frame that emphasizes completely color-blind policies.

The popular wisdom used in 88 percent of the black groups assumes or makes explicit the continued existence of disadvantage and discrimination in the lives of black people; blacks remain, as in the past, a have-not group, and no one argues that affirmative action has changed this fundamental fact of life in America. For close to half of the black groups, affirmative action fails to provide truly equal opportunity and, at the same time, stigmatizes blacks and causes resentment among whites.

About half of the black groups neutralized the resonances of NO PREFERENTIAL TREATMENT by emphasizing the continuing absence of equal opportunity for blacks and other minorities. The others continued to wrestle with the dilemma it presents. They expressed sympathy for poor whites who are also struggling for economic survival and anger at how affirmative action programs set poor whites and blacks against each other. In the symbolic contest between NO PREFERENTIAL TREATMENT and REMEDIAL ACTION over the meaning of equal opportunity, the former holds its own quite well even in black groups.

Among white and interracial groups, however, it is a different contest. Again, there were two patterns of about equal frequency, both endorsing the idea that people should be judged as individuals. Half of the groups did not acknowledge the existence of present-day discrimination against blacks; for them, equal opportunity exists, and there is no excuse for race-conscious programs. The other half of the white groups and all of the interracial groups acknowledged that blacks and other minorities continue to operate at a disadvantage, in spite of affirmative action programs. Acknowledging that full equality of opportunity has not yet been achieved forced them to wrestle with a dilemma and neutralized the resonances of the NO PREFERENTIAL TREATMENT frame.

In sum, two separate symbolic contests were going on in the black and white groups over the resonances of the self-reliance theme. In the black groups, where continuing discrimination is taken for granted, the appeal of color blindness created a dilemma for people. In the white and interracial groups, where the appeal of equal opportunity for all individuals is universal, the knowledge of continuing disadvantage for blacks created the dilemma.

Nuclear power

This issue most obviously engages technology themes, but political power and nationalism themes also have some secondary relevance. The dialectic between theme and countertheme on technology is reflected in direct competition between frames. I noted earlier the images of Hiroshima and Nagasaki, which are never far from the surface in discourse on nuclear power. Such images of vast destruction inevitably resonate with the countertheme.

The PROGRESS package on nuclear power handled the potential tension between nuclear power as a symbol of technological progress and the image of a technology that might destroy its creator through a dualism about nuclear energy. During the period in which it reigned supreme, "atoms for peace" was an uncontested symbol that invoked the progress through technology theme, and the countertheme was safely compartmentalized in the nuclear weapons discourse.[4]

Nuclear dualism broke down during the 1970s, even among many of the keepers of the faith. With the advent of the Carter administration, proliferation of nuclear weapons became a presidential priority issue. To deal with the proliferation problem, Carter tried to promote stronger international control over the spread of nuclear technology, including reactor technology. Although a strong supporter of nuclear power generally, he turned against the breeder reactor lest the plutonium it produced be diverted to weapons use. Atoms for peace and atoms for war no longer appeared to be separate paths. Subliminal mushroom clouds had begun to gather over even official discourse on this issue.

At the same time, dualism was being undermined by the emergence of the safety issue. If a serious accident that releases large amounts of radiation into the atmosphere is possible at a nuclear reactor, then the destructive potential of this awesome energy is not confined to bombs. The additional problem of disposing of radioactive waste from nuclear reactors completed the breakdown of the compartmentalization that earlier had relegated the countertheme to the discourse on nuclear weapons.

Two frames on nuclear power offer strong resonances with the harmony with nature countertheme, but only one of them has significant visibility in media discourse. The environmental wing of the antinuclear movement, epitomized by Friends of the Earth, offers a SOFT PATHS frame. Nuclear power, in this frame, is a symbol of the wrong kind of technology: highly centralized and dangerous to the earth's sensitive ecology. By changing our careless and wasteful way of life to conserve energy as much as possible and by developing alternative sources of energy that are ecologically safe and renewable and have a "human face," we can become a society more in harmony with its natural environment. Split wood, not atoms.

A second frame, RUNAWAY, resonates strongly with the autonomous technology subtheme. Its signature metaphors draw on familiar ones to symbolize a technology that has taken on an independent life of its own. Nuclear power is a genie that we have summoned and are now unable to force back into its bottle, a Frankenstein's monster that might turn on its creator. In a religious version, humans have dared to play God in tampering with the fundamental forces of nature and the universe. He who sows the wind reaps the whirlwind.

Prior to the accident at Three Mile Island (TMI), this frame was invisible in our media samples except for cartoons, but after TMI and Chernobyl it became the single most prominent frame in every medium. In sixty-seven cartoons after TMI, for example, it was represented in two-thirds of them, with the nearest competitor at under 20 percent. In contrast, SOFT PATHS scored under 10 percent in every media sample, with a single exception: It reached a high water mark of 14 percent in opinion columns after TMI. But RUNAWAY and SOFT PATHS complement each other rather than compete in jointly raising the countertheme. Together, they make it much more prominent in media discourse after TMI than the progress through technology theme.

The popular democracy countertheme enters media discourse through the resonance of the NO PUBLIC ACCOUNTABILITY frame. On the one hand, we have the nucleocrats who run the industry and their buddies in government agencies who are supposed to represent the public but, in fact, act as promoters of the industry. On the other hand, we have the people who suffer the consequences in the form of higher electricity costs and risk of life and limb. Nuclear power is a classic case of the "people" versus the "interests."

After TMI, NO PUBLIC ACCOUNTABILITY received quite a bit of media prominence, second only to the RUNAWAY frame discussed earlier. Television is its best medium, where it appeared in 35 percent of the utterances that imply some frame on nuclear power; even among cartoons, where RUNAWAY dominated the discourse, it is the frame of choice in almost 20 percent of them. These figures dropped considerably in our post-Chernobyl sample, however, where it was displayed mainly by invoking comparison between Soviet officials hiding the magnitude of the Chernobyl accident and earlier official dissembling in the United States at the time of TMI.

Finally, there is one pronuclear frame that resonates with the America first countertheme. The ENERGY INDEPENDENCE frame draws a pronuclear meaning from the Arab oil embargo of 1973. The lesson is how dependence on foreign energy sources makes the United States vulnerable to political blackmail. Nuclear energy offers a practical alternative to imported oil. "Do we want to be dependent on the whims of Arab sheiks?" it asks. Nuclear energy, by ensuring independence, allows the United States to control its own destiny.

The ENERGY INDEPENDENCE frame had some visibility in media discourse, particularly in opinion columns, prior to TMI, but it became invisible after that point except in opinion columns, where it was displayed in some form in slightly over 10 percent. The weakness of this frame, then, makes the America first countertheme insignificant in media discourse on nuclear power.

In sum, the most important media resonances on nuclear power are with counterthemes, especially harmony with nature and popular democracy. Resonance with the progress through technology theme remains important, but supporters of nuclear power who would invoke it face the prospect of simultaneously invoking its countertheme. Since the countertheme is now more prominent in media frames on the nuclear power issue, any attempt to make use of technology themes by proponents is likely to backfire.

Resonances in conversations

Many discussions of nuclear power reflect the tension between the progress through technology theme and the harmony with nature countertheme. Overall, the countertheme is more dominant in the thinking of most groups about nuclear power, but some groups reach no working consensus on the issue or waver back and forth between frames. Finally, the popular democracy countertheme comes up in a significant minority of the groups.

The most widely used popular wisdom about nuclear power centers on the inevitability of human error. People understand that the safety of nuclear power depends on official regulations being carried out by ordinary working people like themselves. They frequently exchange stories whose lesson is the gap between official regulations and what actually happens on the work site. In addition, many are skeptical about the willingness of the companies that run the plants to give safety priority over saving costs and increasing profits. Fully one-third of the groups explicitly generalized this popular wisdom in the form of some maxim about the inevitability of human error. The following example is from the same group that discussed affirmative action in Chapter 5.

Characters:

Billie, a delivery van driver, in her fifties.
Anne, a cleaning woman, in her thirties.
Debbie, a bus driver, in her thirties.
Linda, a temporary worker, in her twenties.

(Discussing the initial, open-ended question on nuclear power.)

Billie: I think of all the yo-yos that are around that there just might be one, just one (*pop*) –

Anne: Guess what I read the other day. Of all professions – now, this will curl your hair real good – (*laughter*) nuclear power plant workers have the highest rate of alcoholism, which tells me that they're going to work probably half-pickled. (*laughter*) I mean, it's frightening.

Debbie: That's scary – when you think in terms of what could – what a nuclear power plant – it's terrifying.

Anne: You know, I stopped going to carnivals for the most part for the same reasons – that's my thought on nuclear power plants. I tell my kids – if there's an amusement park that is there permanently, that's one thing. You kind of know it's secure. But you don't know what person set up this ride today. What they were doing last night. (*laughter*) They could have been loaded or high as kites and put the thing together this morning. And I think that about nuclear power plants too.

Linda: It would be nice if, before they decided how we're going to run our lights and get our homes heated, that they would consider human lives a priority. How this is going to affect human lives. But that's the system we're under. They – it's motivated by greed, still.

Debbie: Or even if they do consider that – that human error just gets in the way. I mean, they may not have terrible motives – but then again too, excuse me, I think they're really necessary because we obviously need the energy that they generate. But I think they have to find a way to make them a lot safer than they are.

Billie: Part of it is the conditions in the world – the stress that people are under – which means that it's kind of scary. You don't know if they had a fight in the morning with their wife or if the coffee was too hot. It doesn't take very much for people to get out of control. It really doesn't.

This popular wisdom resonates with the autonomous technology part of the countertheme. As we saw earlier, groups tend to begin their discussions of nuclear power by drawing on media discourse, and the examples they use lead them to this popular wisdom. Both the Chernobyl accident and the *Challenger* explosion had occurred earlier in the year; hence, both nuclear and nonnuclear examples were salient and were frequently used to make the point.

The result is that 80 percent of the discussions developed some version of the RUNAWAY frame on nuclear power, although not necessarily as the only or consensual package. Note that even in the preceding discussion, Debbie takes time out from building the shared RUNAWAY frame to note that she considers nuclear power plants necessary, and Linda attempts, without response, to introduce an alternative theme centered on the greed of the nuclear industry. The appeal of the RUNAWAY frame is only one part of the story.

There are other bits of popular wisdom that were used in about one-fourth of the groups that became part of a pronuclear PROGRESS frame – as either a rival package developed by a subgroup or, in one case, as the exclusive and uncontested frame. The popular wisdom here emphasizes the naturalness of risk as part of life and part of the unavoidable cost of progress. Nuclear power is, implicitly or explicitly, not a different order of risk than we have accepted with other technologies. The following example is from a group we encountered in Chapter 5, discussing troubled industry and affirmative action. On nuclear power, they fall into opposing subgroups, with Michael and Marlene arguing for nuclear power and Marie and Sally arguing against it.

Characters:

Michael, an office manager in a computer company, in his thirties.
Marie, a cashier in a supermarket, in her twenties.
Sally, a clerk at a dry cleaners, in her twenties.
Marlene, a bookkeeper, in her twenties.

(Discussing the initial, open-ended question on nuclear power.)

Michael: I just want to say something about what Marie said about cancer and all this stuff. As I was walking down Charles last night, it was pitch black, and I said, this is a good place to get mugged and killed. And I suddenly thought to myself (*laughter*) – and I suddenly thought to myself, you know, (*laughter*) whenever you die, that's your destiny. Whether or not somebody jumped out and mugged you or you die from a spill, I mean, you're going to die. I mean your time was labeled and you were going to die. Right? I think nuclear power is *great*. The thing that *isn't* great about it is the waste. Now see, this waste, as I wrote on my [questionnaire] there, this is 1986. I'm sure marvelous scientists can put guys in outer space and stuff —

Marie: — and have them blown up too —

Michael: — there must be a way to utilize this waste.

Sally: Whenever there is a leak, it's always passed down the line: "you're responsible, you're responsible, you're responsible —" You know, what about these people that are hurt from it, and their families that are dead, and so forth. So, we'll send them a card. We're sorry —

Marlene: Well, I think the greatest example of really how bad the media can be, there's the Chernobyl accident. I mean, when they had that, the *Boston Herald* and the *Boston Globe* on the *front* page, before they had any official reports at all, said, "Thousands of people killed instantly." Now, nuclear power don't kill you instantly. So, first of all, they were very wrong in that instance. They had everybody in the United States in a panic, literally.

Sally: What's the difference if they died instantly or they died? Thousands of people *did* die because of a mistake that happened there.

Marlene: Look at how many plane crashes there have been. Look at how many people have *died* on planes. That's like saying, let's do away with planes, then, too. And let's do away with cars because thousands of people get killed in cars. More people get killed in car accidents than people dying from nuclear power explosions or leaks a year.

Marie: So far.

Marlene: So far.

Theme and countertheme are put forth by different advocates in the preceding discussion, but a more common pattern is for groups to assert the importance of technological progress while decoupling nuclear power from this theme. They do this by declaring it to be of a different order than these other risks while applying the theme to alternative technologies. The same arguments that Michael uses in the previous discussion about "marvelous scientists [who] can put guys in outer space" are used to argue for developing solar energy or other safe and renewable energy sources as practical alternatives. The appeal of a technofix is still present in many discussions that reject nuclear power as the means of providing it.

About one-sixth of the groups used popular wisdom that resonates with the popular democracy countertheme. Linda's comment about the system's being run on greed suggests this idea, although it failed to become part of a shared frame in her group. Nuclear power, in this frame, is another example of powerful interests pursuing profit with little or no regard for the public interest. The following group is the same one used to illustrate Marjorie's moral indignation about spending money for nuclear power while children are starving in America (Chapter 3) and an especially explicit class discourse on troubled industry (Chapter 5).

> *Characters:*
>
> *Paul, a tire changer, in his thirties.*
> *Daniel, a mover, in his thirties.*
> *Marjorie, a waitress, in her forties.*
>
> *(Discussing the initial, open-ended question on nuclear power.)*
>
> Paul: We don't need 'em. Big business don't give a shit about nobody else.
> Daniel: We don't need them. The bottom line, make money.
> Paul: We could burn, um, tires – junk tires. There's a way to do tires now – it's clean enough to do, but they won't do it because –
> Marjorie: The money.
> Daniel: That's why.

In sum, there is a close correspondence between the resonances in media discourse and conversations. The countertheme of harmony with nature – but primarily its autonomous technology subtheme – is the dominant one in both. The mainstream theme of progress through technology is decoupled from nuclear technology more often than it is invoked in support of it. A second countertheme, popular democracy, has a much more secondary importance but was present in about one-sixth of the conversations. As with troubled industry, counterthemes provide the most important resonances with the most frequently used popular wisdom.

Arab–Israeli conflict

The dialectic between global responsibility and America first is engaged on Arab–Israeli conflict, and it is the countertheme that wins decisively in

media discourse. The theme is strongly reflected in the STRATEGIC IN-
TERESTS frame. This takes for granted the U.S role as a global power
with major geopolitical interests in the Middle East. This region is one
theater of major power competition, a battleground of the Cold War. The
regional participants, in this frame, are strategic assets for the superpowers.
It would be unthinkable for the United States to withdraw from the Middle
East – a return to a Fortress America mentality that is incapable of dealing
with the realities of the twentieth-century world.

The countertheme, America first, resonates with a rival frame, FEUD-
ING NEIGHBORS. The Arab–Israeli conflict, in this frame, is somebody
else's quarrel. The reasons the Arabs and the Jews are fighting are no
more relevant than those of the Hatfields and the McCoys. Each new
outrage creates a new grievance that produces retaliation and keeps the
feud going. U.S. military aid and involvement only make matters worse,
providing ever more powerful weapons that simply increase the devastation
of innocent bystanders.

In the dyadic competition between these two frames, FEUDING
NEIGHBORS easily wins in media discourse (see Chapter 3 and Figure
3.1). STRATEGIC INTERESTS was important from the 1950s through
the mid-1970s, when many commented on the flow of oil and the Soviet
role in the Middle East. But from the 1977 Sadat visit to Jerusalem to the
present, this frame no longer offered any serious challenge to FEUDING
NEIGHBORS in media discourse. With the Soviet Union relegated to a
minor player and oil anxiety transferred to the Persian Gulf, the STRA-
TEGIC INTEREST frame lost its prominence in framing Arab–Israeli
conflict. The collapse of this frame means that, with respect to cultural
resonance, it is the countertheme of America first that increasingly dominates media discourse on Arab–Israeli conflict. The ending of the Cold
War is likely to reinforce this dominance even further.

Resonances in conversations

More than one-third of the groups converged on the same popular wisdom
in understanding Arab–Israeli conflict. It rests on an analogy to conflicts
within their personal experience – particularly fights between siblings,
spouses, and neighbors. Depending on which analogy they choose, there
are some differences in emphasis but also some common lessons. First, the
fight has its own dynamic and is more about itself than about the ostensible
object of the conflict; second, outsiders should remain above the battle
and not take sides.

Applied to the relationships between one's own country and other countries, this popular wisdom has a strong resonance with the America first countertheme. Everyone endorses a peacemaker role if there is one, but military intervention of any sort is likely to make matters worse in this frame. Basically, the United States is an outsider that can do little and should mind its own business. The following group provides a typical example of how a group uses popular wisdom in constructing a frame on this issue:

> *Characters:*
>
> *Charlotte, a bookkeeper, in her thirties.*
> *Floyd, a printing technician, in his thirties.*
> *Dori, a secretary, in her thirties.*
> *Wilma, a kitchen worker, in her twenties.*
> *Alvin, a roofer, in his twenties.*
>
> *(Discussing the initial, open-ended question on Arab-Israeli conflict.)*

Charlotte: Who cares?

(*laughter*)

Floyd: I think the United States should mind their business. I mean, it's like the religion between them two.

Dori: That's right.

Floyd: They're fighting over religion or whatever. But that's a way of life for them. I think they like it that way. They wouldn't know how to deal with it if they wasn't fighting, so I think they should leave them alone, and may the best man win.

Wilma: Think of it as the Hatfields and McCoys.

Charlotte: It'll go on.

(*laughter*)

Alvin: Didn't we get messed up enough times with a couple of wars? I'll say that and I'll leave my nose out of this.

Dori: You said, yeah – he's right. Sticking our nose in where it is not welcome. I'm sure they do not welcome the U.S. sticking their nose in there.

Wilma: They only welcome their money. (*laughs*)

[*Later, after the cartoons.*]

Charlotte: They're using America and they're using Russia too.

Alvin: Think about it. These people are smart because they can play on our emotions so bad that we don't know what side we want to be on. You see my point? They can go to the Russians and say, "We want to get this," and the other side say to the Russians, "We want to get this," and they do the same thing with us. Now, when they first started this war, I'm sure we had nothing to do with it. Neither did the Russians. The second one or the other had something to do with it, then everybody wants to get in the bang bang. Like a fight between two little kids. Your bigger brother comes up and helps you out, and their bigger brother comes up and help him out. It ends up being a big cluster for nothing – over a skate board, and it's just what it's breaking down to.

Slightly more than 10 percent of the groups used some version of a STRATEGIC INTEREST frame in understanding the U.S. relationship to Arab–Israeli conflict, and in several other groups people made passing reference to the relevance of oil or superpower competition, with no development of this idea in the conversation. But only in the following group is there any invocation of the global responsibility theme that is part of this frame.

Characters:

Arlene, a bookkeeper, in her forties.
Maggie, an office worker, in her fifties.

(Discussing the initial, open-ended question on Arab–Israeli conflict.)

Arlene: I don't know, my interpretation, I might be way out. I never read and I don't know too much about anything outside my house, and that's the truth –

Facilitator: Hey, you've got a lot of ideas about this stuff.

Arlene: But foreign policy, from what I understood, is you have to have allies. To get your way in this or that or whatever, and live in this world, you gotta have friends, allies, or what have you. So to me, they try to pick out the one that's going to be most beneficial to us. Let's be realistic. We're not – I used to think the United States was wonderful, perfect, it didn't do anything wrong. That's not true. What we did here with the Indians and everything. I mean we were just as malicious as whatchacallit. So we're not wonderful and we're not perfect, and it's very realistic that we want to survive in this world. So we do this for this guy, it's like "wiping" or whatever – *(laughter)* One hand washes the other. Just like when

> we did this thing [the bombing of Libya] with the terrorists or what
> have you, the only one that stood behind us was Canada –
> Maggie: – the Israeli, Canada, and British people, that was it. That's all.

The use of popular wisdom that draws on an analogy to familiar family and neighborhood conflicts seems to help groups achieve an integrated resource strategy. Almost 40 percent of the thirteen groups who used such popular wisdom linked experiential knowledge and media discourse in a shared frame, whereas less than 10 percent of the other groups used an integrated resource strategy ($p < .05$).

Compared to the one faint invocation of the global responsibility theme in the need for allies, the America first theme echoed through the discussion of close to half of the groups. In general, then, the countertheme dominates the theme in the popular wisdom used by working people to understand Arab–Israeli conflict.

Conclusion

Themes are normative and counterthemes are oppositional, but it is the counterthemes that dominate these conversations among working people on three of the four issues examined here. On two of the four – nuclear power and Arab–Israeli conflict – the counterthemes invoked by popular wisdom are the same as those invoked by the most prominent frames in media discourse. On these two issues, as noted in Chapter 7, media discourse tends to be the first resource used. It is plausible to argue that the prominence of the relevant frames in media discourse stimulates people to bring in popular wisdom with the same cultural resonances.

On troubled industry, however, the prominence of the popular democracy countertheme occurs in spite of, not because of, media prominence. People find supporting examples from the media discourse in spite of the invisibility of the CAPITAL FLIGHT frame that supports their popular wisdom. They find their way first to the countertheme through their experiential knowledge and popular wisdom, and only then to media discourse that supports their emergent frame. Furthermore, on two of the four issues (troubled industry and Arab–Israeli conflict), there is evidence that the explicit use of popular wisdom that supports counterthemes helps a group to formulate a frame that integrates personal experience and media discourse.

The net result is that, for these working people, resonances with counterthemes are central in their understanding of three of the four issues.

The popular wisdom used rarely supports frames promoted by officials that invoke the dominant cultural themes. The strong resonance of counter-themes in these conversations suggests considerable receptivity to critical frames and an entry point for collective action frames with the same resonances. But before turning to such connections, I consider one final question on the relevance of people's varying degrees of engagement with the four issues.

9

Proximity and engagement

Some issues are very close to people's lives, whereas others seem remote. When I first began analyzing media discourse on policy issues, I sought variation on this dimension. Without giving it a great deal of thought, I reasoned that troubled industry and affirmative action were relatively proximate issues, whereas nuclear power and Arab–Israeli conflict were distant ones.

The matter of what is proximate, however, turns out to be more complicated. It should not be confused with the use of experiential knowledge. The fact that people are able to apply their knowledge of how the world works from their own experiences does not necessarily make an issue proximate, since these experiences are typically more general than the issue domain. People may know from their own work experiences, for example, that official safety regulations are often ignored by themselves and their fellow workers without having had any experience with nuclear power plants. The use of experiential knowledge and popular wisdom involves extrapolating from the familiar to issues that are not necessarily proximate.

By the *proximity* of an issue, I mean the degree to which it has direct and immediate consequences for one's personal life. Journalists often reduce this meaning to economic consequences, using such terms as *pocketbook* or *bread-and-butter* issue. There is an implicit assumption here that their pocketbook is what people really care about and, hence, that these are more "real" than abstract issues such as nuclear power and Arab–Israeli conflict. There is a kernel of truth here, but it turns out to be seriously misleading and ultimately indefensible.

Since issues can be framed in multiple ways, it is possible to frame almost any issue as, in part, a pocketbook issue. Much of the affirmative action conversation focuses on jobs and economic opportunities. Nuclear power conversations frequently contain references to people's electricity bills or to property values in nearby towns with nuclear reactors. In talking about

Arab–Israeli conflict, people frequently discuss oil supplies and relate this to gasoline prices and the shortages and lines of 1979.

On the other hand, troubled industry, which one might think of as a prototypical bread-and-butter issue, turns out to provoke a lot of conversation on noneconomic personal consequences. Typically, discussions of hardships deemphasize the direct pocketbook consequences, focusing instead on the effects on self-esteem, family life, and mental health plus the secondary effects on the surrounding community.

It is misleading, then, to talk about pocketbook issues because this is a property of a particular frame, not of the issue as a whole. Frames that emphasize economic consequences may be relatively prominent on some issues, but they are never the only ones available. To assume a priori that an issue is a pocketbook issue imposes a particular frame and obscures the presence of other, competing frames for understanding it.

It is equally misleading to assume that pocketbook consequences are what people really care about. To take the most obvious exception, they are very concerned about their health. In conversations on nuclear power, for example, it is not their electricity bill that engages people but the dangers of radiation and the possibility that they or their children might develop leukemia. People's subjective probabilities make various possible consequences real for them, even when these may seem highly improbable to an outside observer.

Witness, for example, how Arab–Israeli conflict is made proximate in the following example:

> *Characters:*
>
> *Dottie, a computer programmer, in her twenties.*
> *Laurie, a mental health worker, in her twenties.*
>
> *(They are responding to the facilitator's question of whether any-*
> *thing that has happened on the issue of Arab–Israeli conflict*
> *has affected them personally.)*

Dottie: Yeah. I think that – when we bombed Khadaffi, that whole thing was initiated because Khadaffi did a terrorist act against the Israelis in the, um – against the Israelis and the Americans. And I was going to England the week after – (*laughter*) And Khadaffi was bombed. And I was not keen on going to England because I was afraid I was going to get blown up in Heathrow Airport.

Laurie: One of the things that really scared me on that is I guess after his daughter died, he was saying that all Arabs should seek out and kill American children. Like, oh, my God! All I could think of was my little boy. Like, oh, my God! It almost made me want to take down my "baby on board" card thing on the car – it's like a target going down the highway.

(*laughter*)

Dottie: I stay out of the subway system or airports. I mean, really. You can't stop your life. My husband was going to England whether I was going or not. He told me I could stay. And I said that I'd rather be with him if something happened rather than sitting home watching these people who – as horrible as the whole experience would be, I don't think I could stand worrying about it. So I went with him against better judgment. I wanted both of us to stay home but he said, "No way." He said, "I can't, because Khadaffi was bombed, I can't stop my life."

Laurie: My mother goes traveling a lot, and everytime she takes off from Logan Airport or wherever it is in the world that she's on her way to or from, I have wicked anxiety attacks.

The proximity of an issue depends heavily on context. We conducted early trial runs of peer group conversations in the Detroit area in the summer of 1980. A steady stream of plant closings and layoffs was occurring, and unemployment in automobile-dependent towns such as Flint approached Great Depression levels of 25 and 30 percent. The conversations reported here, among participants living in the Boston area, occurred in a place and time with less than 4 percent unemployment and with labor shortages in some industries.

Holding discussions of nuclear power a few months after the accident at Chernobyl increased the proximity of the nearby Seabrook and Plymouth nuclear reactors by raising their salience. Nor can one ignore the bitter racial conflict in Boston over the busing of schoolchildren in understanding the proximity of affirmative action.

Personal consequences, then, are not an intrinsic property of an issue but vary with a context that makes them more or less salient. In sum, issue proximity cannot be assumed but must be analyzed empirically, recognizing that it varies over time and place and that issues may change position as context changes.

Issue proximity

For each issue, the facilitator asked people directly whether they, or their family and friends, were personally affected by "anything that has happened on the issue." But before they were even asked this question, they

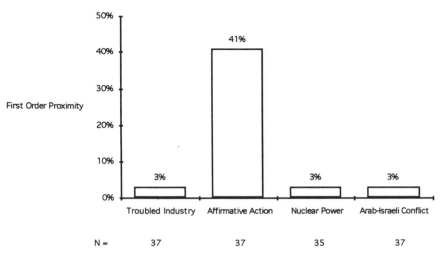

Figure 9.1.   Spontaneous proximity by issue.

were given an opportunity to bring in personal consequences spontaneously in response to the initial, open-ended question. How do the four issues compare on the extent to which one or more people spontaneously brought in personal consequences in their initial discussion of the issue?

As Figure 9.1 shows, affirmative action was by far the most proximate issue for these Boston area working people in 1986; no other issue was even close. In more than 40 percent of the groups, someone brought in personal effects spontaneously compared to only one group (3 percent) on each of the other issues. In a large proportion of these groups (two-fifths), more than one person brought in a personal effect – either positive or negative – on either themselves or a member of their immediate family.

Differences among the other three issues emerge when we consider a more inclusive measure of personal consequences. This measure, which includes both spontaneous mentions and those raised in response to the facilitator's direct question, differentiates three degrees of proximity. First-order effects refer to oneself and immediate family or household members; second-order effects include those on more distant relatives, friends, and acquaintances; third-order effects refer to those that affect one along with a large group of others in the same category. Everyone is affected by nuclear power, some claim, through their electricity bill or by the hazardous waste produced – or would be affected by an accident in a nearby reactor.

Table 9.1 presents the results for the four issues. A group was always coded by the highest degree of proximity claimed, even if other more distant

Table 9.1 *Degree of proximity by issue*[a]

	Troubled industry	Affirmative action	Nuclear power	Arab–Israeli conflict
Proximity				
First order (self/family)	24%	59%	20%	14%
Second order (friends)	57%	24%	11%	16%
Third order (categorical)	0	0	34%	27%
None	19%	16%	34%	43%
N =	37	37	35	37

[a]Including responses to direct question.

consequences were claimed as well. Note that on every issue, a majority of the groups had one or more people who claimed *some* personal consequences. Even on the least proximate issue, Arab–Israeli conflict, only 43 percent disclaimed effects or failed to mention any way in which they were personally affected.

Affirmative action continues to show far more proximity than the other issues, but troubled industry has a high degree of secondary proximity. Although less than one-fourth of the groups had anyone who claimed to have been personally affected, a majority of them mentioned friends or more distant relatives who had been buffeted by the problems of plant closings and layoffs. In contrast, on nuclear power and Arab–Israeli conflict, when they produced any proximity claims at all, they were about as likely to mention only categorical effects as they were to direct attention to anyone known personally. Nuclear power was only slightly more proximate than Arab–Israeli conflict and, in fact, the two issues are quite similar in spite of the recency of the Chernobyl accident and the physical proximity of the well-publicized Plymouth and Seabrook nuclear reactors.

Affirmative action, as Figure 9.2 shows, was of high proximity for both black and white groups. Combining the four issues, there is a slight but statistically significant tendency for white groups to claim more proximate effects ($p < .05$). It is primarily the nuclear power and troubled industry issues that produce this difference; Arab–Israeli conflict has low proximity for both.

Issue engagement

As the conversation moved from issue to issue, the intensity level and the engagement of the participants shifted. On some issues, they seemed to

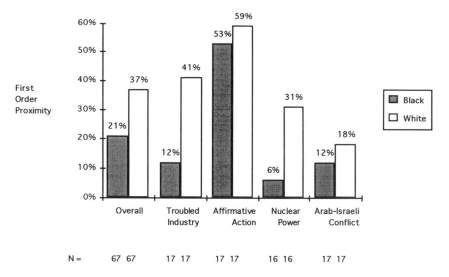

Figure 9.2.   Issue proximity by race.

care a great deal about what they were saying and wanted to make sure they were understood properly. On other issues, they seemed to be anxious to get the task over with and cared little about what they or others had to say about it.

Before the conversation began, participants filled out a questionnaire that asked them three questions about their level of personal engagement in each of the issues: How interested are you in this issue? Have you heard or read much about this issue? When you are with your friends, family, or co-workers, how often would you say you talk about [issue]?

Table 9.2 shows the distribution of answers over the sample of 188 individuals who completed this part of the questionnaire. It shows some suggestive differences from proximity in the rank ordering of issues. Most strikingly, nuclear power was a virtual equal of affirmative action on these measures; in fact, it led all issues in the percentage reporting that they often read about it. The reported engagement in troubled industry was relatively low; only 14 percent claimed to read quite a lot about it, lower even than the figure on Arab–Israeli conflict.

Since the unit of analysis in this study is the group rather than the individual, I constructed a measure of group engagement on the issue based on the questionnaire responses of its members. The group measure combined all three questions, differentiating highly engaged, moderately engaged, and unengaged groups for each issue.[1]

Table 9.2 *Individual interest by issue*

	Troubled industry	Affirmative action	Nuclear power	Arab–Israeli conflict
Responses				
Very much interested	28%	46%	41%	18%
Read quite a lot about it	14%	31%	35%	21%
Often talk about it	7%	19%	9%	1%
Rarely or never talk about it	55%	37%	46%	76%
N = 188				

Table 9.3 *Group engagement by issue*

	Troubled industry	Affirmative action	Nuclear power	Arab–Israeli conflict
Engagement				
Highly engaged	0	27%	0	0
Moderately engaged	59%	49%	86%	38%
Unengaged	41%	24%	14%	62%
N =	37	37	37	37

Table 9.3 shows the distribution of group engagement on the four issues. It provides additional information beyond what the individual level of analysis revealed. There were highly engaged groups only on affirmative action, but nuclear power was the least likely issue to have unengaged groups. Engagement in affirmative action was quite variable among groups, but nuclear power was a moderately engaging issue in close to 90 percent of them. Troubled industry was also a moderately engaging issue (although not as high as nuclear power), whereas more than 60 percent of the groups were unengaged in Arab–Israeli conflict.

Black groups showed higher engagement than white groups on two of the four issues: troubled industry and affirmative action. None of the black groups but more than half of the white groups were unengaged on affirmative action. On troubled industry, 65 percent of the white groups were unengaged compared to only 24 percent of the black groups. There were no racial differences on nuclear power or Arab–Israeli conflict in level of engagement.

Questionnaire measures of this sort always raise some validity issues. Participants are hurriedly checking off a box, not providing the deliberative

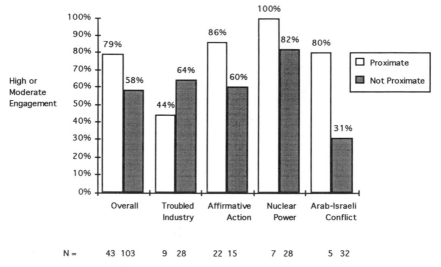

Figure 9.3.   Proximity and engagement by issue.

opinions that they offer in conversation. Does it really give us an indicator
of the likely intensity and engagement of the subsequent conversation?

Unfortunately, it is exactly this intensity that gets lost in the translation
from being there, to listening to an audiotape, to reading a transcript.
Intensity is expressed in body language and in voice intonation. As a rough
validity check, we had a coder who worked with audiotapes as well as
transcripts make a subjective rating of groups on their engagement level
on affirmative action, as well as indicating any "high-intensity moments."
These coder ratings of conversations generally support the validity of the
measure based on aggregated questionnaire responses.[2]

It seems reasonable to hypothesize that how much people care about an
issue will be determined, in part, by its proximity. The more people feel
personally affected, the more engaged they will be in talking about it.
Figure 9.3 suggests that proximity is one factor but not an overwhelming
one. With the exception of troubled industry, the more proximate the issue
was for a group, the higher its level of engagement ($p < .05$). Even without
proximity, a substantial majority of the groups were at least moderately
engaged on every issue except Arab–Israeli conflict. Clearly, proximity is
not a necessary condition for engagement. The reversal on troubled industry is a reminder of the complexity of this relationship. In sum, issue
engagement is no simple function of proximity, although there is likely to
be some positive relationship on most issues.

On affirmative action, it is plausible that proximity leads to engagement;

that is, the feeling of being directly affected in one's personal life stimulates engagement on this issue. But the process can also work in the other direction. On nuclear power and Arab–Israeli conflict, for example, people may become engaged in an issue because of its categorical effects as they understand them from media discourse. They watch stories about nuclear accidents or terrorist hijackings and see people like themselves who are personally affected. They may become engaged for nonproximate reasons and only then begin to recognize or imagine effects on their own lives.

Engagement, proximity, and resource strategy

We saw in Chapter 7 that the resource strategy that groups follow varies from issue to issue. On nuclear power and Arab–Israeli conflict, for example, they almost always began with media discourse; sometimes they brought in popular wisdom and experiential knowledge as well, but only a minority followed an integrated resource strategy. Affirmative action offers the sharpest contrast: Most groups began with experiential knowledge, and a majority integrated popular wisdom and media discourse in constructing a shared frame.

There would appear to be a connection here with how engaging and proximate these issues are for people. Most obviously, affirmative action is both the most proximate in its personal consequences and the issue on which people are most likely to develop an integrated resource strategy. Arab–Israeli conflict is both the least engaging of the issues and one on which people are least likely to develop an integrated resource strategy. We might be tempted to conclude that the more engaging and proximate an issue is, the more likely people are to develop an integrated resource strategy in understanding it. This turns out, however, to need quite a bit of qualification when we look more closely at each issue.

As Figure 9.4 shows, there is a significant overall relationship between issue proximity and the tendency to use an integrated resource strategy ($p < .001$), but it is much stronger for some issues than others. The difference is most dramatic for nuclear power. It is relatively rare for people to introduce personal effects, but when this happens, it virtually ensures that the group will develop an integrated resource strategy; without such first-order proximity, an integrated resource strategy is rare. At the other extreme, proximity seems to make no difference in developing an integrated strategy on troubled industry.

Level of engagement is also significantly related to resource strategy ($p < .05$). Except on affirmative action, as Figure 9.5 shows, the more engaged groups were more likely to integrate media discourse and exper-

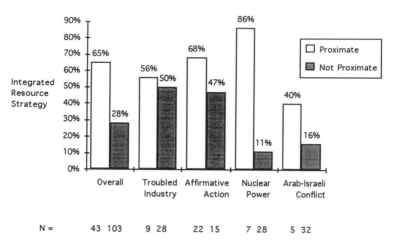

Figure 9.4. Proximity and integrated resource strategy.

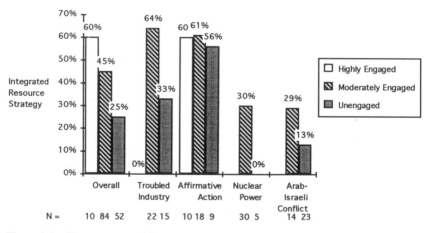

Figure 9.5. Engagement and integrated resource strategy.

iential knowledge. On affirmative action, however, level of engagement
had little or no effect; integrated resource strategies were common at all
levels, even among the unengaged.

There are too few cases to allow us to determine with any confidence if
proximity and engagement have independent effects on an integrated resource strategy, but the results suggest that the relative contribution depends on the issue. On troubled industry, engagement appears to be much
more important than proximity. More than 60 percent of the engaged

groups that lacked proximity on this issue still developed an integrated strategy; only 40 percent of the unengaged groups with proximity used the full range of resources.

On affirmative action, proximity seems to make a difference for the engaged groups but no difference at all for the unengaged ones. There were only three unengaged groups that described proximate effects on this issue, but none developed an integrated resource strategy.

Conclusion

A majority of the groups on all four issues found some consequences for their personal lives. Even for an issue as remote as Arab–Israeli conflict, imagination can bridge the gap between the terrorist attacks that one sees on television and the risk to the baby on board in one's car or to the airplane trip one's mother is about to take. And the gasoline lines of the past serve as reminders of less dramatic effects on one's daily life.

Nevertheless, there are strong differences among issues. Affirmative action was experienced by both white and black groups as an issue that touched their lives directly. Troubled industry was one step removed, not affecting most Boston area residents directly in 1986 but touching the lives of people they knew. Nuclear power and Arab–Israeli conflict, when they were proximate at all, affected people as members of broad categories, but only occasionally did they experience more particular personal consequences.

Proximity was related to engagement on three of the four issues, but only modestly so. It is only one factor in creating interest, and it seems reasonable to hypothesize that engagement on an issue that is stimulated by media discourse can lead to increased attention to proximate consequences, especially second- and third-order effects. Nuclear power, although barely more proximate than Arab–Israeli conflict, was much more engaging to these groups. It was rare for either black or white groups to be unengaged on nuclear power, and for about half of the white groups, it outranked affirmative action in the intensity of their interest.

Proximity and engagement on an issue both contribute to the probability that a group will use an integrated resource strategy in making sense of it. Proximity is especially important on issues such as nuclear power and Arab–Israeli conflict, where the primary resource used by most groups is media discourse. If a group frames the issue in a way that touches their personal lives, this makes them better able to find relevant experiential knowledge to support the media discourse used.

When they are less dependent on media discourse, proximity becomes

less important in whether or not they will integrate the full array of resources. The crucial question here is their success in integrating media
discourse rather than finding a relevant connection to their personal lives.
On this type of issue, engagement seems especially important. If it is
engaging, some of this effort to construct meaning has probably been made
ahead of time by some of the participants. Their prior knowledge of media
discourse makes this resource more accessible for conversational use. If
they are unengaged, they are not only likely to have fewer media resources
available but also to make less effort and care less about how well they
succeed in making sense of it.

10

Developing political consciousness

I hope this book has been an antidote to the conventional wisdom that most political issues and events do not make much sense to most working people. Listening to their conversations over a period of an hour or more, one is struck by the deliberative quality of their construction of meaning about these complex issues. And they achieve considerable coherence in spite of a great many handicaps, some flowing from limitations in the media discourse that they find available and others from their own lack of experience with the task.

These conversations are far removed from the context in which collective action frames are normally developed. I do not claim that these working people have the kind of political consciousness that makes one ready to take up arms against the world's injustices. A small minority of the issue conversations (7 percent) contained all the elements of a collective action frame.

I do argue that people's understandings contain the elements necessary to develop this kind of political consciousness, given the presence of an action context. The raw materials are there, but this varies dramatically from issue to issue. On some issues, they share a sense of moral indignation and injustice, think of themselves as a we in opposition to some they, and have shared models of people like themselves acting to change conditions. On other issues – such as nuclear power and Arab–Israeli conflict – one or more of the crucial elements is generally lacking, and no group puts together a full-fledged collective action frame. Even on affirmative action, where the individual elements are most likely to be present, only 22 percent of the conversations put them all together.

The injustice component of a collective action frame facilitates the adoption of other elements. It increases awareness of social movements that attempt to rectify injustice and encourages sympathy toward their efforts at collective action even when people are not ready to join. It promotes personal identification with whatever collectivity is being wronged and spurs the search for agents who are responsible for the undeserved hardship that members of the recipient group suffer. Hence, it is the key to integrating the three elements into a single collective action frame.

Resource strategy and collective action frames

Using an integrated resource strategy is far from a sufficient condition for developing this political consciousness, but it helps. In 16 percent of the issue conversations that used the full array of resources, all three elements of collective action frames were present compared to only 1 percent in groups that used other resource strategies ($p < .001$).

Media discourse, popular wisdom, and experiential knowledge are all important in developing the crucial injustice component. Experiential knowledge helps to connect the abstract cognition of unfairness with the emotion of moral indignation. It is striking how often the segments of conversation in which injustice frames occur contain some reference to personal knowledge.

Even on nuclear power, where personal knowledge is rarely expressed, it seems to be brought home by a personal experience. Marjorie, whom we quoted earlier to illustrate the expression of moral indignation on nuclear power (Chapter 3), has her anger fanned by images derived from her work with homeless families: " . . . and I had people in the Milner Hotel, mothers with five kids in one room. And we don't have places for them, but we have places to build nuclear plants. That's garbage."

This link to experiential knowledge is especially true for affirmative action. Expressions of indignation seem heavily tied to anecdotes in which a person either witnessed or experienced directly an example of the more general injustice being denounced. Of the twenty-five groups that used an injustice frame on affirmative action, 80 percent expressed it by drawing on experiential knowledge to make the point.

Media discourse is equally important in forging an injustice frame. Experiential knowledge of injustice in concrete form stimulates the emotions, but they may dissipate for lack of a clear target. Media discourse places the experienced injustice in context, making it a special case of a broader injustice. The experiential resource concretizes injustice; the media resource generalizes it and makes it shared and collective.

Popular wisdom also contributes to the development of injustice frames, especially when it resonates with oppositional themes in American culture. As we saw in Chapter 8, the major resonances on three of the four issues are with contentious counterthemes, not with official pieties. By itself, such popular wisdom may evaporate into cynical chic and mean little. But it

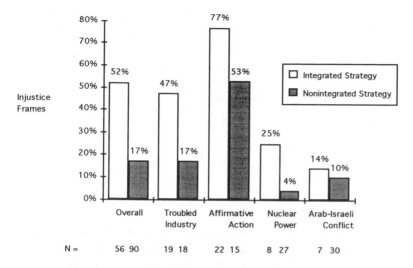

Figure 10.1. Resource strategy and injustice frames.

helps to bridge media discourse and experiential knowledge to produce an integrated resource strategy in support of a critical framing of many issues.

As Figure 10.1 shows, a majority of the groups that followed an integrated strategy on an issue also produced an injustice frame; but only one-sixth of those who failed to integrate experiential knowledge, popular wisdom, and media discourse ended up with injustice frames ($p < .001$). This difference holds for all issues, although the relationship is attenuated, of course, for nuclear power and affirmative action, where both injustice frames and integrated resource strategies were unusual.

Resource strategy is not the only variable affecting the development of collective action frames. We know that the framing of affirmative action is very different in black and white groups. Furthermore, the injustice component contains hot cognitions of moral indignation and an adversarial we. One would expect less emotion when people are less engaged in an issue. What is the role of resource strategy when examined in the context of these other variables as well?

Ragin (1987) suggests a method of analysis, using Boolean algebra, that is especially sensitive to how different combinations of conditions are associated with specific outcomes or processes. I use it here to compare how the racial composition of the group, its engagement in the issue, and its resource strategy combine in the production of collective action frames.

Affirmative action offers the best opportunity for examining the com-

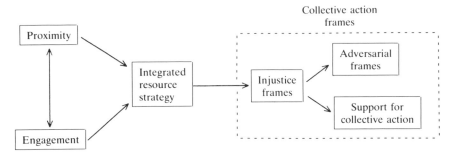

Figure 10.2.   Overall model.

bination for several reasons. First, it is the only issue on which a significant number of collective action frames occur; in addition to the 22 percent that had all three elements, another 40 percent had at least two of the elements. Furthermore, there is significant variance on each of the three conditions on this issue. Racial composition heavily influenced the content of the discussion, and there was significant variability in both white and black groups in their degree of engagement in spite of greater overall engagement in the black groups. About half of both white and black groups followed an integrated resource strategy in discussing it.

The application of Ragin's method shows that collective action frames tended to occur when a group used an integrated resource strategy, regardless of other conditions, as well as in engaged white groups, regardless of resource strategy.[1] An integrated resource strategy is important across the board, including both black and white groups with differing levels of engagement on the issue. There is only one combination in which a majority of the groups developed a full-fledged collective action frame with all three elements. All four of the highly engaged black groups with an integrated resource strategy had this political consciousness.

Figure 10.2 summarizes the overall model suggested by this research effort. Engagement and proximity mutually influence each other and combine to influence the use of an integrated resource strategy. This strategy influences the development of an injustice frame that, in turn, influences the inclusion of the other elements of collective action frames.

Media effects on public opinion

I do not argue that working people are well served by media discourse in their efforts to make sense of the world. The limitations that many media critics point out are reflected in media discourse on the four issues examined here. Media dependence, however, is only partial and is heavily influenced by the issue under discussion. Earlier, I likened people's efforts to make sense of these issues to finding their way through a forest. The various frames offered in media discourse provide maps indicating useful points of entry, and signposts at various crossroads highlight the significant landmarks and warn of the perils of other paths. On certain issues – nuclear power and Arab–Israeli conflict, for example – media discourse is typically their first resort.

Even on these issues, though, they find more than one frame available, leaving them at least a partial choice as well as the necessity of using other resources to complete the task. They control their own media dependence, in part, through their willingness and ability to draw on popular wisdom and experiential knowledge to supplement what they are offered. I began this inquiry with the assumption that on an issue such as nuclear power, media dependence was inevitable, since other resources were unavailable. This is clearly false. Media discourse was rarely the only resource used and was supplemented in most groups at least by integrating it with popular wisdom; more than 25 percent of the conversations on nuclear power brought in experiential knowledge as well.

If media dependence is only partial when media discourse serves as the starting point, it is even less so where experiential knowledge is the primary resource for finding a path through the forest. Lack of dependence, however, does not imply lack of use or influence. Even on affirmative action, where an overwhelming majority of the groups introduced experiential knowledge, most drew on media discourse and popular wisdom as well in constructing a shared frame.

Graber (1988), although she approached the issue of media effects in a different way, simultaneously examined both news content and audience response and reached similar conclusions. Carrying on the tradition begun by Lane (1962), she did a long series of intensive, open-ended interviews with twenty-one participants over a year. At the same time, she analyzed the content of their major sources of news, including the most widely read daily newspaper plus national and local television news.

On media effects, Graber suggests a *modulator model* in which media impact depends on the relationship of the audience to the issue. On many issues, people "round out and evaluate news in light of past learning and determine how well it squares with the reality that they have experienced directly or vicariously" (Graber 1988, 93). All of her panelists, despite inattention, substantial forgetting, and limited learning, had developed a knowledge base about issues currently in the news. "What they knew," she concludes, "and the deductions and inferences that sprang from that knowledge, evidently was not limited to what the media supplied."

These results suggest a reframing in the long-standing debate on the magnitude and nature of mass media effects on public opinion. The effects discussed here are effects *in use*. Instead of treating media content as a stimulus that leads to some change in attitudes or cognition, it is treated as an important tool or resource that people have available, in varying degrees, to help them make sense of issues in the news. When they use elements from media discourse to make a conversational point on an issue, we are directly observing a media effect.

I do not mean to imply that the media element – for example, a spotlighted fact or a particular depiction of a public figure – caused the person to think about the issue in a predetermined way. The causal relationship is complicated and bidirectional, as the tool metaphor implies. One chooses a tool, but some tools are cheap and available everywhere, whereas others can be found only in side streets and out-of-the-way places. One chooses a tool partly for convenience and ease of access but also for its suitability to the job at hand – in this case, to make a particular point in conversation.

The results here suggest that the causal process differs quite a bit from issue to issue and from group to group on the same issue. Media influence depends on which of the three discourse strategies a group is using: cultural, personal, or integrated. It is impossible to say from examining effects in use whether the way people privately think or feel about an issue has been changed by their media exposure, but the results suggest some conditional hypotheses:

> (a) *Cultural Strategies*. People who use cultural strategies to understand an issue are subject to substantial media effects and are heavily influenced by the relative prominence of media frames. Their attitudes and beliefs are relatively unstable and subject to change as media discourse changes.

> (b) *Personal Strategies*. People who use personal strategies to understand an issue are relatively immune to media effects, ignoring or discounting the relative prominence of frames, including even those that support their experiential knowledge and popular wisdom.

> (c) *Integrated Strategies*. People who use integrated strategies are selectively influenced by the relative prominence of media frames, responding to the degree that these frames are consistent with

their popular wisdom and experiential knowledge. They are constrained by omissions from media discourse but relatively immune to differences in the relative prominence of visible frames.

Unanswered questions

Most research projects frustrate us with tantalizing questions that they leave unanswered. This one raises more than its share, about which I can only speculate and make the usual call for further research.

1. How robust are the frames used in these conversations? The results here are based on a single conversation by each group. If the same groups were to discuss the same issues again in a week, would they still frame them in the same way? How about after a few years that include a shift in the relative prominence of different media frames? I have argued that the robustness of a shared frame – that is, its stability over time and its resistance to influence by external stimuli – is greatest when it is based on an integrated resource strategy. But this hypothesis cannot be assessed by looking at a single conversation at one point in time. It remains plausible but untested.

2. Would the conversations of people in a different social location be different? Much has been written about differences between men and women in their ways of knowing (see Gilligan 1982; Belenky et al. 1986). Does the kind of "connected knowing" described by Clinchy (1989), based on empathy and attachment, lead groups of women to use different resource strategies in making sense of these issues? Do women use media discourse less or integrate it in a different way than men? Do they rely on experiential knowledge more or use a different type? Are they more likely to adopt injustice frames but less likely to include an adversarial element? Are working women's conversations different from those of college-educated women with respect to resource strategies and collective action frames?

I had initially hoped to learn more about gender differences. The sampling design called for equal numbers of men and women as contact persons. But it was not always easy for the initial contact person to recruit enough friends to form a group and, even with considerable nagging on our part, they did not always follow through on their initial commitment. Our pretest experiences forced us to abandon most of our efforts to restrict the other people whom they enlisted. The result was too few all-male or all-female groups to detect any meaningful differences between men's and women's ways of knowing about politics.

The decision to focus our limited resources on working people was a deliberate one. As I suggested in Chapter 1, the mystery for most mainstream social scientists is how the mass public manages to have opinions about so many matters about which they lack the most elementary knowledge. Critical social scientists, influenced by the Marxist tradition, worry about workers' inability to recognize their own objective interests. In short, the unanswered questions in the literature focused on how working people make sense of politics. So we chose to concentrate on people from this social location.

Now I wonder how different the conversations of college-educated people might be. Are they more likely to attend to the media spectacle and to rely on media discourse as a primary resource? Are they less likely to draw on popular wisdom and experiential knowledge and, therefore, to use integrated resource strategies in the framing process? Are they more likely than working people to be affected by shifts in the relative prominence of media frames on an issue? If they rely less on experiential knowledge, are they less likely to generate the kind of righteous indignation that helps to produce injustice frames?

3. To what extent are the relationships observed here dependent on the absence of an action context? Political consciousness is forged in the process of collective action, but I have examined a series of conversations that are far removed from opportunity. The process changes dramatically when action is a more immanent possibility. I wonder if the variables identified as important here are still important as the context changes and if they operate over time in the manner suggested here.

Does it really matter if people initially have the raw materials of collective action frames, since these may be readily supplied in the course of political struggle? Do people who normally rely on media discourse to understand a given issue switch to experiential knowledge and popular wisdom when faced with an action context? If people rely on experiential knowledge to understand an issue, do they become more attentive to the media resource in an action context? Is injustice still the key to uniting the three elements of collective action frames, or do processes of collective identity and agency become more central in an action context? In sum, one cannot assume that the relationships discovered here in a context divorced from the opportunity for collective action would necessarily hold in a different context.

Strategic implications

There are implications here for those interested in actively furthering the ability and willingness of working people to influence the conditions of their daily lives through some form of collective action. I have focused on one aspect of this capacity: the particular form of political consciousness embodied in collective action frames.[2] The strategic implications are expressed below as advice to movement activists who seek grass roots support and participation among working people:

1. Pay attention to the link between media discourse and experiential knowledge. Relevant experiences, be they direct, vicarious, or the generalized sort embodied in popular wisdom, are not enough. They may be sufficient to guide people to some coherent package on an issue but, to become agents who influence the conditions that govern their daily lives, they must connect their understanding with a broader public discourse as well. Without integrating their understanding across levels, relevant events and actors in the news will remain a side show, and a frequently bewildering one, having little to do with their daily lives. It is under these conditions that, to quote Gans again (1988, x), "Washington, New York and the other centers of American society are, for many people much of the time, on other planets."

Discussions of troubled industry, in particular, frequently approximate this condition. In most groups, the participants know people who have been laid off and have a vivid appreciation of the consequences of plant closings for the individual, family, and community. But a very large gap remains between this understanding and broader framings of industrial policy that dominate much of the media discourse. It is a bridgeable gap, but few groups have the resources to bridge it successfully on their own, and it is not likely to happen spontaneously. The result was that only 5 percent of the troubled industry conversations developed into full-fledged collective action frames.

Note, however, that the problem of linkage varies from issue to issue. Some understandings are overly dependent on media discourse. The difficulty people face here is connecting their media-based understanding of the issue with their everyday lives. Understanding remains abstract and emotionally distant without the elements of collective identification and moral indignation that flow from experience. Integration does not happen spontaneously unless special conditions produce it – as they can, for example, when events in the news directly disrupt or threaten to disrupt their daily lives. More typically, the relevance is indirect and some cognitive leap is necessary to bridge the gap.

The organizer's task is more difficult on such issues. Abstract argument about complex indirect and future effects will not forge the emotional linkage even if people are convinced intellectually. Two alternative strategies seem more promising than presenting arguments about general causes and effects:

> (a) Search for existing experiential knowledge that can be shown to be relevant for a broader collective action frame. It helps here if organizers share the life world of those who are being encouraged to make the linkage. Then they can draw on their own experience in pointing out connections with some confidence that others will have similar stories of their own. Some relevant experiences are universal enough to transcend a broad range of social backgrounds.

> (b) Create situations where people can gain experiential knowledge of injustice. Public discourse facilitates knowledge through vicarious experience when it personalizes broader injustices by using exemplary cases to embody them. Hence, the concrete experience of Anne Frank conveys the meaning of the Holocaust in an experiential mode that no amount of factual information on the 6 million victims of Nazi death camps can convey. Social movement organizations frequently try to make the link by offering witnesses whose firsthand accounts provide listeners with vicarious experiential knowledge.

Simulations and role-playing exercises can provide a powerful form of experiential knowledge. In an effective simulation, people may become so engaged in their roles that their experiences seem more direct than vicarious. The intensity of the experience is real; only the world in which it occurs is make-believe. If participants are able to see the connection between this simulated world that they experience and the world represented in public discourse, they will have achieved a form of integration.[3]

2. Pay attention to the potential relevance of counterthemes. Popular wisdom acts as a bridge between public discourse on an issue and lessons drawn from experience. Issue frames gain strength through a symbolism that resonates with broader cultural themes and counterthemes embodied in popular wisdom. Counterthemes are particularly relevant for challenger frames. Appeals to apple pie and motherhood symbols are harmless enough and may even be helpful in neutralizing the manipulation of mainstream themes by authorities and political adversaries. But one shouldn't underrate the strong appeal of counterthemes among working people.

The dominant frames on every issue studied here except for affirmative action resonate with counterthemes more strongly than with themes. This strong appeal of counterthemes lays the groundwork for a critical consciousness about the issue. It gives the political talk of working people a contentious quality, even when it is expressed in the form of cynicism rather than a collective action frame.

Symbolic strategies should aim at showing the connection between a collective action frame, the broader cultural counterthemes with which it resonates, and the experiential knowledge encapsulated in popular wisdom. This does not complete an integrated resource strategy for people; they themselves must do the additional work of linking their personal and shared experiential knowledge with public discourse. But the task is considerably easier for them if some helpful bridges are provided.

3. Avoid the hot button approach. There is a well-laid cultural trap into which movement activists sometimes fall. They frame their primary task as marketing a product for consumers. The product is a cause in which they sincerely believe but that, for a variety of reasons, they must "sell" to others. The constituency for this mobilization effort is thought of as a set of potential buyers whose response, consisting of a vote, donation, signature, or other token, marks a successful sales effort. The logic of this approach leads one to look for a more effective marketing strategy, expressed through catchy symbols that tap an emotional hot button and trigger the desired response.

Emotion is an important component of collective action frames, as I have emphasized. Perhaps it is quite possible to trigger a burst of moral indignation by finding the right photograph or clever slogan. The problem with the hot button approach is not that it doesn't work but that it directly undermines the goal of increasing people's sense of agency.

Collective agency is also a central part of collective action frames; it can hardly be encouraged by treating potential participants as passive objects to be manipulated. This simply decreases any tendency toward the development of a collective identity and sympathy with some sustained effort at social change. It provides a good reason to extend the pervasive cynicism about those who run the society to include those who supposedly challenge their domination.

To increase a sense of agency, symbolic strategies should attempt to draw out the latent sense of agency that working people already carry around with them. They frequently express a sense of powerlessness or frustration, but they rarely come across as docile. Organizers need to assume that a sense of agency is at least dormant and capable of being awakened. Their task is to listen for it and to nurture it where it occurs spontaneously. One doesn't transform people who feel individually powerless into a group with a sense of collective efficacy by pushing hot buttons.

4. *Learn to listen carefully.* People are not, as Giddens (1986, 72) reminds us, "cultural or structural fools. . . . All social actors, no matter how lowly, have some degree of penetration of the social forces which oppress them." They use their insight in a practical way to resist some of the demands and to create a bit of free space for themselves. Their understanding is frequently partial and incomplete, but their insights are validated by their personal experience with social institutions. Organizers whose life world is different would do well to recognize that they have much to learn from the experiential knowledge of working people.

Careful listening is one of life's rarities – a free lunch. Not only does one learn in the process, but creating occasions in which working people have an opportunity to explore their understanding of public issues is itself a form of "cultural action." Freire's (1970a, 1970b) writings on cultural action emphasize the creation of a sense of empowerment. Teaching literacy, for example, is not a matter of teaching a specific skill but of liberating the whole person, creating a new consciousness of the world and people's place in it. Cultural action implies treating others as colearners and participants, not as vessels into which one pours enlightenment. It is a validating experience for people to have their opinions on public affairs taken seriously and to develop a shared understanding of an issue.

Taking people seriously goes beyond asking questions and passively accepting the answers. All frames are not equally useful for understanding events, and there is nothing wrong or disrespectful in challenging people's beliefs by suggesting alternative frames. Ideally, organizers are learning and testing their own understanding in interaction with thoughtful people who use their own experiential knowledge as one important basis for making sense of the world.

We saw ourselves as engaged in research, not cultural action, but we uncovered evidence that taking part in it sometimes did have a modest impact on participants' sense of themselves as active agents. At the end of the long discussion, we asked people a few questions that invited them to reflect on the experience. As I described in Chapter 2, most people enjoyed the experience, but a few groups suggest something more. They indicate that participation gave them voice and increased their sense of confidence about their understanding of the world. They found it liberating simply to share their views with others and have them taken seriously by outsiders such as ourselves.

It seems especially appropriate, in a book with the themes featured here, to give participants the final word:

> *Characters:*
>
> *Lucas, a worker in a shelter for the homeless, in his twenties.*
> *Thomas, a tailor, in his thirties.*
> *Evelyn, a nurse, in her thirties.*
>
> *(They are responding to the facilitator's question about how comfortable they felt during the discussion.)*

Lucas: At first, you know, everybody's worried about what they're saying. Then, after a while you just – you don't care. You just say it anyway.

Thomas: It makes you think. . . .

Lucas: It was – it was good.

Thomas: Once you get into it.

Lucas: Yeah, once you get into it and start answering the questions, and you start thinking – like Thomas was saying, you start thinking about things, you know; you become aware. You find that you – you get a little insight on what other people around you think on key issues because lots of times you don't always discuss those issues. . . .

Evelyn: I think it's been a very positive – a *very* positive experience because it got us all together, and we sat down as a group and explored some issues. That's how it builds awareness in terms of when we have problems that affect us all, that we can't solve them by ourselves. Coming together in a family sort of small setting like this, it gives you insight on what you can do to make a difference when something is wrong in your life or in your community.

Appendix A: Methodological issues

This appendix presents the details of the research design used here and discusses some of the implications of the choices made.

Recruiting and sampling working people

We do not have a perfect probability sample but a less satisfactory quota sample. It was not our purpose to estimate the frequency of some characteristic in the population, but the great advantage of a probability sample is that, by eliminating the factor of self-selection, it randomizes error from uncontrolled and perhaps unmeasurable variables. Whatever subtle differences distinguish those who are willing to participate in the research are randomized and not unique to the particular sample.

We made a serious attempt in a pretest to select our contact people using a probability sample. To achieve this, we were willing to surrender the diversity of working-class occupations that we ultimately achieved and to focus on a narrower segment of nonprofessional hospital workers. With the cooperation of relevant unions, we were able to obtain work lists for a major hospital in Boston and to draw a random sample of names to contact.

It was no easy matter, however, to convert these names into actual groups. Participants in this research were not asked merely to answer a few questions then and there or to fill out a questionnaire at their leisure, but to arrange a meeting with friends in their home. One doesn't casually let strangers into this intimate social space. At a minimum, the recruiter must establish some relationship of interpersonal trust, something that is extremely difficult to accomplish over the telephone, even for the skillful recruiters with community organizing experience that we utilized.

Face-to-face recruitment presented formidable obstacles, since people lived in many different communities around the Boston area and many had moved from the address on our list. They worked different shifts at the hospital and were difficult, if not impossible, to contact at work. A substantial minority did not speak English or spoke it with difficulty.

Even when we succeeded in establishing sufficient trust for participants to consider participation, it was no simple matter to bring this to fruition. Many agreed after initial hesitation and then dragged their feet in calling friends or found it difficult to arrange the time; scheduled groups fell through at the last moment, at great expense and frustration for the research staff. In the end, we were able to convert only about 10 percent of our pretest sample into an actual group; by Herculean efforts we might have been able to raise this to 15 percent but no more. With a response rate at this level, the element of self-selection was clearly still present, and we could make no pretense of having a probability sample.

The frustrations of this pretest experience led us to abandon the quest for a probability sample, accepting the limitation that our participants would be self-selected. Within this limitation, we sought heterogeneity on several different variables. On race and gender, we sought approximately equal numbers of blacks and whites and men and women among the contact people.

We had formed an impression that there was a tendency to "invite up" – that is, the contact persons would select their better-educated friends to invite. Indeed, this did happen to such a degree in three groups that a majority of the participants were college graduates, and we did not include them in our sample. But once these three groups were eliminated, no overall tendency to invite up existed. When we compared the educational level of the contact people with that of the people they invited, we found that an identical 58 percent of both groups had no more than high school education. The remainder all had some college education, but less than 15 percent of the invitees with some college actually graduated.

Nor was there any significant difference between the contact people and the invitees in their level of self-reported general interest in the news. The questionnaire asked them: "People differ in how much they follow what's going on in the news. Some people seem to follow what's going on most of the time, while others are not that interested. How about yourself? Would you say you tend to follow what's going on in the news: (a) most of the time, (b) some of the time, (c) only now and then, or (d) hardly at all?" Overall, some 43 percent of the invitees checked "most of the time," whereas 38 percent of the contact people chose this category; almost identical percentages of 43 percent and 41 percent claimed that they follow the news "some of the time."

I often report the frequency with which some idea element appears in the conversations of the thirty-seven groups. Since the universe from which these conversations are drawn is a hypothetical one of potential conversations and since the participants do not comprise a probability sample, it is worth asking what these numbers mean.

They are intended to provide information on the robustness of any given result. They tell us whether what is said is consensual, appearing independently of the race and gender composition of the groups; whether it is a majority view in groups of different types or restricted to a particular type; whether it occurs in a minority of groups but is not a rarity or an idiosyncratic expression of a few unusual ones; or, whether it never appears at all. These are important differences even if one takes the exact numbers with a grain of salt.

Similarly, I provide information on the statistical significance of some relationships – for example, between the racial composition of the group and the occurrence of a particular frame or idea element in the conversation. This is not mere ritual or a confusion of substantive significance with statistical significance. It is important to know if a relationship of a given magnitude is one that we would rarely expect to occur by chance in samples of this size; statistical significance provides some reassurance that we are not building a theoretical argument around the feckless interpretation of chance results.

Focus groups

The focus group technique has been widely used in market research and political election campaigns. There is a large practitioner literature concerned with passing on tricks of the trade, but it is riddled with assumptions that need not apply to social science uses. The social science literature that seriously analyzes the method is sparse. The best effort by far is that of Morgan (1988), who reviews the methodological issues in a thoughtful and balanced way, placing it in the context of other social science methods such as participant observation and survey interviews.

Morgan considers focus groups as both a self-contained data-gathering technique and in conjunction with other methods. "The hallmark of focus groups," he argues (1988, 12), "is the explicit use of the group interaction to produce data and insights that would be less accessible without the interaction found in a group." We hoped to gain several advantages over individual interviews in using the technique to understand how people construct meaning about public issues:

1. To talk about issues with others, people search for a common basis of discourse. It is difficult to converse across frames, since they imply different ways of looking at the world. Finding a mode of discourse

in conversation means finding a working frame that can be shared by
the other participants. Different working frames may be used at different points, but during any given segment, the demands of discourse
will push a group toward the adoption of a single frame.

2. Focus groups, compared to survey interviews, allow us to observe the
    natural vocabulary with which people formulate meaning about the
    issues. As participants bring their everyday knowledge to bear on these
    issues, we are able to observe the commonsense conceptions and taken-
    for-granted assumptions they share – to use Schutz's (1967) term, their
    intersubjectivity.[1] This process rests, Schutz argues, on the assumption
    that others see the world in the same way and, hence, is defined
    socially, not individually. The key variables in the degree of intersub-
    jectivity are personal contact and similarity of socialization. It is more
    problematic across societal cleavages such as race, class, and gender
    than within them. Hence, the closer focus groups come to natural peer
    groups, the more easily will this world of everyday knowledge emerge.

3. Through challenges and alternative ways of framing an issue, partici-
    pants are forced to become more consciously aware of their perspec-
    tive. "Collective attempts to create or expand a perspective are
    inherently limited to groups," Morgan (1988, 29) observes. Differences
    inevitably arise and frames become elaborated in either reconciling
    these differences or explicitly recognizing disagreement. Furthermore,
    our particular discussion procedure involved confronting people with
    a number of different perspectives on each issue through political car-
    toons that they were asked to discuss.

Focus groups, then, seem especially likely to provide insight into the
process of constructing meaning. As Morgan sums it up, they "are useful
when it comes to investigating *what* participants think, but they excel at
uncovering *why* participants think as they do." Many of these same advantages apply to conversations in natural settings, but the focus group
contrivance allows us to observe a concentrated interaction on a topic in
a limited period of time, with the opportunity to raise questions and per-
spectives that would not naturally occur.

Peer group conversations as a variation

The generic category of focus groups contains a number of different variations, differing in the size of groups, the acquaintance relationship among
participants, the setting of the conversation, and the level of facilitator
involvement. Usage among market researchers tends to restrict the term

focus group to reflect conventional practices in their field, ignoring the different purposes that social scientists might have. Hence, Krueger (1988, 18, 25) writes that "a focus group is typically composed of seven to ten participants who are unfamiliar with each other" and " . . . is ideally composed of strangers – people who will likely not ever see each other again." The moderator, whose claim to special skills and talent must be sold to clients who finance the research, typically takes an active role, sitting at the head of a table like a teacher in a seminar, drawing out different participants in turn. The interaction may resemble a group interview more than a discussion.

None of these characteristics hold in the peer group conversations used here and, to avoid confusion, I have chosen a different term for this variation, recognizing it as part of the broader genre. The groups constructed here

1. Are smaller, consisting of four to six people. Two groups had only three members and four groups had more than six, but the average size was five,
2. Are held on the participants' turf rather than in a bureaucratic setting,
3. Involve familiar acquaintances rather than strangers, and
4. Play down the facilitator's role in keeping the conversation going.

Interaction among strangers or close friends follows different rules. Many focus groups involve strangers, and the setting as well may push the interaction style away from the playful bantering of familiar acquaintances. Although there is always an element of public discourse in this methodology, the sociable interaction component is variously encouraged or discouraged by facilitator style, group size, setting, and topic.

The lesson is not that peer group conversations are superior to other variations of the focus group methodology. They have special elements that are not necessarily present in other variations. Users of these alternatives need to examine the appropriateness of the norms governing these other situations for their own research purposes. For the purposes here, it is no problem that people have an awareness of a gallery as long as we do not confuse their conversation with a purely private one among friends and recognize the differences that apply in interpreting our results.

The facilitator and observer would typically arrive about a half hour ahead of the scheduled beginning of a discussion to arrange chairs, set up the tape recorder, and take care of other preliminary tasks. Participants were asked to fill out a short questionnaire in advance, asking them a few questions to determine their prior interest in the issues being discussed and

eliciting standard social background information. Of course, not everybody
had filled it out in advance or remembered to bring it; those who had not
were asked to complete it before the discussion began.

We considered using videotape but were concerned about its intrusive-
ness, especially under conditions that we did not control or know in advance. Furthermore, the lore in the practical literature warned us against
it. "Videotaping is obtrusive and simply not worth the effort. I have found
that it invariably changes the environment and affects the participant spon-
taneity," Krueger (1988, 87) cautions. I am not convinced that such categorical generalizations hold under all conditions, but they seemed
especially applicable for a conversation in a participant's living room when
many already felt anxious about discussing public affairs.

In transcribing audiotapes, we adapted a notation developed by Jefferson
(1978) and widely used by conversational analysts. We soon discovered
that many of these conventions were unnecessary for our particular purposes and added significantly to the cost of transcription. In the end, we
used a greatly simplified version. In cases where the written transcript was
ambiguous, we occasionally consulted the original audiotape to supplement
the available information.

Facilitator Instructions

Once participants had completed the questionnaires, the facilitator turned
on the tape recorder and asked people to introduce themselves, saying
their name, what work they do, and what they like to do in their spare
time. Issues were always discussed in the order listed here, and facilitators
were asked to read the descriptions as written:

1. (Troubled Industry) One topic in the news has been the problem of
   troubled industries. Sometimes businesses shut down and they may or
   may not start up again. Some examples include:

   > The decline of shipbuilding, like the Quincy shipyard.
   > The problems in the auto industry a few years ago, as with Chrysler.
   > The closing of a lot of factories in New England that were making
   > clothes and shoes.

   There is disagreement over what the government should do (if anything)
   to help the companies or the workers and communities that are involved.
   When you think about this issue of troubled industry, what comes to mind?

2. (Affirmative Action) Another topic in the news is the issue of affirmative action programs for blacks and other minorities. There is disagreement over what kinds of programs we should have (if any) to

increase the hiring, promotion, and college admission of blacks and other minorities. When you think about this issue of affirmative action, what comes to mind?

3. (Nuclear Power) Another issue in the news is nuclear power plants. There has been disagreement over how much we should rely on nuclear power plants as an energy source. When you think about this issue of nuclear power plants, what comes to mind?

4. (Arab–Israeli Conflict) Another topic in the news has been the conflict between the Arabs and Israel. There has been disagreement over what our government should do with respect to this conflict, if anything. When you think about this issue of Arab–Israeli conflict, what comes to mind?

Following the open-ended question on each issue (question one), and before proceeding to another issue, the facilitator asked these four follow-up questions:

> *Question two* (the "proximity" question): Would you say that any-thing that has happened on this issue of _____ has affected you personally or has affected your friends and relatives?

> *Question three* (the "social cleavage" question): We've talked about ourselves and the people we know and how we are affected by _____; now let's talk about whether larger groups of people might have an interest in this issue. What groups in this country might stand to gain or lose by what policies are followed on _____?

Participants often asked to have this question repeated or its meaning clarified. The facilitator was instructed *not* to give examples but to say, "We mean any group larger than a family" and to accept all examples that participants offered as legitimate answers. If there was hesitation, the facilitator also encouraged responses by saying, "Some of the groups may seem obvious."

> *Question four* (cartoon question). The facilitator handed around the sets of cartoons, saying, "Now I am going to ask you to look at some cartoons about _____. Take a look at cartoon number _____. The cartoonist seems to be saying [read from bottom of cartoon]. What do you think about this?

Our objective here was to present different ways of framing the issue, some of which might be unfamiliar to participants. The cartoon was one device, but since we recognized the high probability that cartoons that did not express their preferred frames would be misunderstood, we added a verbal description to underline the intended frame. The complete set of cartoons used and the attendant frame descriptions are included in Appendix B.

> *Question five* (summary position): You've already said a lot about the issue of _____, but just to sum up, what do you think should be done about _____?

At the end of the discussion of the four issues, the facilitator invited participants to reflect on the situation by asking a few evaluation questions:

a. We're going to be doing a lot more of these groups, and now that you all have done this, we thought maybe you could help us out by telling us your reactions. How comfortable did you feel talking about these issues?
b. Do people you know talk very much about political issues or things in the news?
c. Do you have any suggestions about what we could do to make it better for future groups?

Sampling media discourse

Our media samples represent two different modalities: news accounts and explicit commentary. The accounts tell a story and frame the information presented, particularly in the headings, leads, and closings. Numerous interpretive comments are sprinkled throughout the accounts in the form of quotations from sources or excerpts from interviews.

More specifically, we collected four media samples: (1) television network evening news broadcasts on ABC, CBS, and NBC; (2) newsmagazine accounts and commentary from *Time, Newsweek,* and *U.S. News and World Report;* (3) editorial cartoons; and (4) opinion columns. Our sample included everything that appeared during the relevant time period.

We went to substantial lengths to ensure that our cartoon and columns represented *all* of those published during the time period examined. We sampled the ten largest circulation daily newspapers in each of five regions: Northeast, Southeast, Southwest, Midwest, and West. The *New York Daily News, New York Times, Philadelphia Inquirer, Washington Post,* and *Boston Globe* were included among the ten from the East; the *Miami Herald, Atlanta Journal, Louisville Courier, Baltimore Sun,* and *New Orleans Times Picayune* were included from the Southeast; the *Chicago Tribune, Chicago Sun Times, Detroit News, Detroit Free Press, Kansas City Star, St. Louis Post Dispatch,* and *Milwaukee Journal* were included from the Midwest; the *Phoenix Republic, Houston Chronicle, Houston Post, Dallas Morning*

News, and *Dallas Times Herald* were included from the Southwest; and the *Los Angeles Times, San Francisco Chronicle, Portland Oregonian, San Diego News Tribune, Denver Post,* and *Seattle Times* were among those included from the West.

To find out how close our sample of columns and cartoons were to representing the complete set in all newspapers, we calculated how much each successive wave of five newspapers contributed to our final sample. For affirmative action, for example, the last two waves contributed two additional cartoons, increasing our sample by only 4 percent; they also contributed ten additional columns, increasing this sample by 11 percent. Looked at another way, 12 percent of the cartoons and 19 percent of the columns in the last ten papers were items not already included in the sample. Clearly, our sample approached saturation.

In dividing our newspaper sample into regions, we intended to explore possible regional differences, but the nature of syndication makes such a comparison virtually meaningless. For example, Tom Wicker may be on the staff of the *New York Times,* but his columns on affirmative action appeared in one or more papers in our sample in *every* region. Although not every commentator is carried equally in each region, we found no significant regional differences in what was displayed on affirmative action. We carried out less complete checks with respect to other issues, but with similar results.

The Vanderbilt Television Archive began recording the evening news broadcasts of the three major networks on August 5, 1968. Hence, our television sample is complete only for critical discourse moments after this date. For events after 1981, we used a smaller group of sixteen newspapers to include about 70 percent of what we would have obtained from the full set.

Measurement

The primary quantitative measure used is the *prominence* of an issue frame or one of its associated elements. This simple statistic is the ratio of actual displays to the total opportunities for display, expressed as a percentage. It allows us to compare the relative prominence of different frames over time and to chart their emergence and disappearance in national media discourse. Frames are called *visible* if they reach a threshold of at least 10 percent prominence on any one of the four media samples. Some frames from other forums – especially social movement forums – are invisible in media discourse or become visible only at certain critical discourse moments.

We wrestled with the technical issue of whether or not to use a weighted prominence measure in which each display was multiplied by a figure representing the audience size of the media source. Each display represents an opportunity to be exposed to a frame, and the measure should reflect how pervasive a frame is and how likely it is to be encountered in a random selection of media offerings. By this reasoning, a display is more culturally available if more units of it are produced. A display in a paper that runs off 1 million copies ought to get ten times the weight of one that appears in 100,000 copies. On the other hand, one might argue that media prominence simply measures the popularity of different frames among a set of journalists; in this case, each usage represents a single opportunity for display, and there is no need to weight displays by circulation.

It turns out that this is a distinction without a practical difference. The variance in displays among networks and newsmagazines is so small and the audience size is so similar that weighted and unweighted measures of prominence are virtually identical. The situation is more complicated for cartoons and columns, which, being syndicated, appear in multiple sources. When we examined weighted and unweighted measures for selected events, we found no differences in prominence scores for any frame that were greater than 5 percent. Hence, we used the simpler, unweighted measure of prominence.

The unit of analysis here differed for accounts and commentary. For cartoons and opinion columns, each was considered a single opportunity. Most cartoons displayed a single frame, but displays of competing frames were common in opinion columns as well as multiple displays of the same frame. We counted a frame as being displayed even when the displayer was clearly not an advocate and had no intention of furthering its influence. Indeed, a frame was sometimes displayed for the purpose of rebuttal or mockery; in such cases, we used an additional code to indicate a negative display. Note that the possibility of several frames being displayed in a single column means that the total prominence scores for the set of frames typically adds up to more than 100 percent.

For television and newsmagazine commentary, the relevant unit was any utterance that was part of a frame on the issue. Hence, any given broadcast or newsmagazine account included many opportunities for display.

Parts of the analysis, especially of visual imagery and changes in *how* a frame is expressed, are more qualitative and interpretive. Here I attempt to present enough rich textual material so that readers can form their own independent judgment on the validity of any interpretation.

Selection of critical discourse moments

We attempted to identify all points that would produce a minimum of five displays for each medium. Using the *New York Times* index, we were able to identify a number of possibilities before settling on those points finally selected. For issues such as Arab–Israeli conflict, there were many possibilities, but on other issues, some of the points we initially chose were insufficient to meet even this modest criterion for inclusion.

We ended with the following critical discourse moments by issue:

Troubled industry

1. Lockheed loan request and debate (May 1971 and July 1971).
2. Carter administration six-point plan for the steel industry (December 1977).
3. Chrysler loan debate (November 1979).

Affirmative action

1. The introduction of the Philadelphia Plan (September 1969).
2. Presidential campaign and reevaluation of the Philadelphia Plan (September and December 1972).
3. The Supreme Court Bakke decision (June 1978).
4. The Supreme Court Weber decision (June 1979).
5. The Supreme Court Memphis Firefighters decision (June 1984).

Nuclear power

1. Eisenhower's "Atoms for Peace" speech to the United Nations (December 1953).
2. Citizen's Committee Report on the Future of Nuclear Energy (February 1956).
3. Nixon energy speech (December 1973).
4. Seabrook demonstration and Carter nonproliferation initiative (May 1977).
5. Accident at Three Mile Island (March 1979).
6. Accident at Chernobyl (April 1986).

Arab–Israeli conflict

1. Israeli independence (May 1948).
2. Sinai War (November 1956).
3. Six Day War (June 1967).
4. October War (October 1973).

5. Sadat visit to Jerusalem (November 1977).
6. Camp David accord (September 1978).
7. Sadat assassination (October 1981).
8. U.S. peacekeeping forces sent to Lebanon (September–October 1982).
9. Shultz shuttle for proposed international peace conference (February–March 1988).

Compiling

Once sample materials were assembled for a time period, a trained compiler examined them to identify relevant portions. This procedure differed somewhat for each medium. In newspapers, for example, the compiler looked only at the editorial and op ed pages, ignoring other sections.

Many graduate students and undergraduates were involved in compiling the materials. To ensure that they all used the same criteria of relevance, my colleagues and I reviewed a body of material and established a set of rules for inclusion. Hence, compilers were trained on material that had already been independently identified as relevant and were scored for their ability to meet this established standard. When they met the criterion of 80 percent inclusion, they were allowed to review new material. Regular spot checks were conducted thereafter, consistently yielding inclusion scores of better than 90 percent. Furthermore, an examination of fourteen items that one compiler had included and another had ignored indicated that only one contained any codeable display of a frame. Omissions, then, were few and apparently occurred primarily on items that were marginal or irrelevant.

Coding reliability

Having identified relevant passages, coders then entered information into a computer file in machine-readable form, using an interactive program and video display terminal. The entry included a direct quote, identifying information, and material on context. Coders were instructed to include any elements that seemed relevant even if they were uncertain of which frame was implied (if any).

Individual passages were coded using a three-digit code in which the first digit referred to the overall frame and the others to more specific idea elements that implied it (see Appendix C for the codes used). It is important to emphasize that the coder was not asked to code an overall frame (genotype) but a much more specific idea element (phenotype). For example, there was a specific code, within the REMEDIAL ACTION frame, for reference to a history of slavery and oppression of black people. It was not necessary for the coder to make a judgment about which frame was implied by the coding category; this was built into the structure of the code. Some categories within a frame were later collapsed when coders were unable to distinguish among them. All categories used in the final analysis have reliability scores of at least 80 percent.

Coders did not have to make a judgment on which frame a writer or speaker advocated. Some displays may be used for the purpose of rebuttal. Coders scored a frame as having been displayed even when the displayer was clearly not an advocate and had no intent of furthering its influence but included an additional code to indicate negative displays.

Although the audio portion of television was treated in the same manner as the print media, we also prepared a "deaf" visual transcript – that is, a description of what is seen by an observer who cannot hear the sound. Using independent transcribers, some of whom could hear the audio and some of whom could not, we found that the deaf transcription provided considerably richer and more subtle detail for qualitative analysis. Visual transcripts were analyzed directly by the author without prior coding.

For opinion columns, we treated the column as a whole as the unit rather than individual passages coded within it. We asked, in effect, whether a given frame had been displayed in the entire set of passages rather than in any individual one. Reliability at this aggregate level was well above 90 percent, reflecting the fact that coders may disagree on some individual quotes without this disagreement affecting the aggregate code.

All cartoons were coded directly and independently by myself and a senior colleague rather than delegating this task to regular coders.

Appendix B: Cartoon set for peer group discussions

1.   The cartoonist seems to be saying that with the government, the banks, and labor all pulling together with management, automobile sales are moving up again.

2. The cartoonist seems to be saying that it's not really fair for the government to be giving special help to some companies while others have to make it on their own.

3. The cartoonist seems to be saying that Detroit's auto industry is under severe attack from Japanese and German automakers much like the United States was under attack from these countries in World War II. Reprinted by permission: Tribune Media Services

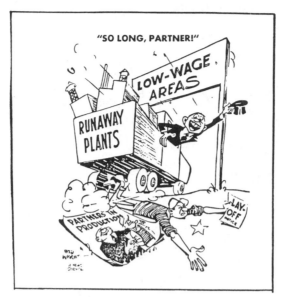

4. Fred Wright. Copyright, United Electrical, Radio and Machine Workers of America (UE). The cartoonist seems to be saying that companies are ready to forget all about their partnership with workers and to take off for areas where they can pay lower wages whenever it suits their interests.

5. The cartoonist seems to be saying that affirmative action makes the race fairer by removing the unfair handicaps of the past. SARGENT, Copyright 1979, Austin-American Statesman. Reprinted by permission of Universal Press Syndicate. All rights reserved.

"Yes, your qualifications are excellent,
but frankly there were other considerations."

6.   The cartoonist seems to be saying that affirmative action guidelines make it so hard for whites to get hired that even someone as well qualified as Uncle Sam himself probably couldn't get the job anymore.

THE BALANCING ACT

7. The cartoonist seems to be saying that it is hard to protect everyone from discrimination while at the same time allowing affirmative action programs to take race into consideration in hiring and college admissions.

8. The cartoonist seems to be saying that rich liberals want to give special breaks to blacks at the expense of whites who also need a break. Reprinted with permission.

9. The cartoonist seems to be saying that opponents of nuclear power are against progress and would probably have opposed the invention of the ox and cart if they had been around then. Reprinted by permission: Tribune Media Services.

10.   From HERBLOCK ON ALL FRONTS (New American Library, 1980). The cartoonist seems to be saying that nuclear power companies are more concerned with making big profits than with making sure their nuclear reactors are safe.

"The impudence! Accusing me of an unhealthy lifestyle?!
Why, I've the highest standard of
living in the world!"

11.   The cartoonist seems to be saying that relying on nuclear energy may bring wealth but it is much less healthy for our lifestyle than relying on natural energy like wood and wind.

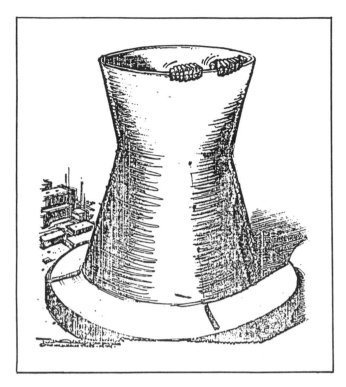

12.   Paul Conrad. Copyright, 1979, Los Angeles Times. Reprinted with permission. The cartoonist seems to be saying that in using nuclear power we may be producing a monster that we can't control.

13. The cartoonist seems to be saying that the Arab–Israeli conflict is part of a big Middle Eastern chess game between the Russians and the United States in which each is trying to use its allies to gain an advantage over the other.

ANOTHER DAVID DID IT.

14. *The Detroit News*, October 11, 1973, reprinted with permission. The cartoonist seems to be saying that Israel is surrounded by Arab enemies that want to destroy it.

15. The cartoonist seems to be saying that the continuing crossfire between Arabs and Israelis is threatening to plunge the whole world into war.

16. The cartoonist seems to be saying that both Palestinians and Jews have a right to be there, and they could both be comfortable and at peace in countries of their own.

WOX

17. The cartoonist seems to be saying that the United States trains and guides Israel to intimidate the Arabs in order to maintain control over the rich resources of the Middle East.

Appendix C: Working frames and codes

For each issue, we developed a set of working frames that were used in the analysis of the media and transcripts. We recognized that if we relied on the mass media samples for this task, we would run the risk of missing frames that, although culturally available, have no visibility in media discourse. Since the absence of certain frames in media discourse was important in the overall analysis, we used a broader definition of *cultural availability*.

A frame was considered culturally available if there was any organization or advocacy network within the society that sponsored it. The initial source for frames, then, was not general audience media but more specialized publications by individual and organized sponsors, both public and private. We took particular care to include the publications of challengers, since it is here, we hypothesized, that we were most likely to discover candidates with little or no media prominence.

In the case of affirmative action, for example, we examined the opinions of the Supreme Court justices in the Bakke and Weber cases, as well as various speeches and statements by government officials. We examined many of the 155 amicus curiae briefs filed in the Bakke case by established organizations, making particular use of the one filed by the Anti-Defamation League of B'nai B'rith.[1] We examined the writings of neo-conservatives on affirmative action appearing in *Commentary, The Public Interest, Public Opinion,* and *Policy Review,* plus important books such as Nathan Glazer's *Affirmative Discrimination* (1975). The major challengers on the affirmative action issue are on the right. The Ku Klux Klan, John Birch Society, and other like-minded groups offered their views in publications such as *The Crusader, National Vanguard,* and *American Opinion.*

We used different sources but essentially the same procedure on the other three issues as well. From such sources, we constructed a working list of frames that were revised and supplemented in applying it to mass media materials. I make no claim that these frames reflect an underlying *objective* structure; they are merely one useful way of viewing the discourse, a heuristic for discovering and systematizing the prominence of issue frames and their change over time.

It is difficult to be fair in the statement of a frame that is not one's own. An adequate statement should meet the fundamental ground rule that it is accepted as fair by an advocate. We attempted to satisfy this rule by relying on the exact language of advocates and sponsors, quoting directly as much as possible.

The working frames for each issue are presented here in two forms. Because they are most easily grasped as a gestalt, I state them first in the form of a few brief paragraphs, suggesting the core organizing idea and employing some of the language and catch phrases by which it is typically suggested. The frames are then stated in the form of a three-digit code used in coding specific texts.

TROUBLED INDUSTRY

Free enterprise

To increase the activity of the state in the sphere of economic liberty is a foolish mistake for which we would pay with both our liberties and our prosperity. The market system has a self-correcting character. The weak and inefficient lose out to the strong and efficient. One must allow this market mechanism to operate without messing things up with federal intervention. Government planning and coordination is a form of state capitalism and creeping socialism. It was tried in Europe and did not work.

Weaker companies fail and plants shut down, but towns with plant closings have manageable and short-lived problems. Youngstown, Ohio, and Seattle, Washington, were able to survive plant closings and economic contractions and adjust. It is cowardly and unfair to let thousands of small businesses fail all the time, only to intervene when big business is involved. The government should maintain a responsible fiscal policy and make sure that the rules are followed. Otherwise, they should allow the free market to sort out the weak from the strong.

There are two special variations of this frame. An antigovernment *variation emphasizes the cost imposed by unnecessary and overzealous government regulation as the primary source of the problems that industries face.*

These government regulations were imposed through the political power of the Nader juggernaut with its Earth Day mentality, mindless of the costs of regulation. These costs inevitably fall unequally on companies with different sizes and situations, giving them an unfair handicap in the market competition. We should get government off the back of industry.

An antilabor *variation emphasizes the costs imposed by powerful unions.*

Through the tyranny of big labor, wages are driven up faster than productivity, making American products no longer competitive on the world market.

Partnership

Healthy industry means a healthy America. We are all in the same leaky lifeboat, and everybody needs to row and bail to keep us afloat. We need a new attitude of cooperation among business, labor, and government: a new social contract. The central issue is how government can play the most helpful role, in cooperation with business and labor, to restore American industry to full health.

There are ample precedents for government aid and coordination, both here and abroad. Witness Japan, Inc., and the numerous ways in which the Japanese government helps Japanese industry to compete better in the world market. In this country as well, government aid to business is common and not an unusual event.

The root cause of the current problems suffered by basic American industries is their declining share of the world market. This decline has multiple origins, including decaying physical plants, high interest rates, poor management decisions, costly government regulation, and high labor costs. Who is to blame is not important; doing something about it is. It would be irresponsible to allow a major corporation to fail in light of the massive human and economic costs that inevitably would flow from a failure. It would cause a ripple effect throughout the economy, causing other failures, unemployment, and economic hardship.

There are government-led *and* business-led *variations of this frame. In the former, the government should serve as coordinator and active planner of an industrial policy. In the latter, the government should serve as facilitator and provider for the private sector.*

Capital flight

Millions of working people have lost their jobs, with devastating effects on their communities, particularly in the northeastern and midwestern industrial heartland. Yet they have no say in the crucial decisions that affect their lives. The job loss is a result of investment decisions made by private corporations without public accountability. The so-called American corporations that make these decisions are, in fact, multinational corporations that make decisions on a global basis in order to maximize their profits. The basic pattern of these investment decisions has involved a flight of capital from the industrial heartland to the southern rim of the United States and, increasingly, to the Third World.

The purpose of this capital flight is a search for a docile, unorganized, or cowed labor force. In the United States, this means moving from states with unionized to nonunionized labor; in the Third World, it means investing in countries with authoritarian governments that suppress working-class organization, frequently with violence. We need democratization and public control of these investment decisions. Plant closing legislation on a national basis might be a useful step. Government support of some form of employee ownership might also be appropriate. But one must be wary of corporations that milk a plant for profit and then try to sell the corporate cow to the workers. This is lemon socialism.

Foreign invasion

In World War II, we fought the Germans and the Japanese on land and sea in a battle for survival. The weapons then were things like battleships and bombers; now they are things like cars and steel. We are facing a foreign invasion, and we are in a new battle for survival. Buy American. When you buy a foreign car, you are taking a job away from an American worker. In a battle for survival, everyone has a civic duty to help our country win the war. The government should do its part by limiting the imports of foreign products, produced by cheap foreign labor, that are flooding our shores and undermining our basic industries.

General coding rules

These rules refer to the coding for all of the working frames and they will not be repeated.

A. Each code consists of three digits. The first digit refers to the frame or variation; the second digit refers to a weak form or a strong form of the frame; the third digit refers to the specific idea element within the frame.

B. All relevant items are coded, whether or not they imply a frame. A 900 series is used for items that don't imply a frame.
C. The weak form -1- has not been used if the strong form -2- was codeable.

Codes

Preparation and background. This code centers on the policy issue of what the government should do, if anything, about companies and industries that are in trouble and about the communities and people affected. We focus on three basic industries: steel, automobile, and transportation.

The code is based on four central frames: *partnership, free enterprise, foreign invasion,* and *capital flight.* These are then broken down into more specific idea elements (for example, "It's unfair to help big businesses and let little ones fail"). Read the descriptions of the frames a few times so that you have the general frames in mind and can look under that general rubric in the code for the particular subcategory that fits. The first digit of the code refers to the frame.

The commentary that is coded here is from three different time periods: 1971, 1977, and 1979. Most of the 1971 commentary focuses on the controversy over a federal loan to the (then) troubled Lockheed Corporation. At about that time, there was also a wave of strikes in basic industries and a recent bankruptcy of the Penn Central Railroad, which draws some relevant commentary. The 1977 commentary focuses on the problems of the steel industry and the troubled community of Youngstown, Ohio. The 1979 commentary focuses mainly on the controversy over a federal loan to Chrysler.

A lot of the commentary is about the central irony of this issue: that apostles of free enterprise are asking for government handouts. The irony rests on the fact that people do not always match their actions to their professed beliefs. Note that the *beliefs* being invoked here are from the free enterprise frame. Hence, you will find this irony in the subcategories of this frame.

1 Partnership

111 If we let the company fail, it will drag too many others down with it and create too much havoc with the economy. It will cost more in the long run. It will hurt national defense.

112 Temporary aid (including import quotas) will help a company get back on its feet, where it can be productive again. It turns out to

be a good investment. Cases of companies (e.g., Lockheed, Chrysler) that paid back the loan and became profitable again.

113 If we are going to aid a company, it should be enough to make sure that the company can survive and pay it back.

114 Government aid is important for unions and to protect workers' jobs.

115 Saving jobs is more important than any abstract principles involved.

116 Opponents of government aid are kicking a victim when he's down.

117 Opponents of government aid are antibusiness obstructionists.

118 Management and labor need to make sacrifices to justify government aid.

119 A bankruptcy will have bad consequences (but no implication is drawn or solution suggested).

120 Let's help the failing company this time but avoid setting a precedent.

131 Government frequently helps business. Partnership is not a new thing (e.g., the old Reconstruction Finance Corporation). The "arms-length" relationship between government and business is a myth.

132 Everyone should pitch in and work together for recovery: government, labor, banks, and management.

133 We need a New Reconstruction Finance Corporation.

134 We need a new industrial policy.

135 We ought to imitate or learn from the Japanese, with the government helping business and coordinating industrial policy.

2 Free enterprise

211 Bailouts are a ripoff of taxpayers and consumers. They are public charity or handouts.

212 A loan to a failing company is poor business, throwing good money after bad.

213 The taxpaying public shouldn't have to bear the brunt of bad management decisions.

214 The failing company itself should not be helped, but we should try to cushion the effects on other companies hurt by its failure.

215 Blaming industry problems on foreigners is scapegoating. The idea of "dumping" is a myth and an excuse.

216 Japan (or some other country) is outperforming us fair and square. They're more efficient and work harder.

217 Complaining about government regulations is just an excuse.

231 Giving government aid undermines the free enterprise system on which our economy is based. It sets a bad precedent.

232 The central irony: Apostles of free enterprise are asking for a government handout.

233 Companies want "socialism for the rich" or "welfare for the rich."

234 It's unfair to let little companies fail all the time and then to bail out a big company.

235 The companies that fail deserve to fail because of poor management. Bailing them out is rewarding poor management.

236 Bailouts (or import quotas) have hidden costs. They keep inefficient companies in business, and this costs the consumer more.

237 If you give special aid to one company, other companies that are having trouble will expect it. It's unfair to the competition.

238 Import quotas interfere with the operation of the free market.

239 Negative economic consequences from a company failure are temporary and manageable. Competitors will pick up the business, and the lost jobs will be recovered.

240 The only role of the government is to restore competition and to make sure that foreign competitors follow the rules and don't have special advantages.

241 Helping out a troubled company will encourage dependency on government and will give it too much power.

242 If the government gets too financially involved with companies, it will develop a conflict of interest.

243 The Japanese claim to be for free trade, but they don't really practice it. Instead, they put obstacles in the way of foreign companies and give unfair government subsidies to Japanese companies trading abroad.

244 We're heading for a corporate state (like fascist Italy) or toward state capitalism.

245 Bailouts and government subsidies may be good politics, but they are bad economics.

3   Free enterprise: Antiunion variation

   311   Unions are smothering companies with excessive wage demands and featherbedding.

   312   Unions are forcing costs on companies that make it impossible to meet foreign competition.

4   Free enterprise: Antigovernment variation

   411   Getting government off the back of business is what's needed, not government handouts.

   412   Government regulations and bureaucracy have made companies uncompetitive, and it is the government's responsibility to pay the costs it has imposed on business.

   413   Environmental regulations are making American business uncompetitive.

5   Foreign invasion

   501   Temporary import quotas are necessary to meet foreign competition (but no imagery of war or battle is included).

   502   Foreign companies are dumping their product on the American market, selling below cost (but the negative effects on Americans are not made explicit).

In the stronger version that follows, there is more than simply an acknowledgment of foreign competition. The imagery of a battle for survival is important as is the idea of a war or a physical fight.

   511   The problem is an assault or invasion by foreigners.

   512   Import restrictions are necessary for survival.

   513   Buy American. Buying foreign products is unpatriotic.

   514   We have to get tough with foreigners.

   515   Foreign countries cheat and don't play by the same rules that we use.

   516   The dumping of foreign goods is taking jobs away from Americans.

6   Capital flight

   611   Companies want government money but no public accountability.

   612   We should help the workers buy out the company and run it.

613 Worker takeovers of badly run or failing companies are no panacea; this is lemon socialism.

614 Better to help the hungry poor than the hungry rich; better to spend money directly on the unemployed than to hope that it will trickle down through a failing company.

631 Corporations are shifting capital to nonunion, low-wage areas of the country.

632 Multinational corporations are shifting capital from the United States to Third World countries with low wages and repressive regimes.

633 Multinational corporations are bringing about the deindustrialization of America.

8 Additional frames

801 Company is characterized as part of the military–industrial complex but is not being condemned thereby.

811 Nationalization. If the government is going to bail out a company or industry, it might as well take over and run it.

821 The company is getting help because it is part of the military–industrial complex.

9 No frame implied

911 No framing of the issue of troubled industry.

912 Predictions about outcome. There is a good chance (or a poor chance) that the aid will (will not) go through.

913 Someone opposes or supports aid, but no reason is given.

914 Political parties (or politicians) are trying to gain by playing politics with the issue.

915 Strikes are causing problems for the economy (but whether labor or management is responsible for the strike is not clear).

916 Important principles are involved in the struggle over what to do about the particular company.

AFFIRMATIVE ACTION

Remedial action

The core issue is whether race-conscious programs should be used to redress the continuing effects of a history of racial discrimination. "In order to get beyond racism, we must first take into account race. There is no other way. And in order to treat some persons equally, we must treat them differently" (Justice Harry Blackmun, opinion in the Bakke case, 1978). Racism has a long history, and our present institutions are still permeated with its influence. Affirmative action is the present phase of a long struggle to achieve genuine equality of opportunity and to overcome chronic minority underrepresentation and institutional racism. It's too late to act color-blind.

"Reverse discrimination" (for this frame) is simply the latest battle cry in a long tradition of historical resistance to efforts to bring blacks into the mainstream of American life. It plays the same reactionary role in the current struggle that "states' rights" played in the earlier struggles for voting rights and equality of treatment in public accommodations. Institutional racism is not a thing of the past. "How can there be reverse discrimination when the black and brown population of California is 25 percent but the [minority] medical school population is only 3 percent?" (Benjamin Hooks, executive director, NAACP, on *CBS News,* July 4, 1978). "Bringing the Negro into the mainstream of American life should be a state interest of the highest order" (Justice Thurgood Marshall, opinion in the Bakke case, 1978). By encouraging and enforcing vigorous affirmative action programs, we can accomplish this.

Delicate balance

The core issue is how to maintain a proper balance, helping old victims of discrimination without creating new ones. We need to strive for racial equality while at the same time upholding the right of individuals to be protected from discrimination on the basis of race. Providing opportunities to those who have been denied them is fine, but this should not become preferential treatment. The rights of different groups are in conflict. The trick is to find the proper balance whereby an old wrong can be overcome without creating a new one.

It is fine to consider race as *a* factor in admission and hiring, but not as *the* factor. The difference between a quota and a goal is subtle but real. Quotas cross the line between striving to include more members of a minority group and actually excluding other individuals on the basis of race. An admission program such as Harvard's is fine because race is taken into consideration in a positive way, along with many other factors. But a program such as the one at the University of California (Davis) is not because it sets aside certain slots *only* for minorities. The former attains the necessary delicate balance; the latter does not.

No preferential treatment

The consideration of race or ethnicity, however benignly motivated, is not the American way. Race-conscious policies inevitably lead to preferential treatment and unfair advantages for some at the expense of others. "What cannot be, and should not be, countenanced is thinking in blood" (Bennett and Eastland 1978, 34). "A quota is a divider of society, a creator of castes, and it is all the worse for its racial base, especially in a society desperately striving for an equality that will make race irrelevant" (Bickel 1975, 133).

The idea of a "white majority" is a myth. America contains all kinds of ethnic groups that can claim varying degrees of past discrimination. Most people are "tossed salads." If the government continues "to divide the majestic national river into little racial and ethnic creeks, . . . the U.S. will be less a nation than an angry menagerie of factions scrambling for preference in the government's allocation of entitlements" (George F. Will, *Newsweek*, July 10, 1978, 84). The core concept of justice should be equal opportunity for individuals, not statistical parity for government-approved groups.

Between quotas and goals, there is a distinction without a difference. Goals are quotas in covert form, and institutions will inevitably be forced to treat them as quotas to avoid being charged with discrimination. Cosmetic surgery cannot hide the "ugly whore of minority racism" (*The Crusader,* August 1978, 3). Public policy should be exercised without distinction of race or national origin.

Within this general frame, there are four somewhat different variations. The first of these is reverse discrimination. *The emphasis here is on how affirmative action programs* exclude *individuals on the grounds of race and, hence, violate the right to be judged as individuals.*

"Injuries are suffered in fact, claims made and burdens carried, by individual persons. . . . The sacrifice of fundamental individual rights cannot be justified by the desire to advance the well-being of any ethnic group" (Cohen 1979, 44). When affirmative action comes to mean statistical requirements based on race or ethnicity, this abandons the "first principle of a liberal society, that the individual and the individual's interest and good and welfare are the test of a good society" (Glazer 1975, 220). Affirmative action programs are a form of "benign Nuremberg laws" (Glazer 1978). How long will it be before we start seeing signs saying, "No whites need apply?"

The second variation is undeserving advantage. *The emphasis here shifts from who is excluded to the unfair advantage of those who benefit from affirmative action.*

Affirmative action gives minorities something they have not earned and do not deserve. Whatever happened in the past is over; this is now. Other groups had handicaps to overcome and did not get any special treatment. There should be no "special Americans"; the same rules should apply to all.

"There are some of these do-gooders, with official hats or without official hats, who feel that the so-called minority groups should be provided a short cut to attaining the [necessary] skills. . . . Well, you and I know there is no shortcut" (George Meany, *U.S. News and World Report,* October 6, 1969, 72). Those for whom racial equality was once demanded are now to be more equal than others. Standards are lowered to admit undeserving minorities. "If minority applicants fail to pass routine tests, . . . then the tests [are] deemed discriminatory and standards lowered to accommodate those who are not proficient" (Guidry 1979, 33).

One particular version of this variation emphasizes the hypocrisy and arrogance of affirmative action bureaucrats and the unholy alliance between the liberal establishment and black militants.

The cost of affirmative action is carried by white, middle Americans, the silent majority. Affirmative action advocates are "Jews and wealthy corporation lawyers and upper-echelon bureaucrats and bankers and socialites [who] pride themselves on being on a first-name basis with their Vietnamese gardeners and with the black bartenders at their clubs, but they despise working-class White Americans." We can understand the Supreme Court's ruling against Brian Weber and for Allan Bakke by remembering that "black quotas for medical schools . . . gore the Jews' ox and the ox of the white 'smart set' [instead of] the ox of the despised white masses" (*National Vanguard,* August 1978, 7).

"Affirmative action serves only to allow the bureaucrats to subjugate American enterprise and make upward mobility dependent upon their whim." These bureaucrats now "goosestep over personal rights with dictatorial abandon, ordering racist and sexist harassment and cutthroat tactics that would have made Mussolini blush" (Guidry 1979, 34). Affirmative action is ultimately a hustle that allows the liberal elite to buy the political support of minorities at the expense of ordinary middle Americans.

The third variation is blacks hurt. *The emphasis here is on the injury to the minorities who are the supposed beneficiaries.*

Special programs reinforce common stereotypes, since they imply that certain groups need special help to succeed in life. Affirmative action stigmatizes the minorities it is supposed to help. "The individual admitted under the quota will bear the stigma of one who could not 'make it' under standards applicable to his fellow students. And fellow students of the same race will be stigmatized by the suspicion, however mistaken, that they were enrolled for professional study under diluted standards of admission" (Anti-Defamation League, amicus brief in Bakke case, 1978, 16).

Affirmative action deprives minorities of credit for their genuine achievements. "The message that comes through loud and clear is that minorities are losers who will never have anything unless somebody gives it to them" (Thomas Sowell, *Time Magazine,* July 10, 1978, 15). The result is that "those black people who are already competent... will be completely undermined as black becomes synonymous – in the minds of black and white alike – with incompetence, and black achievement becomes synonymous with charity or payoffs" (Sowell 1972, 292). In effect, this perpetuates racism rather than allowing it to die a natural death.

The last variation is divide and conquer. *The emphasis of this populist subpackage is on the centrality of class or economic disadvantage rather than race or ethnicity.*

Poor whites are a minority too. "Just because you're white, that doesn't mean that you've had it made in America the last 200 years" (Leonard Walentynowicz, spokesman for the Polish-American Congress, *U.S. News and World Report,* July 9, 1979, 71). A mind is a terrible thing to waste, whether it is a black mind or a white one. Affirmative action divides those who have a common interest.

With all the furor over who gets into medical school, "no one seems to notice that the rich are still being assured of their quota" (Jack Anderson column, *Atlanta Journal,* July 6, 1978, 6). Bakke and Weber took on the establishment on behalf of the little guy. It is easy for those who do not pay the price to favor affirmative action. In the end, only the rich benefit, and even the minorities who are supposed to benefit get exploited.

Codes

Preparation and background. In these codes "Plan" refers to the Philadelphia Plan, Davis Plan, Kaiser Plan, Bethlehem Steel Plan, and so on. Items were not coded 3——if they could be coded any of these other numbers: 4—, 5—, 7—, or 8—.

1 Remedial action

11 – (weak form) A pro–affirmative action position is implied, but the frame must be inferred from the position.

111 Decision left most affirmative action programs intact; at most, a minor setback for affirmative action, civil rights, or black progress.

112 Decision was a blow against civil rights and black progress; the Supreme Court didn't go far enough, equivocated, is impeding black progress; the administration isn't doing enough to support civil rights or black progress, or to overcome discrimination and imbalance; *Brown v. Board of Education* is an exemplar contrasting the earlier commitment with current reneging and equivocation.

113 Decision gave the green light to affirmative action, and was a victory for civil rights and black progress; the Supreme Court (or the administration) is helping black progress and civil rights, is allied with the black cause. Decision will discourage so-called reverse discrimination lawsuits, will put to rest the issue of reverse discrimination.

114 Charge that racial discrimination and racism exist (or did in the past) *but are not explicitly linked to affirmative action programs;* note made that the civil rights movement was (is) an effort to overcome discrimination *without specific reference to affirmative action plan.*

115 Civil rights movement is alive and well; protests and pressure will continue, are necessary.

116 Affirmative action programs (or quotas) are not reverse discrimination; the Supreme Court says they are okay, fair, legal, consistent with the Civil Rights Act; quotas are no big deal; a lower court was asked to reconsider a decision against an affirmative action program; no practical alternative to quotas; no real difference between Harvard and Davis programs.

117 Decision (or plan) will bring hope to blacks and other minorities; will motivate them and encourage them.

118 Decision (or plan) will increase job opportunities or admissions opportunities for blacks and other minorities.

119 Governmental preference is common, no stranger to our legal life.

12 – (strong form) Core idea that affirmative action is an effort to remedy an imbalance or discrimination is explicit or clearly implied.

121 Plan is an effort to remedy past discrimination; data on discrimination and lack of progress presented in the context of an affirmative action plan. In the past, blacks were last hired, first fired.

122 Plan is an effort to correct racial imbalance or chronic minority underrepresentation; an effort to bring blacks into the mainstream, an inclusion effort; an effort to overcome the racial crisis, to achieve racial equality, to open opportunities previously closed.

123 Color blindness is insufficient; it's too late to be color-blind; one must take race into account to overcome racism.

124 Conflict is between advocates of black inclusion and equality and racists; opponents of affirmative action are racists, bigots, people who discriminate or condone discrimination.

125 It's ironic that the Civil Rights Act, which was intended to remedy past discrimination, is interpreted by some to forbid affirmative action.

126 If there isn't pressure, voluntary efforts to remedy past discrimination will flag.

127 Hypocrisy, fraudulence, phoniness, and unfairness of affirmative action opponents and of the reverse discrimination claim in the face of black misery and oppression; Bakke pretending to be oppressed when he really isn't; opponents pretending to be concerned about lowering standards, the work ethic, and so on to hide a racist intent; the idea that reverse discrimination is a myth.

129 The metaphor of a handicap race.

2 Delicate balance

21 – (weak form)

211 Two groups are in conflict, but there is no suggestion that one has more legitimacy than the other; both groups have equal rights.

212   Clumsy balance. Supreme Court tried to give something to every-
      body and left no one satisfied; produced a strange hybrid, polka
      dots.

213   *Brown v. Board of Education* is an exemplar to draw a contrast
      with current cases; current cases raise different sets of issues.

214   Quotas are okay only if applied to those guilty of past
      discrimination.

215   Employers (or admissions officers) are (were) caught in the mid-
      dle, forced to walk a tightrope; faced with potential lawsuits from
      each side.

216   Decision is a sensible compromise.

217   There is a conflict between seniority and affirmative action.

22 – (strong form)

221   Two legitimate groups or principles are (or need to be) balanced;
      equal right between contesting sides is implied; Supreme Court
      as a referee or arbiter, trying to find the proper balance that is
      fair to both sides; both sides won.

222   Efforts to overcome racial imbalance (or discrimination) are le-
      gitimate, but they shouldn't involve quotas or methods that pit
      one group against another or exclude whites.

223   Goals and quotas are different; the distinction between them is
      meaningful; considering race as one factor is different from a rigid
      quota.

224   Some affirmative action plans exclude whites, but others don't;
      the Davis plan excluded whites, but the Kaiser plan (or Harvard
      plan) doesn't.

227   Quotas are all right equivocally, as a temporary measure until an
      imbalance is corrected and only when the opportunity for whites
      is also present; not a general remedy.

228   Harvard admissions program as an exemplar showing that a well-
      balanced admissions policy is possible.

229   Georgia Tech admissions program as exemplar to teach same
      lesson as no. 228.

230   Special recruitment efforts for minorities are fine as long as they
      are not tied to goals, quotas, or timetables.

231   Being for the principle of seniority isn't being against affirmative
      action, civil rights, or black progress.

3   No preferential treatment: General

This parent frame should be used only if it is impossible to code one of the variations, 4—, 5—, 7—, or 8—.

31 – (weak form)

311   Racial imbalances are not due to discrimination but to motivation or to other legitimate individual differences.

312   Quotas are bad (no reason specified); against the American tradition.

32 – (strong form)

321   Color blindness principle. No consideration of race or ethnicity is proper; not the American way, unconstitutional. Plan means racial favoritism for blacks; Constitution prohibits favoritism.

322   Everyone should receive the same treatment; same rules should apply to everybody; no special Americans.

323   People will be put out if some get preference because of race.

324   If preferential treatment is given to some groups, others will want it and claim it; Supreme Court can't decide which ones deserve it; a given group claims that they too want affirmative action for their group.

326   Civil Rights Act implied color blindness and no racial criteria, not preferential treatment and quotas; decision turns the Civil Rights Act on its head, distorts its meaning.

327   Violating an individual's seniority is unfair, regardless of race.

4   Reverse discrimination

41 – (weak form)

411   Plan (embodying quotas) violates the Civil Rights Act.

412   A white person charges discrimination; court rules that the white person was discriminated against because of race.

413   Plan characterized as "reverse discrimination," "unconstitutional racial quota," or "discrimination in reverse" (with nothing stronger codeable).

414   Decision was blow against (or for) reverse discrimination, against affirmative action "idiocies"; against rigid quotas.

415   Battle over reverse discrimination will continue, more whites will take up cause, will spur white civil rights movement.

417   The Memphis firefighters decision upheld "civil rights."

42 – (strong form)

421   Plan fails to judge people as individuals; violates individual rights; decision will encourage (or discourage) treatment of people as individuals.

422   Plan (quotas) excludes people on the basis of race; whites are excluded by it; whites will lose out to less qualified minorities; description of how an individual white was excluded solely because of his race; "No whites need apply" will become the rule; whites will be (are being) hurt.

423   No meaningful distinction between quotas and goals, purely semantic; racial criteria are inherently discriminatory; use of racial criteria is racism; only color blindness is nondiscrimination.

424   Affirmative action will lead to absurdities in which individual differences in ability and preference are ignored; hypothetical or actual absurdities are used as exemplars.

425   Jews will be especially hurt, adversely affected; *quotas* are a code word for Jews, reminding them of how quotas were used in the past to exclude them, raising fears that they will be used this way again.

426   The white people who are excluded or hurt by affirmative action are not themselves guilty of racial discrimination and shouldn't have to pay the price of affirmative action.

427   Pendulum has (or may have) swung too far the other way; one needs to find a middle ground; two wrongs don't make a right; one shouldn't fight the wrong of discrimination against blacks by discriminating against whites.

428   Reverse discrimination may be well motivated, but it is still discrimination and illegal; mercy discrimination is morally different, but it is still discrimination.

429   Only the individuals who actually experience discrimination can or should require affirmative action.

5 Undeserving advantage

511   Affirmative action is a hustle.

52 – (strong form)

522   Blacks get things they haven't earned or aren't qualified for; they want something for nothing, but there are no shortcuts.

523 Blacks now have a better chance than whites, are advantaged, get more than is justified.

524 Blacks have gained things by unfair intimidation, pressure.

526 Blacks blame discrimination for their personal failures.

53 – (liberal scam variation)

531 Bureaucrats, officials, do-gooders, Supreme Court are imposing their ideas, ripping people off, acting arbitrarily, forcing integration and racial balance inappropriately.

532 Unholy alliance between liberal establishment and black militants; middle Americans pay the cost.

7 Blacks hurt

71 – (weak form)

711 Blacks don't need any special programs; they can make it on their own.

72 – (strong form)

721 Affirmative action deprives blacks of credit for their individual achievement by leaving the suspicion that they didn't really earn it; denies their humanity and individual worth; reinforces stereotypes; stigmatizes them.

722 Affirmative action saps the motivation and productivity of blacks by making them feel that they don't have to make an effort to get ahead; that they are entitled to rewards without effort.

8 Divide and conquer

811 Whites haven't necessarily had advantages or had it easy; many poor whites have encountered discrimination.

82 – (strong form)

821 The real issue is *class,* not race. Poor whites are a minority too. Affirmative action divides those who have a common interest.

822 Blacks get things handed to them at the expense of white Americans who are themselves struggling to make it.

823 Bakke and/or Weber took on the establishment on behalf of the little guy.

824 Poor, struggling whites pay the price of affirmative action and are the real victims.

825 The rich are still getting their quotas.

826 Liberal hypocrisy: It's easy for those who don't pay the price to favor affirmative action.

827   In the end, only the rich benefit. Even the minorities who are supposed to benefit end up getting exploited.

9   No frame implied

911   Court decision ambiguous, uninterpretable, gave no clear direction; only thing clear is more litigation; Supreme Court was inconsistent on Bakke and Weber; only clear thing is that Bakke can go to medical school.

912   Supreme Court acted in cowardly fashion, but the reasons are unclear or unstated.

913   Too many people are mixing into the problems of the construction industry.

914   George McGovern is identified with quotas; McGovern rejects quotas.

915   Some Americans don't want to work (but this is not tied to affirmative action).

916   Admission process is not universalistic.

917   If manpower programs are cut, it will hurt blacks.

918   Private employers are governed by the Civil Rights Act, not by the Constitution.

919   Decision (plan) won't affect whites adversely.

920   Admissions officers will have to decide what the decision means; admissions officers should have wide latitude to decide.

921   Description of cases that are pending or decided by the courts.

922   Harvard is too unusual to use as an exemplar for affirmative action programs in general.

923   The decision means "Last hired, first fired." The court ruled that seniority is more important than affirmative action.

924   Seniority and/or job security is important for workers.

NUCLEAR POWER

Progress

If the electric chair had been invented before the electric light, would we still be using kerosene lamps? There has always been resistance to technological progress by nervous nellies who see only the problems and ignore the benefits. Resistance to nuclear energy development is the latest version of this irrational fear of progress and change, the expression of modern pastoralists and nuclear Luddites. Certainly nuclear energy development is not free of problems, but problems can be solved, as the history of technological progress shows. The failure to develop nuclear power will retard our economic growth and renege on our obligation to the poor and to future generations. If coercive utopians prevent us from moving ahead now with nuclear energy, the next generation is likely to be sitting around in the dark, blaming the utilities for not doing something this generation's officials would not let them do.

The Three Mile Island (TMI) accident showed that the safety systems worked even in the face of a string of improbable errors. A total core melt-down was prevented, and most of the radiation released never breached the containment building. Furthermore, we learned from the experience and have improved safety even more. Chernobyl has taught us equally sanguine lessons. It shows the wisdom of the American nuclear industry in building large, fortified containment structures as a safety precaution. U.S. nuclear reactors have multiple protective barriers, called *defense in depth*. American nuclear reactors cannot be compared with their Soviet counterparts any more than their political systems are comparable. Furthermore, even in this most serious of accidents, it turns out that initial claims of thousands killed reflected mere hysteria, egged on by antinuclear activists.

Energy independence

The lesson is how dependence on foreign sources for vitally needed energy can make the United States vulnerable to political blackmail. Nuclear energy must be understood in the context of this larger problem of energy independence. To achieve independence, we must develop and use every practical alternative energy source to imported oil, including nuclear energy. Nuclear energy, plus domestic oil, natural gas, and coal, remain the only practical alternatives to a dangerous and humiliating dependence on foreign, particularly Middle Eastern, sources. These foreign sources are unstable and unreliable and are likely to make unacceptable political demands. Do we want to be dependent on the whims of Arab sheiks? Ultimately, independence is the cornerstone of our freedom.

Soft paths

Split wood, not atoms. Nuclear energy presents us with a fundamental choice about what kind of society we wish to be. Do we wish to continue a way of life that is wasteful of energy, relies on highly centralized technologies, and is insensitive to ecological consequences? Or do we want to become a society more in harmony with its natural environment?

Nuclear energy relies on the wrong kind of technology – centralized and dangerous to the earth's long-run ecological balance. We need to pursue alternative, soft paths. We should change our way of life to conserve energy as much as possible and to develop sources of energy that are ecologically safe and renewable and that lend themselves to decentralized production – for example, sun, wind, and water. Small is beautiful.

No public accountability

If Exxon owned the sun, would we have solar energy? The root of the problem is the organization of nuclear production by profit-making corporations, which minimizes accountability and control by the public. Spokesmen for the nuclear industry are motivated to protect their own economic interests, not the public interest. One cannot rely on what they say. Company officials are frequently dishonest, greedy, and arrogant. Who killed Karen Silkwood?

The nuclear industry has used its political and economic power to undermine the serious exploration of energy alternatives. Public officials, who are supposed to monitor the activities of the industry, are all too often captives of it. They function more to protect the industry than to protect the public.

Not cost effective

When one compares the costs and benefits of nuclear energy with the alternatives, it makes a poor showing. Nuclear power, through nobody's fault in particular, has turned out to be a lemon, and it is foolish to keep pouring good money after bad by supporting the continued development of nuclear energy.

Runaway

We didn't understand what we were getting into with nuclear power. We thought we could harness it to maintain our standard of living. Now we are committed to it and will sooner or later have to pay a price of unknown dimension. We have unleashed it, but we can no longer control it. Nuclear power is a powerful genie that we have summoned and are now unable to force back into its bottle, a Frankenstein's monster that might turn on its creator. Nuclear power is a time bomb waiting to explode. Nuclear energy is not simply one of several alternative energy sources but something more elemental. It defies a cost–benefit analysis. Radiation is invisible, and one may be exposed to it without knowing it; its harmful effects may not show up right away but may strike suddenly and lethally later. Radiation can create grotesque mutants.

In a religious version, humans have dared to play God in tampering with the fundamental forces of nature and the universe. He who sows the wind reaps the whirlwind.

Devil's bargain

Nuclear power turns out to be a bargain with the devil. There are clear benefits, such as inexhaustible electricity and an energy supply that doesn't depend on the whims of OPEC. But sooner or later, there will be a terrible price to pay. We are damned if we do and damned if we don't. And the deeper we get in, the harder it is to get out.

Codes

Preparation and background. In this series of codes it was necessary to be conservative in making inferences. This is a tough rule to apply. Here are two examples:

a. "To the company that runs the power plant, a mass evacuation would make TMI look like a monster more dangerous than useful." No clear company deception or withholding of information is implied here, but merely a concern with public relations. Since the monster metaphor is explicit, code it as 4.22.

b. "Scientists now agree that the danger is lessened: They can't say why it got better, and they can't say with certainty that it will never happen again." Code this 3.22 rather than 4.21. There is too much of an inference here to interpret this statement as saying that nuclear power is out of control.

The code 9.11 was used if the meaning of a quote was unclear or if it didn't print out properly. Items were not coded 3— if they could be coded 4— through 8—.

1 Progress
    1.11 There is no practical alternative to nuclear power; we need it.
    1.12 Nuclear energy can provide a lot of our power; we can't do without it.
    1.13 Other sources of energy all have serious problems.

1.14 Officials will protect the public from harm, are concerned with protecting the public. The situation is under control.

1.17 The TMI or Chernobyl accident was not that serious; media coverage exaggerated the risk.

1.18 Nuclear power isn't so different from other forms of energy.

1.19 Nuclear energy hazards are just another of life's many hazards; not that different.

1.21 Underdeveloped nations can especially benefit from peaceful uses of nuclear energy.

1.22 Nuclear energy can (will) liberate us. Although it can be used to destroy (with weapons), it can also give us the abundant energy we need for the good life.

1.23 Nuclear power is necessary for economic growth, maintaining our way of life, standard of living; the choice is between nuclear energy and going back to a more primitive time of technological backwardness. We owe it to future generations to develop nuclear power.

1.24 The problems of nuclear power are solvable ones; they will be solved by effort and research; the question isn't whether to rely on nuclear power but at how fast a rate; nuclear power can (will) become more cost effective.

1.25 TMI shows that the system works; a serious accident didn't happen because the backup systems functioned to prevent it.

1.26 Nuclear power opponents are "coercive utopians" or a "new class" trying to impose their values and vision on others; nuclear opponents are protesters in search of a cause.

1.27 Nuclear power opponents are hysterical, afraid of change, opposed to technological progress, naive and panicky, neo-Luddites, pastoralists.

1.28 "Too cheap to meter" quote.

1.29 Safety record of nuclear power plants is excellent.

1.30 Chernobyl is contrasted with TMI to make the point that radiation was contained at TMI; Chernobyl couldn't happen here.

1.31 U.S. plants are different from and safer than Soviet plants.

1.32 Lessons for a safer future can be learned from TMI and Chernobyl; new procedures will be instituted that will reduce future risks.

2 Energy independence

    2.11   Rising oil prices have put a premium on nuclear power and other energy sources; have made them more attractive.

    2.12   Nuclear power is a better alternative than foreign oil (reasons implied rather than spelled out).

    2.21   The choice is between nuclear power and dependence on foreigners (especially Arabs).

    2.22   Nuclear power protects us from being blackmailed and exploited by others (especially Arabs).

3 Specific problems (but no general frame implied)

    3.11   No nukes (reasons unspecified); nuclear power is bad, plants should not be built (reasons unspecified).

    3.12   Radiation is harmful; can cause diseases, birth defects.

    3.13   Recovery from problems caused by TMI will be slow, costly, very expensive.

    3.15   The nuclear future is past, has ended; TMI is the beginning of the end for nuclear power.

    3.16   Earthquakes could cause problems for reactors.

    3.17   Evacuation plans are inadequate.

    3.18   Nuclear energy has serious problems.

    3.20   Nuclear energy is scary.

    3.22   Nuclear power plants are hazardous; need to be made safer than they currently are. Accidents can happen and might happen in the future.

    3.23   The nuclear waste problem is still unsolved; danger of accidents in transporting nuclear wastes.

    3.24   Nuclear proliferation (from breeder reactors) is a potential problem; danger of terrorist attack on nuclear plants.

    3.27   We should put more money into the development of solar energy; a Manhattan project for solar energy.

    3.28   People are being kept in the dark, information withheld, not getting the full story; claims that a plant is safe are made, but can they be believed?

    3.29   Contradictory information is given on what is happening (or what happened); claims contradict each other.

    3.30   Plant workers are not sufficiently protected.

4   Runaway

    4.11   TMI problems are new, unexpected ones, not something we have under control and understand.

    4.12   Nuclear technology is so complicated that one can't anticipate all of the problems that will arise.

    4.13   Link to nuclear bombs, destruction; Hiroshima, mushroom clouds.

    4.14   TMI is like the movie *The China Syndrome.*

    4.21   Officials may think (or say) that they have nuclear power under control, but they really don't. Nuclear energy is out of control, has a momentum of its own. We don't know what we have unleashed.

    4.22   Monster metaphor. Nuclear power is a monster (e.g., Frankenstein's monster) that is lying in wait and may wreak havoc upon us.

    4.23   Genie metaphor. Nuclear power is a genie that has been let out of its bottle.

    4.24   Dangers of nuclear power are hidden, invisible; like sitting on a time bomb; one doesn't even know if one has been injured until many years later.

    4.27   Jokes about being irradiated and other forms of gallows humor about nuclear catastrophes.

    4.29   The only safety is running like hell, praying, using good luck charms, and the like; there is really no place to run.

    4.32   Play on the concept of the China syndrome.

    4.33   Jokes about mutants.

    4.34   Dangers are too great to calculate in a cost–benefit analysis.

    4.35   It's ridiculous to say that the system worked at TMI just because the accident wasn't worse than it was. The system broke down, didn't work.

    4.36   Slogan: "Chernobyl is everywhere."

    4.37   Image of a reactor out of control, spewing dangerous radiation.

5   Soft paths

    5.11   If we conserve more and use our energy more efficiently, we won't have to change our way of life.

5.13 Radioactive wastes are part of the general problem of toxic wastes and environmental pollution that is plaguing our society.

5.21 Wrong type of technology; contrasted with alternative energy sources such as solar, wood, thermal, and wind energy; contrasted with ecologically safer, renewable, decentralized sources.

5.22 Conservation and changes in lifestyle as alternatives to nuclear energy.

5.23 Nuclear power plants threaten ecology and the environment; threaten marine life.

5.24 If we didn't have a lifestyle that wasted so much energy on needless gadgets, we wouldn't be endangering the planet with nuclear energy.

6 No public accountability

6.13 Initial reports underestimated the seriousness of the TMI accident; the TMI company misled the public and officials about the possibility and/or seriousness of the accident; information on safety hazards has been consistently underestimated.

6.15 TMI company lax, incompetent, too slow to react.

6.16 TMI company trying to escape responsibility for errors, passing on costs to consumers. Class action suits charge company with liability.

6.17 Company officials are more concerned about their public image than they are about the public's safety.

6.18 Russian secrecy about the Chernobyl accident was comparable to American secrecy about TMI.

6.19 There is insufficient public accountability by those who control nuclear power.

6.21 Corporate greed leads (led) to cutting corners, sloppy construction, rushing into operation prematurely; profits emphasized at the expense of safety.

6.22 Government regulation is ineffective, part of the problem; regulators are dominated by industry, have buddy–buddy relationships.

6.23 Nuclear companies are arrogant, contemptuous of the public, and insensitive to legitimate concerns.

6.24 Nuclear companies have a conflict of interest; private nuclear companies generally have an incentive to withhold negative information about nuclear power to protect their interests.

6.25   Karen Silkwood is used as an exemplar to draw the lesson of a company covering up safety violations.

6.26   United States is trying to keep benefits of nuclear power technology from other nations to make profits bigger for American companies.

6.28   Nuclear companies and utilities ignore human costs in order to make as much money as possible.

7   Not cost effective

7.11   It was once said, unrealistically, that nuclear power would produce electricity "too cheap to meter."

7.21   Nuclear power is not cost effective; the trade-off between risks/ costs and benefits is unfavorable; no sense continuing with it. Hasn't proved to be as cheap as was originally hoped.

7.25   List of problems, implying that collectively they make nuclear power an impractical alternative.

7.26   Coal and other fossil fuels are more practical, cost-effective alternatives to nuclear power (but no mention of "soft paths" such as solar energy).

8   Devil's bargain

8.11   NIMBY position: Nuclear power is okay, but not in my backyard.

8.21   Pros and cons are balanced. Nuclear power is needed (necessary), but also has the potential to destroy and should be treated warily.

8.22   The energy independence dilemma: Our dependence on foreign oil makes us vulnerable to exploitation and blackmail, but nuclear power has too many problems of its own to make it a satisfactory solution to this problem.

8.23   The devil's bargain metaphor: We are committed to nuclear power and we may need it, but eventually there will be an enormous price to pay. It's a Faustian bargain.

8.24   Nuclear power has us trapped in a dilemma. We can't live with it, and we can't live without it. We're damned if we do and damned if we don't.

8.25   Swamp or quagmire metaphor: We've gotten ourselves in, and now it is hard or impossible to get out.

9   No codeable frame

9.11   Unclear what the quote is saying or claiming.

9.12 Causes of the TMI accident are unclear; there is confusion about what is happening, but no attribution of blame is made.

9.13 People are anxious and nervous about nuclear power; the future of nuclear energy is unclear.

9.14 The TMI accident will cause increases in utility rates, economic hardship, and other problems for residents of the area.

9.15 The immediate solution to the problem of TMI is unclear.

9.16 A combination of technical and human errors was responsible for the TMI accident.

9.17 Opposition to nuclear power is growing.

9.18 Fatalism. Accidents will happen. If one's time has come, that's it; no point in worrying about it. Like an act of God.

9.19 Other countries are more dependent on nuclear energy and need it more than we do.

9.20 Pure gag. No frame on nuclear power.

9.21 More careful regulation is needed.

9.22 More research is needed.

9.23 Russians are given to secrecy, as shown by their not being forthcoming about the accident at Chernobyl.

ARAB–ISRAELI CONFLICT

Feuding neighbors

The Arabs and Israelis are fractious peoples. Like the Hatfields and McCoys, each is convinced that it is aggrieved. Each new attack keeps the feud going, stimulating further retaliation by the other side. In such a blood feud, neither side deserves much sympathy, and claims of justice and entitlement can be safely ignored. A plague on both houses.

The problem is that such a local quarrel can spread to engulf the whole world. Take World War I as an exemplar. A local assassination in the Balkans set off a chain of events that eventually drew the major powers into a world war. American concern should be with the innocent bystanders who are hurt in such a feud and with the danger that it will spread into an even larger conflict. For visual images, try a time bomb or a tinder box that any stray spark can set aflame.

The root cause of the conflict is the destructive cycle of hostile acts that stimulate a hostile response, and the unwillingness of both sides to forget the injuries of the past and make peace. The Camp David accord was a hopeful sign, since it represented at least a partial reconciliation and an end to the feud. The participants should learn to live and let live. Let bygones be bygones. The United States should try to mediate the dispute as best it can, but it should avoid taking major risks that would involve America directly in the fighting in the Middle East.

Strategic interest

Action in the Middle East must be seen as part of the global chess game with the Soviet Union. The example of Soviet military aid to various countries of the Middle East and North Africa are examples of Soviet designs. The lesson is clear: The Soviet Union is actively seeking to expand its influence in the Middle East. The Soviet role in the conflict is exclusively a mischievous one. The Soviet Union gains by exploiting the indigenous conflict in the region for its own imperial aims.

The core issue is how best to pursue U.S. strategic interests in the Middle East vis-à-vis the Soviet Union. Without Soviet exploitation of the issues, Arab–Israeli conflict would be resolvable or, at the least, could be contained and localized. The most profound danger to world peace is a Soviet success in the Middle East that would upset the world balance of power, thereby greatly increasing Western vulnerability and the Soviet temptation to exploit it.

Arab intransigence

On one side, a few million Israelis. On the other side, twenty Arab countries with a population of 100 million. Through ingenuity, resourcefulness, and courage, the beleaguered Jewish settlement in Palestine was able to forestall the attack of five Arab armies. David versus Goliath.

The world must believe those who say that they want to push the Jews into the sea or destroy the state of Israel. Hitler made his intentions clear, but the West watched without resisting as he acquired the means and began carrying out his designs. Never again. With a state of their own, Jews have the means of organizing their own self-defense.

Zionism is the national movement of the Jewish people, and the UN resolution condemning it as racism was an obscenity. It reflected the political power of a large bloc of implacable enemies of Israel in the UN. The UN does not function as a neutral arbiter interested in peace but as a partisan instrument of the Arab side in the conflict. Although Goliath cannot use his size advantage to crush David militarily, he can use it to win political victories. Arab leaders, who proclaim their undying enmity to and hatred of Israel, brandish weapons and are feted in the halls of diplomacy.

The core of the conflict is the unwillingness of the Arab world to accept Israel's right to exist. The Sadat visit to Jerusalem was a historic breakthrough that went to the root of the issue. But Sadat was isolated in the Arab world, and his death was greeted with open joy in most Arab countries. The conflict will not end as long as Arab zealots, unwilling to make peace with Israel, continue to be the dominant force in most of the Arab world. The United States has a moral obligation to help Israel survive in a hostile environment and to encourage the Arab countries to accept Israel's right to exist.

Israeli expansionism

Israel is an expansionist European settler state and an alien presence in the Middle East. It serves as an instrument of American control over the resources of the Middle East and the Arab people. The Zionist entity is the attack dog of its American master. It is comparable to other settler states that have tried to maintain dominance over the indigenous population of a region. Witness South Africa or Rhodesia.

Zionism is racism. Arab violence in opposition to it is a symptom and a response to injustice. The members of the Palestine Liberation Organization (PLO) are freedom fighters, using the only means available to a stateless people. Sadat, by making a separate peace with Israel without requiring progress on the Palestinian issue, betrayed the Arab cause. By removing the threat of war, he left the Palestinians and their Arab allies at the mercy of the Zionist entity, armed to the teeth with the latest American technology.

The root of the conflict is Israeli intransigence and a desire for more territory, as well as the effort of the United States to maintain domination of the region. American military support increases Israeli intransigence.

Dual liberation

There are two national liberation movements in the Middle East, in conflict over the same land. Palestinian Arabs and Jews can both make a legitimate historical claim. But history is less important to human justice than present human reality. Whatever should have happened 2,000 years ago, or 200 years ago, or 20 years ago, today both an Israeli people and a Palestinian people exist. Any workable solution must respect the national aspirations and right to self-determination of *both* peoples. A conflict between two incompatible rights can be solved only by compromise. Israel *and* Palestine, not one or the other.

Palestinian and other Arab spokesmen must accept Israel's right to exist as a Jewish state in the Middle East. Israel, at the same time, should accept the fact that the Palestinian issue is not merely a refugee problem. It should recognize that a Palestinian national movement can be satisfied only by some form of Palestinian state. All people have a right to self-determination. The United States should work toward a compromise in which Israel's right to exist within secure, recognized borders is accepted and a Palestinian state is created. Land for peace.

Codes

Preparation and background. This code centers on the policy issue of what the United States should do, if anything, about the Arab–Israeli conflict in the Middle East. The events in this strip are enormously complicated and frequently involve issues other than Arab–Israeli conflict. For example, some of them occur near national elections, and there is commentary about the potential impact on American domestic politics. Some are commentaries on conflicts other than the Arab–Israeli one – for example, on Anglo–American conflict.

It is important to remember that not all commentary on the relevant events is commentary about the issue of Arab–Israeli conflict. If in doubt, use the following strategy: When you encounter an idea element that resembles something in one of our frames, ask yourself whether the idea is being suggested in the context of Arab–Israeli conflict (that is, ask yourself if the statement directly addresses this conflict). I will refer to this as the *context rule.*

The code is based on five central frames: *strategic interest, feuding neighbors, Arab intransigence, dual liberation,* and *Israeli expansionism.* Within these frames, we also consider variations – for example, Israeli-leaning and Arab-leaning variations of *strategic interest;* a Western imperialist variation of *Israeli expansionism,* and a Jewish conspiracy variation that can be part of different parent frames. The first step in learning the code is to read over these frames descriptions a few times. As usual, the first digit of the code refers to the frame, and the second and third digits refer to more specific idea elements under the general rubric.

References to the Arab oil weapon should be treated as a topic on which different frames have something different to say, rather than as an indicator of any particular frame.

The commentary you will be coding covers nine different time periods. So that you understand the general context, they are discussed briefly here:

1. May 1948: the establishment of the state of Israel and the Israeli war of independence. In 1947, the UN voted to end the British mandate in Palestine and to partition the land between the Jews and the Arabs there. The Soviet Union and the United States both supported this act, and it was accepted by the Jewish community in Palestine. The Arab states did not accept partition. The British tended to side with the Arabs, putting them in conflict with the United States, which tended to support Israel.

2. October–November 1956: the Sinai War. There are four national actors in this war: Egypt, Israel, Britain, and France. The latter three attacked Egypt and were opposed by the United States *and* the Soviet Union. This bizarre set of alliances makes this a confusing and difficult event to code. The easiest method is to distinguish the Israeli–Egyptian dispute from the one that the British and French had with Egypt over the nationalization of the Suez Canal. It is the British–French versus Egypt dispute that gets most of the attention and is, for us, *irrelevant.* We become concerned with the commentary *only when it focuses on the Israeli–Egyptian part of the dispute.* Note also that this event coincides with the Soviet invasion of Hungary, and commentary on this event, most of it irrelevant, may be combined with commentary on the Sinai War. There was also a Soviet threat to send "volunteers" into the Middle East to help the Egyptians, and this draws both relevant and irrelevant commentary. The context rule is important here to determine relevance.

3. June 1967: the Six Day War. Commentary about the fighting and who is winning is not relevant for us. Commentary about the origins of the conflict and what should be done about it after the war is over is likely to be relevant.

4. October 1973: the October War (or the Yom Kippur War). This event coincides with the Watergate scandal and draws irrelevant commentary on the implications of events in the Middle East for the outcome of this scandal.

5. November 1977: Sadat visit to Jerusalem. No special problems.

6. September 1978: Camp David accord. No special problems.

7. October 1981: the assassination of Sadat. No special problems.

8. September 1982. Two separate weeks during the war in Lebanon are included. The first corresponds to the Reagan plan, the evacuation of the PLO from Lebanon, and the introduction of U.S. peacekeeping forces. The second corresponds to the assassination of Bashir Gemayel and the massacre in the Sabra and Shatilla refugee camps in Lebanon.

9. March 1988: two weeks corresponding to the Schultz diplomatic initiative; this occurs about three months into the *intifada.*

1   Strategic interest

If the theme that there is a larger global power game that provides the key to understanding what is happening in the Middle East came up, those comments were not coded as part of this code. For example a comment about the conflict between England, France, and the United States or about the cold war in general, making no connection to the Arab-Israeli conflict, would not be coded here.

111   The United States has important interests in the Middle East (but not put in the context of the cold war). The United States has interests tied up with both sides in the conflict.

112   There are important natural resources such as oil at stake in the Middle East (but not put in the context of Soviet control of these resources or the cold war).

113   The Suez Canal is strategically important in the East–West struggle.

121   Actions in the Middle East are part of a global conflict with the Soviet Union; must be seen as part of the cold war. The core issue is how best to pursue America's interests vis-à-vis the Soviet Union. The defense of the free world is at stake.

122   The Soviet Union is exploiting the Arab–Israeli conflict to gain control and advantage over the United States and other Western countries in the Middle East. Its role there is a mischievous, not a constructive, one.

123   Russia has a long history of trying to take over countries in the Middle East and expand its empire there. Examples from the past are given.

124   The beauty of the Camp David accord is that it excluded the Soviet Union from the process.

125   There are indigenous conflicts in the region, but they could be contained and localized if it were not for the Soviet exploitation of them.

126   The most profound danger to world peace is the kind of Soviet success in the Middle East that would upset the world balance of power, thereby increasing Western vulnerability and the Soviet temptation to exploit it.

128   The United States (and other Western countries) have their vital oil supply at stake in the conflict. War in the Middle East threatens

the disruption of our oil lifeline. (Note: The threat is from the *outbreak of hostilities* rather than from Arab blackmail.)

129　Soviet hypocrisy: pretending to be for peace and justice while cynically furthering their selfish interests.

13 – Arab-leaning variation.

131　It is important to support our friends in the Arab world (with weapons if necessary) or they will turn to the Soviet Union.

132　It is important to support our friends in the Arab world or we will no longer have access to their oil.

133　It is important to support our friends in the Arab world, since there are many Arab countries (and only one Israel) and many more Arabs than Israelis.

134　The Arab oil weapon is a new fact of life that shifts our strategic interest. We should make special efforts to keep on good terms with oil-producing Arab states, even if this means ending our "special relationship" with Israel. Our policies should reflect the increased importance of this objective.

14 – Israeli-leaning variation.

141　It is important to support Israel because it has proved to be an effective, reliable, stable ally in the struggle with the Soviet Union.

142　Arab countries make unreliable, ineffective allies.

143　To prevent vulnerability to economic blackmail, we should make special efforts to reduce our dependence on Arab oil. Otherwise, our strategic interest may be compromised.

144　Arab oil boycott threatens vital U.S. strategic interests.

145　Arab defeat is a defeat for the Soviet Union, defeat for Soviet policy.

15 – Jewish conspiracy variation.

Use this code only when a statement is put in the context of U.S. strategic interest.

151　The United States is prevented from pursuing its true strategic interests in the Middle East by the power of the Israeli lobby and/ or American Jews.

2   Feuding neighbors

*Look for the theme that this is a fight that doesn't concern the United
States unless we inadvertently get dragged into it. General expressions of the
goal of keeping the peace are insufficient unless put in the context of Arab–
Israeli conflict. Do not, for example, include the idea that the Anglo–French–
Egyptian conflict might spread and lead to World War III.*

211   Innocent bystanders are being hurt (but no implications about
      who is to blame or what the conflict is about).

212   The Sadat visit and the Camp David accord were helpful steps,
      since they represent at least a partial reconciliation and end to
      the feud.

213   The event (e.g., Sadat assassination) suggests how fragile peace
      is in the Middle East and how unstable the region is.

214   Neither side really seems to want peace.

215   The conflict hasn't gone away. The differences that divide the
      Arabs and the Israelis are still there.

216   The two sides are behaving reasonably, trying to patch up their
      long-standing differences; event is a ray of hope, a step toward
      peace; Carter is struggling to get the peace process going.

221   The United States should try to mediate the dispute but should
      be careful not to take any major risks that would involve us
      directly in the fighting in the Middle East.

222   The reasons that the Arabs and Israelis are fighting isn't impor-
      tant. It's a feud in which each new attack creates a new grievance,
      produces retaliation, and keeps the feud going.

223   Neither side deserves sympathy. A plague on both their houses.

224   The issue is whether this local conflict will spread to engulf the
      whole world.

225   Examples of other local conflicts that spread (for example, an
      assassination in the Balkans that set off a chain of events that
      drew the major powers into World War I).

226   Hatfield–McCoy metaphor or another metaphor of a meaningless
      feud.

227   The conflict is self-perpetuating. It is about itself. It is a cycle of
      conflict in which hostile acts stimulate hostile responses. The wars

are senseless, don't settle anything, and just lead to more wars in the future.

228 The Middle East is a tinder box that any spark can ignite or a bomb that might go off at any minute.

229 The warring parties should forget the injuries or injustices of the past and make peace. Live and let live. Let bygones be bygones.

231 Blood is being spilled in the Holy Land; endless strife and feuding in the land of the Bible.

232 The fractious peoples and countries of the Middle East need a strong, mature authority to keep them from destroying each other and dragging in the rest of the world.

233 The UN offers a possible path to peace.

234 Innocent Lebanese people suffer from the war.

235 Israel victory was a Pyrrhic one; it cost more than it gained.

237 U.S. taxpayers pay the price for trying to keep the peace in the Middle East.

238 U.S. peacekeepers in Lebanon are trapped, in danger.

239 The United States shouldn't side with either party in this senseless conflict.

240 War in the Middle East threatens to wreck detente.

241 The superpower competition and the Middle East arms race threaten world peace; superpowers shouldn't meddle in Arab–Israeli conflict, make matters worse.

242 Superpowers should act in concert to pursue peace in the Middle East.

243 The United States makes matter worse by arming both sides.

244 The UN has handled situation badly, failed to act as real peacekeeper.

3 Arab intransigence
311 The Jewish people have a long history of oppression (but not explicitly linked to Arab–Israeli conflict).

312 The legitimacy of the partition of Palestine by the UN resolution and, hence, the legitimacy of the state of Israel. (Note: If the Arab refusal to accept the resolution is mentioned, then code it 322.)

313 Israel is worthy of American moral support as the only democracy in the Middle East.

314 Israel is worthy of American moral support because of the Holocaust.

If there is a linking of Arab hostility with the Nazis, then code it 325.

316 The creation of the state of Israel is a healthy, positive development.

317 The creation of the state of Israel is the fulfillment of a promise from God; it has biblical sanction.

318 Contrast between Israeli efforts to develop the land and Arab neglect; between Israeli economic progress and Arab backwardness.

321 The David and Goliath metaphor, with Israel as David. (Note: Don't confuse this metaphor with a later play on it: "David has become Goliath"; see code 528.)

322 Arab refusal to accept the UN resolution that partitioned Palestine into Jewish and Arab territory shows Arab responsibility for the conflict. Contrast between Israel's acceptance of partition and willingness for peace and Arabs rejection of it.

323 The one-sidedness of the conflict, with 100 times as many Arabs as Jews and twenty Arab countries against tiny Israel. Israel as surrounded by enemies who would destroy it.

324 The desire of the Arabs to destroy Israel and to push the Jews into the sea. Arab unwillingness to accept the existence of a Jewish state in the Middle East.

325 The relevance of the Holocaust and Hitler's attempt to destroy the Jews for the Arab–Israeli conflict. "Never again."

326 The unfairness of equating Zionism, the national movement of the Jewish people, with racism.

327 The UN is controlled by Israel's enemies. It functions as a partisan instrument of the Arab side rather than as a broker interested in peace. Arab political warfare against Israel in the UN.

328 Examples or quotations from Arab leaders who proclaim their undying enmity to and hatred of Israel.

329 Examples of terrorist acts against Israeli civilians to illustrate Arab intransigence and hostile intentions.

331 Sadat visit was an important breakthrough, but Sadat was repudiated by other Arabs and eventually assassinated. His death was greeted with joy in most Arab countries. Arab hard-liners hope for failure of the peace efforts; lack of acceptance of Camp David accord by Arab hard-liners; PLO as an obstacle to peace.

332 Arab zealots, unwilling to make peace with Israel, have the upper hand, and moderate voices in the Arab world are suppressed.

333 Arab political and economic warfare against Israel prior to Sinai War or Six Day War, including the closing of the Suez Canal to Israeli shipping, terrorist or *fedayeen* raids from Egypt, and the blockade of the Strait of Tiran in the Red Sea.

334 Arab economic boycott against Israel.

335 The Arab oil weapon increases the threat to the survival of Israel, since it adds a potent economic weapon to the political and military weapons that the Arabs have always used against Israel.

341 Arabs are tricky, devious, untrustworthy.

342 Arabs are hypocritical in expressing a desire for peace; they haven't given up the idea of destroying Israel.

343 PLO setback in Lebanon hasn't made them give up their dream of destroying Israel; PLO survives and is still venomous.

344 Arabs blame others, try to escape responsibility; delude themselves; make war and bring suffering on themselves.

4 Dual liberation

It is easy to confuse this frame with the feuding neighbors *frame. The essential difference is that this frame emphasizes two* rights *in conflict, whereas* feuding neighbors *emphasizes two wrongs or, more accurately, fighting about nothing important. For example, the idea that the Arabs and Israel should work out their* unspecified *differences and stop fighting is* feuding neighbors. *It becomes dual liberation only with the additional idea that there is something legitimate that they are fighting about. For* dual liberation, *the conflict is real, and not just the result of misunderstanding.*

Note also that both *sides' rights must be acknowledged before this frame applies. To emphasize Israel's right to exist by itself implies Arab intransigence, whereas to emphasize only Palestinian rights implies Israeli expansionism (see the next frame). It is only by including both that the dual liberation frame is invoked.*

411 Some compromise is necessary (but no clear indication of two rights in conflict).

412 The Palestinian issue is more than simply a refugee problem, since it includes a legitimate Palestinian desire for some form of self-determination.

413 The UN partition of Palestine is a just solution. (Note: If this idea is used to make the point of Arab lack of acceptance of Israel, this would be coded as 322.)

421 The conflict is between two national liberation movements with a legitimate historical claim to the same land. Palestinian Arabs and Jews both have historical rights.

422 Two peoples exist and have rights – Israel and Palestine. Any workable solution must respect the national aspirations and rights to self-determination of *both* peoples.

423 Israel has a right to live within secure, recognized borders, and the Palestinians have a right to a national home or state of their own.

424 Examples of other warring peoples who have come to live in peace with each other through compromise and partition.

425 Desirability of simultaneous, mutual recognition of the rights of both sides. Palestinians and Arab states should simultaneously accept the right of Israel to exist, and Israel should accept the principle of some form of Palestinian state.

426 The Sadat visit and the Camp David accord improve the atmosphere and are an important step toward Arab recognition of Israel but, to bring peace, the Palestinian issue must also be addressed.

427 The United States should promote a compromise in which Israel's right to exist within secure, recognized borders is accepted and some sort of Palestinian state is created.

5 Israeli expansionism

We include two basic variations of this frame. One of them, Western imperialism, *presents Israel as a tool of the United States; the other,* Jewish conspiracy, *presents the United States as a tool of Israel through Jewish control of American foreign policy. There are many references to imperialism in the British–French–Egyptian dispute in 1956, but code these only when Israel is brought in as an agent of British–French imperialism.*

Western imperialism

511 Some Arab countries act in collusion with American oil companies and as American client states. (Note: The lineup here changes, currently including Saudi Arabia, Jordan, the oil emirates, and Egypt.)

521 Israel is an instrument of American imperialism, being used to maintain control over the resources of the Middle East and to dominate the Arab people.

522 Israel is an instrument of Anglo–French imperialism.

523 Israel is a colonial settler state like South Africa. It is used to maintain dominance over the indigenous population of the region by an outside Western minority.

524 Zionism is racism.

525 The members of the PLO are freedom fighters, using the only means available to a stateless people. Their violence is understandable, and is justified in seeking national liberation and justice for the Palestinian people.

526 Sadat betrayed the Arab cause by making a separate peace with Israel without requiring progress on the Palestinian issue. He left the Palestinians and their Arab allies at the mercy of the Zionist entity.

527 Israel is a client state of the United States, which arms it to the teeth with the latest American military technology.

528 Israel is constantly expanding, trying to take over more and more Arab territory and to dominate its Arab neighbors.

529 Israel is a powerful bully. David has become Goliath.

Israeli intransigence

531 Israel resists efforts at peace; has no real interest in peace.

532 Israel complains about its press coverage and tries to restrict the press because it doesn't like the ugliness that it sees in the mirror.

533 The United States lets Israel push it around, against its own real interests and principles of justice. Israel is the tail that wags the American dog. No one can control Israel.

534 Israel is brutal and unjust in its treatment of Palestinians.

535 Even American Jews are appalled at Israeli brutality and treatment of Palestinians.

536 Israel has reduced Lebanon to rubble.

537 Palestinians are now the victims, as the Jews once were.

538 Israel tries to escape responsibility for massacres and other destructive acts.

539 Israeli hard-liners are an obstacle to peace.

6 Jewish conspiracy

611 There is a Jewish (or Israeli) lobby with a lot of influence on American foreign policy. (But there is no clear implication that this influence is sinister, or is more than it should be, or is used to produce undesirable ends.)

621 American Jews place loyalty to Israel above loyalty to the United States. All Jews care about is Israel.

622 Jews control the banks and mass media in America, and use this undue power to sway American foreign policy inappropriately in a pro-Israeli direction.

9 No frame codeable

911 Uninterpretable comment.

912 Implications for American domestic politics are emphasized, with no codeable statement about Arab–Israeli conflict.

913 American policy is inconsistent and in disarray.

914 Peace is possible. We need a fresh start toward peace. (But no clear frame is implied on how it can be achieved.)

915 Descriptions of or comments on how the fighting or war is going, on who is winning or losing, but with no larger frame on the conflict implied.

916 There is intense diplomatic maneuvering to resolve the crisis.

917 The Western alliance is in disarray.

918 The Anglo–French–Egyptian conflict may lead to World War III.

919 Arab states don't really care about the PLO.

920 Israelis are critical of their own government's actions.

921 Phalangists as villains, but not identified with Israel.

922 Airborne warning and command systems (AWACS) sale is anti-Israel.

923 Sadat is a peacemaker; the world mourns the death of Sadat as a man of peace.

924 Comments on Kissinger, but with no general frame on Arab–Israeli conflict.

925 Irony that some people who oppose the war in Vietnam support helping Israel in its Middle East war.

926 Arabs are in disarray, lack unity.

927 UN is ineffective, mistaken in its peace efforts, trying to claim credit that it doesn't deserve.

928 Anti-Semitism in the United States is discredited.

929 Carter is inept.

Notes

Chapter 1

1. Snow and Benford also define collective action frames as "emergent," but this seems an unwise inclusion. Changes in political consciousness can occur at various points, sometimes well in advance of mobilization. They may have already emerged by the time mobilization occurs, awaiting only some change in the political opportunity structure to precipitate action. In other cases, they may emerge gradually, developing most fully after some initial collective action. Emergence should not be made a matter of definition.
2. Affirmative action for women involves some overlap as an issue domain, but with some important differences. The overall symbolism and meaning are sufficiently distinct that it requires separate analysis; our attention here is focused on affirmative action for racial and ethnic minorities. Unfortunately, this leaves us without an issue that would appear to engage a gender cleavage. However, surveys of public attitudes on nuclear power going back to the 1950s show a large and consistent gender gap, with women much more opposed to nuclear power than men. Nelkin (1981) has a particularly insightful treatment of this gender gap on nuclear power.

Chapter 2

1. Actually, we conducted many more, but as in any research project, we treated some of these as pretests, lost some materials through technical failures, and disqualified some groups because, after the fact, we learned that they failed to meet our selection criteria.
2. This stratum is generally estimated at anywhere from one-fifth to one-third of the population. See Neuman (1986) for a good discussion of the "three publics," including a politically involved group of 10 to 15 percent and a very large "middle mass" who are marginally attentive to politics but accept the duty to vote and the norm that it is important to keep informed to some degree about current events. Neuman warns against the dangers of confusing this middle mass with the apolitical stratum that does not vote or attend to politics at all.
3. For exact wordings of these questions, see Appendix A.
4. All names of participants used in this book are invented ones.
5. Eisenstadt (1984), working with David Riesman and Robert J. Potter, carried out research in the late 1950s designed to map the domain of sociable interaction, and many of her categories and observations are helpful here. To use her distinction based on the types of relationships among participants, the participants in our peer groups can best be described as "familiar acquaintances." Familiar acquaintances see each other frequently, but not necessarily as a result of personal choice. Rather, they are thrown together by virtue of work, neighborhood residence, or construction of a group for social researchers. The norms governing their sociable interaction, she argues, are different from those operating among close friends, strangers, or other kinds of acquaintances.

6. "In purely sociable conversation," Simmel (1950, 52) observes, "the topic is merely the indispensable medium through which the lively exchange of speech itself unfolds its attractions. . . . For any conversation to remain satisfied with mere form it cannot allow any content to become significant in its own right. As soon as the discussion . . . makes the ascertainment of truth its *purpose* . . . it ceases to be sociable and thus becomes untrue to its own nature."

7. Eisenstadt (1984) uses a similar concept to describe a conversational style that she labels *conventional nihilism*. In it, people understate their private commitments to others and to institutions as they join in making fun of them. "The conversation dramatized and distorted the negative characteristics, making them grotesque, and therefore funny," she writes. Her examples include stories about the army, graduate student conversations about their professors at the university, and conversations about doctors. These nihilistic assaults, she observes, were usually directed against powerful targets on whom the speakers shared a dependency. Typically, they were expressed in the legendary style referred to previously.

8. The details of how and what we sampled are contained in Appendix A.

9. This limitation means that some of the differences that one observes over time may be a reflection of different types of critical discourse moments. An accident at a nuclear power plant, for example, is a very different kind of event from a site occupation by protesters. Of course, some observations may hold for very different types of critical discourse moments. It is also possible, in some cases, to compare differences over time where the type of critical discourse moment is held constant – for example, different Supreme Court decisions on affirmative action.

Chapter 3

1. One should not make too much of this difference. The affirmative action issue is an indirect vehicle for black indignation compared to direct manifestations of economic inequality such as unemployment and substandard housing.

2. The other media samples show a very similar overall pattern.

Chapter 4

1. As indicated in Appendix A, a frame is considered visible if it has a prominence of at least 10 percent on one of the four media samples.

2. It takes only one person with such an experience to make it part of the conversation. Less than 5 percent of the participants bring in such incidents. Of course, others may have had them at some point but did not see them as relevant to the discussion.

3. *Time* magazine, Dec. 5, 1977, p. 58.

4. James Reston column, Dec. 2, 1977.

5. Nicholas von Hoffman column, Dec. 10, 1977.

6. Art Buchwald column, Dec. 11, 1977.

7. *Time* magazine, July 10, 1978.

8. *NBC News,* June 27, 1979.

9. The *New York Times,* Aug. 25, 1981, p. 1.

10. *Time Magazine,* June 25, 1984, 63.

11. *NBC News,* June 12, 1984.

12. Media Institute (1979).

13. Jeremiah Murphy column, May 2, 1977.

14. *Time* magazine, Oct. 29, 1973, p. 56.

Chapter 5

1. I regret not having chosen an issue with a greater potential for making gender relevant – for example, abortion. Although public opinion polls show a very large and consistent gender gap on nuclear power (with women being much less favorable than men), gender is never treated as a relevant social cleavage in discussions of nuclear power.

2. Lofland (1989) and McCarthy and Wolfson (1992) write of *consensus movements*, the latter defining them as "organized movements for change that find *widespread support for their goals* and *little or no organized opposition* from the population of a geographic community." The movement against drunk driving provides an example. But widespread support for the broadest goals of a movement doesn't tell us much about whether there will be organized opposition. This depends on how a group translates its goals into action imperatives. Within the same movement, different social movement organizations vary in how they frame the issue and in the form and targets of their action. The peace and environmental movements provide examples of a range of more consensual and more adversarial groups. It seems more useful to speak of consensus *frames* or consensus *strategies* rather than to treat this as a property of movements.

3. J. Gamson (1989) develops this argument in his analysis of the dynamics and activities of the AIDS activist group ACT-UP and its struggle with the problem of the "invisible enemy." Cohen (1985) and Melucci (1989) emphasize the centrality and importance of issues of collective identity in movements that emphasize cultural change and target civil society.

4. See Bluestone, Harrison, and Baker (1981) for a nontechnical presentation of this frame directed at labor movement activists and their allies.

5. As indicated in Appendix A, visibility is defined as a prominence score of at least 10 percent on any one of the four media samples.

6. Participants frequently used the second person plural rather than the first person plural to refer to themselves. For example, "They will take whatever they can get from you everytime if you let them" is treated as equivalent to "They will take whatever they can get from us everytime if we let them."

7. This also occurs in one white group. White groups do not use racial categories explicitly, but may do so implicitly in the use of such categories as *common people* or *working people*. The extent to which such symbols exclude people of color is unclear, and Halle's (1984) evidence suggests that they frequently may imply white working people.

8. I refer here to adversaries within American society. An American–Japanese adversarial frame is quite visible on troubled industry, and Soviet–American and Arab–Israeli adversaries are central in framing that issue.

Chapter 7

1. See Chapters 2, 3, 4, and 5.

2. Groups often use different shared frames at different points in the discussion, employing some quite briefly while elaborating others at length and at many points. I counted as their shared frame the one used most extensively in the total conversation in analyzing the resources used to construct it.

Chapter 8

1. I use the term *theme* in two slightly different ways – inclusively to refer to themes and counterthemes together, and as shorthand for the mainstream or dominant member of the pair. The context indicates which of these meanings is intended.

2. These pairs are not intended to be exhaustive. They are chosen because of their relevance for at least one of the four issues considered here.

3. We encountered both of these groups earlier in Chapter 3, discussing affirmative action.

4. Gamson and Modigliani (1989, 14) note one significant exception to this compartmentalization. In the late 1950s and early 1960s, a movement against the atmospheric testing of nuclear weapons called public attention to the long-range dangers of radiation. Some of this increased awareness about radiation dangers spilled over into concern about nuclear reactors. But the dualism was reestablished with the signing of the Limited Test Ban Treaty of 1963, which ended atmospheric testing of nuclear weapons.

Chapter 9

1. To be exact, highly engaged groups were defined as having (a) two or more people who often talk about it (and less than half who rarely or never talk about it); (b) at least half who read some or a lot about it; and (c) at least half who are very interested in it. Unengaged groups had (a) half or more who rarely or never talk about it (and fewer than two who often talk about it); (b) at least half who rarely or never read about it (or fewer than two who read about it quite a lot); and (c) less than half who are very interested in it. Any groups that met neither the high engagement nor the unengaged definition were coded as having moderate engagement.

2. These measures did not meet the intercoder reliability criterion of 80 percent, but there is no reason to suspect any systematic bias, since all coders made their ratings independently, without knowledge of the questionnaire responses. They flagged two or more high-intensity moments in 70 percent of the conversations of highly engaged groups on affirmative action; in unengaged groups, two or more high-intensity moments were identified in only 44 percent. Coder ratings of overall engagement level showed similar results. In groups scoring high by the questionnaire responses, coders rated the engagement level high 60 percent of the time in the conversations, compared to 33 percent high in the groups scoring low from questionnaire data.

Chapter 10

1. The Boolean approach uses binary data. There are two conditions or states: true (or present) and false (or absent). Hence, all measures must be transformed into dichotomies. Since the engagement measure used here has three categories and the distribution for whites and blacks is quite different, I used a different cutting point. The presence of this condition in black groups means high engagement (compared to moderate engagement); in white groups, the presence of this condition means either high or moderate engagement (compared to low engagement).

Table 10.1 *Conditions for collective action frames on affirmative action*

| | Condition | | Outcome | Frequency |
B	*E*	*I*	*CA*	*N*
0	0	0	0	4
0	0	1	1	5
0	1	0	1	2
0	1	1	1	6
1	0	0	0	4
1	0	1	1	5
1	1	0	0	4
1	1	1	1	$\frac{4}{34}$

B = race of group: 1 = black; 0 = white (interracial groups excluded).

E = engagement: 1 = high for black groups, high or moderate for white groups; 0 = moderate for black groups, unengaged for white groups.

I = integrated resource strategy: 1 = present; 0 = absent

CA = collective action frame: 1 = at least two of the three defining elements are present in a majority of the groups; 0 = anything else.

Ragin's method begins with the construction of a truth table for every possible combination of the three conditions. An entry of "1" indicates that the condition is present; "O" means that it is absent. The outcome variable – in this case, a tendency to develop collective action frames – is considered present if a majority of the groups in this combination of conditions exhibit it. Table 10.1 uses the weaker measure of collective action frames: the presence of any two of the three elements.

This truth table indicates that five of the eight combinations produce this outcome in a majority of the groups. There are straightforward rules in the Boolean approach for simplifying complexity. The most fundamental of these rules, as Ragin states it, is: "If two Boolean expressions differ in only one causal condition yet produce the same outcome, then the causal condition that distinguishes the two expressions can be considered irrelevant and can be removed to create a simpler, combined expression." Applying this minimization rule to Table 10.1 gives the following equations (where uppercase indicates presence and lowercase indicates absence). The initial equation,

$$CA = beI + bEI + BeI + BEI + bEi$$

reduces to,

$$CA = I(be + bE + Be + BE) + bE = I(b + B) + bE$$

which reduces to

$$CA = I + bE$$

2. See Ryan (1991) for an excellent discussion of the full range of strategic issues for organizers in the complex transaction between movements and media.

3. Most of my evidence for this assertion comes from my experiences with SIMSOC, a game simulation of a society with great inequality and power differences (Gamson 1991). Wherever possible, I attempt to maximize learning by inverting roles that people play in their daily lives. When adults who normally exercise considerable power and control are placed in weak and dependent positions in the game, they frequently claim new insights based on their personal experience of powerlessness.

Appendix A

1. This argument is elaborated in Calder (1977).

Appendix C

1. This was actually a collective brief, with B'nai B'rith being joined by an AFL-CIO local, the Jewish Labor Committee, the Jewish Commission on Law and Public Affairs (COLPA), and UNICO (an Italian-American community service and public affairs organization).

References

Alger, Horatio. 1962. *Ragged Dick*. New York: Macmillan.

Alinsky, Saul. 1972. *Rules for Radicals*. New York: Random House.

Alperovitz, Gar and Jeff Faux. 1982. "The Youngstown Project," pp. 353–69, in Frank Lindenfeld and Joyce Rothschild-Whitt (eds.), *Workplace Democracy and Social Change*. Boston: Porter Sargent.

Belenky, Mary F., Blythe McVicker Clinchy, Nancy R. Goldberger, and Jill M. Tarule. 1986. *Women's Ways of Knowing: The Development of Self, Voice, and Mind*. New York: Basic Books.

Bennett, W. Lance. 1975. *The Political Mind in the Political Environment*. Lexington, MA: D.C. Heath.

1988. *News: The Politics of Illusion*. New York: Longman.

Bennett, William L. and Perry Eastland. 1978. "Why Bakke Won't End Reverse Discrimination: 1," *Commentary* 66: 29–35.

Berelson, Bernard, Paul Lazarsfeld, and William McPhee. 1954. *Voting*. Chicago: University of Chicago Press.

Bickel, Alexander. 1975. *The Morality of Consent*. New Haven, CT: Yale University Press.

Bluestone, Barry, Bennett Harrison, and Lawrence Baker. 1981. *Corporate Flight*. Washington, DC: Progressive Alliance.

Boyer, Paul. 1985. *By the Bomb's Early Light*. New York: Pantheon.

Calder, Bobby J. 1977. "Focus Groups and the Nature of Qualitative Marketing Research," *Journal of Marketing Research* 14: 353–64.

Canovan, Margaret. 1981. *Populism*. New York: Harcourt Brace Jovanovich.

Carbaugh, Donal. 1988. *Talking American: Cultural Discourse on DONAHUE*. Norwood, NJ: Ablex.

Chilton, Paul. 1987. "Metaphor, Euphemism, and the Militarization of Language," *Current Research on Peace and Violence* 10: 7–19.

Clinchy, Blythe McVicker. 1992. "Ways of Knowing and Ways of Being," in Andrew Garrod (ed.), *Emerging Theories in Moral Development*. New York: Teacher's College Press.

Cohen, Carl. 1979. "Why Racial Preference Is Illegal and Immoral," *Commentary* 67: 40–52.

Cohen, Jean L. 1985. "Strategy or Identity: New Theoretical Paradigms and Contemporary Social Movements," *Social Research* 52: 663–716.

Converse, Philip. 1975. "Public Opinion and Voting Behavior," Vol. 4, pp. 75–169, in Fred Greenstein and Nelson Polsby (eds.), *Handbook of Political Science*. Reading, MA: Addison-Wesley.

Dahl, Robert. 1967. *Pluralist Democracy in the United States.* Chicago: Rand-McNally.

Diamond, Edwin. 1975. *The Tin Kazoo: Television, Politics, and the News.* Cambridge, MA.: MIT Press.

Edelman, Murray J. 1988. *Constructing the Political Spectacle.* Chicago: University of Chicago Press.

Eisenstadt, Jeanne Watson. 1984. "Studies in Sociability," unpublished manuscript, 24280 Jerome, Oak Park, MI 48237.

Eliasoph, Nina. 1990. "Political Culture and the Presentation of a Political 'Self'," *Theory and Society,* 19: 465–94.

Ellul, Jacques. 1964. *The Technological Society.* New York: Knopf.

Epstein, Edward J. 1973. *News from Nowhere.* New York: Random House.

Fantasia, Rick. 1988. *Cultures of Solidarity.* Berkeley: University of California Press.

Fink, Rychard. 1962. "Introduction" to Horatio Alger's, *Ragged Dick.* New York: Macmillan.

Flacks, Richard. 1988. *Making History.* New York: Columbia University Press.

Freire, Paulo. 1970a. *Pedagogy of the Oppressed.* New York: Continuum.

1970b. "Cultural Action for Freedom," *Harvard Educational Review* Monograph Series, No. 1.

Gamson, Josh. 1989. "Silence, Death, and the Invisible Enemy: AIDS Activism and Social Movement 'Newness,' " *Social Problems* 36: 351–67.

Gamson, William A. 1991. *SIMSOC (Simulated Society),* 4th ed. New York: Free Press.

, Bruce Fireman, and Steven Rytina. 1982. *Encounters with Unjust Authority.* Homewood, IL: Dorsey Press.

, and Kathryn E. Lasch. 1983. "The Political Culture of Social Welfare Policy," pp. 397–415 in Shimon E. Spiro and Ephraim Yaar (eds.), *Evaluating the Welfare State.* New York: Academic Press.

, and Andre Modigliani. 1987. "The Changing Culture of Affirmative Action," Vol. 3, pp. 137–77, in Richard D. Braungart (ed.), *Research in Political Sociology.* Greenwich, CT: JAI Press.

1989. "Media Discourse and Public Opinion on Nuclear Power," *American Journal of Sociology* 95: 1–37.

Gans, Herbert. 1979. *Deciding What's News.* New York: Pantheon.

1988. *Middle American Individualism.* New York: Free Press.

Giddens, Anthony. 1986. *Central Problems in Social Theory.* Berkeley: University of California Press.

Gilligan, Carol. 1982. *In a Different Voice.* Cambridge, MA.: Harvard University Press.

Glazer, Nathan. 1975. *Affirmative Discrimination.* New York: Basic Books.

1978. "Why Bakke Won't End Reverse Discrimination: 2" *Commentary* 66: 36–41.

Goodman, Paul. 1970. *New Reformation: Notes of a Neolithic Conservative.* New York: Random House.

Graber, Doris. 1988. *Processing the News.* New York: Longman.

Guidry, William B. 1979. "Affirmative Action," *American Opinion* (March), 19–34.

Gurevitch, Michael and Mark R. Levy (eds.). 1985. *Mass Communication Review Yearbook,* Vol. 5. Beverly Hills, CA: Sage.

Halle, David. 1984. *America's Working Man.* Chicago: University of Chicago Press.

Harding, Vincent. 1981. *There Is a River: The Black Struggle for Freedom in America*. New York: Harcourt Brace Jovanovich.

Illich, Ivan. 1973. *Tools for Conviviality*. New York: Harper and Row.

Iyengar, Shanto. 1991. *Is Anyone Responsible?: How Television Frames Political Issues*. Chicago: University of Chicago Press.

and Donald R. Kinder. 1987. *News That Matters*. Chicago: University of Chicago Press.

Jefferson, Gail. 1978. "Explanation of Transcript Notation," pp. xi–xvi, in Jim Schenkein (ed.), *Studies in the Organization of Conversational Interaction*. New York: Academic Press.

Katznelson, Ira. 1981. *City Trenches*. Chicago: University of Chicago Press.

Krueger, Richard A. 1988. *Focus Groups: A Practical Guide for Applied Research*. Newbury Park, CA: Sage.

Lane, Robert E. 1962. *Political Ideology*. New York: Free Press.

Lofland, John. 1989. "Consensus Movements: City Twinning and Derailed Dissent in the American Eighties," pp. 163–96 in Louis Kriesberg (ed.), *Research on Social Movements*, Vol. 11. Greenwich, CT: JAI Press.

Lovins, Amory B. 1977. *Soft Energy Paths*. New York: Harper Colophon Books.

Lowi, Theodore. 1967. "The Public Philosophy: Interest Group Liberalism," *American Political Science Review* 61: 5–24.

1971. *The Politics of Disorder*. New York: Basic Books.

Marshall, Gordon. 1983. "Some Remarks on the Study of Working Class Consciousness," *Politics and Society* 12: 263–301.

McAdam, Doug. 1982. *Political Process and the Development of Black Insurgency*. Chicago: University of Chicago Press.

McCarthy, John D. and Mark Wolfson. 1992. "Consensus Movements, Conflict Movements, and the Cooptation of Civic and State Infrastructures," in Aldon Morris and Carol Mueller (eds.), *Frontiers of Social Movement Theory*. New Haven, CT: Yale University Press.

McCarthy, John D. and Mayer N. Zald. 1977. "Resource Mobilization in Social Movements: A Partial Theory," *American Journal of Sociology* 82: 1212–34.

McCracken, Samuel. 1977. "The War Against the Atom," *Commentary* 64: 33–47.

1979. "The Harrisburg Syndrome," *Commentary* 67: 27–39.

Media Institute. 1979. *Television Evening News Covers Nuclear Energy: A Ten Year Perspective*. Washington, DC: Media Institute.

Melucci, Alberto. 1989. *Nomads of the Present*. Philadelphia: Temple University Press.

Merelman, Richard M. 1984. *Making Something of Ourselves: On Culture and Politics in the United States*. Berkeley: University of California Press.

Miller, Mark Crispin. 1988. *Boxed In: The Culture of TV*. Evanston, IL: Northwestern University Press.

Moore, Barrington, Jr. 1978. *Injustice: The Social Bases of Obedience and Revolt*. White Plains, NY: M. E. Sharpe.

Morgan, David L. 1988. *Focus Groups as Qualitative Research*. Newbury Park, CA.: Sage.

Mueller, Klaus. 1973. *The Politics of Communication*. New York: Oxford University Press.

Nelkin, Dorothy. 1981. "Nuclear Power as a Feminist Issue," *Environment* 23: 14–20, 38–39.

Neuman, W. Russell. 1986. *The Paradox of Mass Politics*. Cambridge, MA: Harvard University Press.
Oberschall, Anthony. 1973. *Social Conflict and Social Movements*. Englewood Cliffs, NJ: Prentice-Hall.
Pole, J. R. 1978. *The Pursuit of Equality in American History*. Berkeley: University of California Press.
Ragin, Charles C. 1987. *The Comparative Method*. Berkeley: University of California Press.
Reinarman, Craig. 1987. *American States of Mind*. New Haven, CT: Yale University Press.
Ryan, Charlotte. 1991. *Prime Time Activism*. Boston: South End Press.
Schumacher, E. F. 1973. *Small Is Beautiful*. New York: Harper and Row.
Schutz, Alfred. 1967. *The Phenomenology of the Social World*. Evanston, IL: Northwestern University Press.
Scott, James C. 1985. *Weapons of the Weak*. New Haven, CT: Yale University Press.
Sennett, Richard. 1980. *Authority*. New York: Knopf.
Simmel, Georg. 1950. *The Sociology of Georg Simmel*. New York: Free Press.
Slater, Philip E. 1970. *The Pursuit of Loneliness*. Boston: Beacon Press.
Snow, David A. and Robert D. Benford. 1988. "Ideology, Frame Resonance, and Participant Mobilization," Vol. 1, pp. 197–217, in Bert Klandermans, Hanspeter Kriesi, and Sidney Tarrow (eds.), *International Social Movement Research*. Greenwich, CT: JAI Press.
    1992. "Master Frames and Cycles of Protest," in Aldon Morris and Carol Mueller (eds.), *Frontiers of Social Movement Theory*. New Haven, CT: Yale University Press.
Sowell, Thomas. 1972. *Black Education: Myths and Tragedies*. New York: McKay.
Turner, Ralph H. and Lewis M. Killian. 1987. *Collective Behavior,* 3rd ed. Englewood Cliffs, NJ: Prentice-Hall.
Weaver, Paul. 1981. "TV News and Newspaper News," pp. 277–93, in Richard P. Adler (ed.), *Understanding Television*. New York: Praeger.
Williams, Raymond. 1950. *Culture and Society*. New York: Columbia University Press.
Williams, Robin M., Jr. 1960. *American Society*. New York: Knopf.
Willis, Paul. 1977. *Learning to Labor*. Westmead, U.K.: Saxon House.
Winner, Langdon. 1977. *Autonomous Technology*. Cambridge, MA: MIT Press.
Wolfe, Alan. 1977. *The Limits of Legitimacy*. New York: Free Press.
Wolin, Sheldon. 1981. "Editorial Statement," *Democracy: A Journal of Renewal and Radical Change* 1: 2–4.
Wright, Erik Olin. 1985. *Classes*. London: Verso.
Zajonc, Robert B. 1980. "Feeling and Thinking: Preferences Need No Inferences," *American Psychologist* 35: 151–75.

Index